Urban Design Methods

Integrated Urban Research Tools

Undine Giseke, Martina Löw,
Angela Million, Philipp Misselwitz,
Jörg Stollmann (eds.)

jovis

A.1

urban design as a changing profession

Undine Giseke, Martina Löw, Angela Million,
Philipp Misselwitz, Jörg Stollmann

In recent years, we have witnessed an unprecedented surge in public, academic, and policy debates focusing on cities and urban areas. Urbanization is seen as one of the key risks to planetary sustainability globally, with an estimated 2.5 billion additional urban dwellers by 2050, particularly in developing countries, dramatically increasing carbon footprints through the anticipated building activities and traffic, causing rising environmental degradation through the dramatic expansion of built-over areas, and increasing the risks and destabilization related to uneven development and new levels of expected urban poverty. Yet at the same time urbanization continues to produce imaginaries of hope. To most of us, cities are associated with improved and more inclusive access to resources and policy arenas, as well as with arrangements that produce societal innovations, including new forms of living and the transition towards sustainability. We realize that the urban and natural systems are inextricably linked by a complex circulation of materials, dissolving the old categorical and spatial boundaries between the city and its "outside." Against this backdrop, cities and urbanization processes take center stage in political and policy debates and ideas such as the Right to the City, the involvement of the civil society, the decentralization of decision-making, and stronger mandates are gaining ground (see WGBU 2016 and United Nations 2017).

Ironically, the more we talk about cities, the more we realize how much we don't know. Paradoxically, the growing certainty that the city holds the key to achieving global sustainability is paired with an increasing awareness of complexity and lack of clarity in how we define a city or the urban on a conceptual and practical level. What is a city, and where do we draw its limits when we realize that they are embedded in complex social, ecological, and economic metabolisms and flows? How do processes of digitalization, mediatization, translocalization, and polycontextualization change the urban and our perception of urbanity? We tend to consider urbanization as a limitless societal transformation process at global scale – a planetary phenomenon (Brenner and Schmidt 2014). But how can we then establish more effective and just governance and management systems which must be put into practice in situated political, cultural, geographic, and social conditions?

The ongoing and profound transformation processes challenge not only our conceptual understanding of what cities and urbanities are, but also, crucially, the traditional urban-oriented disciplines such as architecture, urban planning, landscape architecture, spatial planning, and urban sociology. The rise in the complexity of urban systems has fueled an ever-increasing fragmentation of expertise and skill sets, which is further reflected in the disciplinary fragmentation of academia. Going beyond interdisciplinary challenges to think and act in relation to the city, urban transformation processes force us to question the assumed centrality of expert knowledge itself.

At a global scale, it is urban informality rather than institutionalized planning that has established ways of governance, with urbanization shaped by the everyday actions of city-dwellers themselves (Roy and Al Sayyad 2004). In developed countries, furthermore, citizens are increasingly declaring their right to fully participate in decision-making about and in the demanding process- and actor-oriented approaches to urban development.

While many questions concerning the tangible effects of those open processes are yet to be addressed, the growing number of pioneering movements and experimental planning and design approaches introduce alternative modes of spatial production. Depending on the context, such approaches have drawn on local particularities, cultural perspectives, and administrative structures; in some cities, among them Berlin, the approaches rely on strong collaborative traditions. If the co-production of urban space promises to be both more socially inclusive and broader in its perspective than existing and established participatory or bottom-up planning processes, we need a new, transdisciplinary understanding of urban knowledge – one that includes, beyond expert technical knowledge, a broad range of different knowledge cultures, including the embedded and situated knowledge of citizens themselves.

Confronted with overlapping roles, and with a reality they experience as messy, planning and design professionals often feel overwhelmed. This volume attempts to discuss how the challenge of gaining a broader understanding of urban knowledge, urban co-production, and inter- and transdisciplinary research and practice might lead to new approaches to pedagogy, research, and design responses within critical practice. Urban design – *as an integrative field of study, profession, and course of action* – takes a clear stance for inter- and transdisciplinary co-production as well as for a systemic understanding of the challenges of our still-urbanizing world.

Urban Design as an Inter- and Transdisciplinary Field of Study

In 2006, four institutes at TU Berlin – the Institutes of Architecture, Landscape Architecture, Urban and Regional Planning, and Sociology – started a joint teaching experiment. They established the MSc in Urban Design program as the first interdisciplinary urban-oriented master's of its kind in Germany, based on the assumption that mono-sectoral approaches are insufficient in preparing young professionals for the ever-increasing complexity of urbanization and a radically transforming field of practice. In the program, urban design is understood as a new field of reflection and practice in which multiple disciplinary approaches converge, and where, therefore, new didactic approaches are required in order to build appropriate capacities and develop creative solutions.

We benefit from the well-established wealth of methodological expertise and know-how within each of the four distinct disciplinary traditions. Their specific methods are adept at covering the concise and isolable aspects of the urban, while the common work across disciplinary boundaries reveals the interdependencies of urban dynamics and allows us to combine both basic and applied research approaches in teaching practice.

This applies, for example, to our attempt to bridge the conventional gap between the social sciences and design disciplines. We deny any hierarchical relationship between observing, non-normative social sciences and projective, implementation-oriented urban design. Instead, we orchestrate conversation and cooperation between participants in order to expand the range of insights. The urban designers thus gain a better awareness of how to generate and deal with data and empirical material in order to understand their subject. Urban design is in need of a methodological debate to scrutinize its ways of knowledge generation and, in turn, strengthen its accountability and possibilities for critique. In parallel, social science methods often fall short when it comes to a spatialized understanding of reality. Through cooperation with urban designers, social scientists are introduced to the non-linear and iterative modes of urban, architecture, and landscape design processes and the ways in which they impact the production of space.

This volume presents the most important insights, gained in the form of methods and tools developed through this integrative work at the intersection of the disciplines. While some of these insights refer back to long-standing traditions, others reach out to emerging schools of thought. The overview is necessarily extensive, but despite this is still not comprehensive.

Co-producing Space, Co-producing Knowledge

While the production of urban space is expected to steer towards inclusivity in democratic discourses, basic professional education is only now starting to query the contested socio-economic and political conditions within which design tasks are situated. Uncovering the frequently naturalized – yet intrinsically political – dynamics of gentrification, privatization, and financialization at the root of urban transformation cannot rely solely on multidisciplinary expertise, nor on tapping local actor-specific knowledge. It requires the co-production of knowledge from within a constellation of different actors and networks. We therefore foster this understanding in the urban design field of study by way of a co-operational, multi-scalar, and trans-disciplinary approach.

In the long-winded processes of co-producing knowledge, the resource of time emerges as the main challenge. In conditions of rapid change, the need for readily available and assimilated databases and methodological tools for sourcing, analyzing and interpreting qualitative and quantitative data is crucial. This is precisely one of the issues that this volume, as well as the overall urban design curriculum, aims to address.

Urban Design as a Diversifying Profession

Are planners and designers inevitably condemned to always lag behind and be only retroactively asked to intervene? Or is it in fact possible to reconceptualize the city as a contested field, and to deliberately choose and shape one's own role, scope, and range of responsibilities – including by identifying potential alliances and sites of intervention? The disparity between education and profession is hard to ignore. Urban design as a field of study addresses the complex socioeconomic, political, and ecological conditions within which professional actors act in order to reframe the urban designer as a trans-disciplinary urban professional. To that end, we must also question the frequently privileged social and educational background of the designers themselves, which is often disconnected from the everyday life of most of the citizens they plan and design for. Urban design as a course of action starts with reflection and introspection long in advance of a specific commission.

Design as Transformative Knowledge Production

Part of this introspection should be directed at one's own design attitude. Shaped by individual background, history, and experiences, the designer's attitude and agency have to be put under closer scrutiny, especially as they become part of academic knowledge production in research-based design or research-by-design projects. The designer's attitude and agency can be critically examined not only through the lens of theoretical perspectives, but also against the real, transformative outcomes of a specific design task. As convoluted and opaque as it may at first seem, design ultimately brings about a tangible, physical change and a sense of purpose; this need to be reflected upon, negotiated, and made transparent.

Notwithstanding our insufficient knowledge of the world that we aim to transform, we as urban designers are confronted with the very real consequences of current forms of design practice on the built environment. Alongside other methods of complexity reduction, we promote a systemic understanding of spatial phenomena that accounts for a variety of interrelated factors, which may range from the local up to the planetary scale and involve the socioeconomic, political, and ecological spheres. The aim of a systemic understanding is to identify possible points of intervention where design, even as a small-scale change, can resolve a specific problem and simultaneously have far-reaching transformative effects.

Having abandoned the illusion of a universal framework for action, urban design faces an overwhelming task; diverging and fragmented operating practices create further structural obstacles. This volume's main contribution is to collect a range of current practices and decipher the underlying methodological thinking; it offers an orientation, embraces the multitude of perspectives, and ultimately hopes to provoke reflection on one's own role, frame of action, and attitude. As such, this volume is a repertoire of instruments and tools with broad disciplinary origins. These tools have been applied in project- and research-based teaching within the curriculum of the MSc in Urban Design in order to foster and advance the attitudes that trained urban professionals carry to the field of practice. We are convinced that the field of Urban Design will become a key arena in helping to find creative and locally appropriate answers for steering and shaping our cities and urbanized regions towards sustainability and social justice.

Brenner, N. and Schmid, C. "The 'Urban Age' in Question." In **Implosions/Explosions. Towards a Study of Planetary Urbanization**, edited by N. Brenner, 310–337. Berlin: Jovis Verlag, 2014.
Brenner, N. and Schmid, C. "Towards a new epistemology of the urban?" **City 19**, issues 2–3 (2015): 151–182, DOI: 10.1080/13604813.2015.1014712
Brenner, N., Schmid, C. "Planetary urbanization." In **Urban Constellations**, edited by Matthew Gandy, 10–13. Berlin: Jovis, 2012.
Roy, A., AlSayyad, N., eds. **Urban Informality: Transnational Perspectives from the Middle East, Latin America and South Asia**. New York: Lexington Books, 2004.
WBGU – Wissenschaftlicher Beirat der Bundesregierung Globale Umweltveränderungen. **Der Umzug der Menschheit: Die transformative Kraft der Städte**. Berlin: WBGU, 2016.
United Nations. **New Urban Agenda**. [Online]. 2017. Available at www.habitat3.org Accessed April 22, 2020.

A.2

some notes about interdisciplinarity

Future Urbanists: Embrace Complexity, Co-Make Flexible Pluralities.

Andreas Brück

Today we live in liquid times (Baumann 2000) where a mode of constant crisis triggers small, short-term, and ad-hoc answers to a multitude of problems – financial crises, housing crises, climate crises, sociopolitical crises, and their manifolds. In a modern age focused on quantification and standardization, we struggle to deal with uncertainty and complexity. However, urban professionals "should not claim the instant ability to solve complex problems" and instead "be exploratory and inclusive" (Hall and Tewdwr-Jones 2010, 268). "Planning is becoming *plural*" as "drivers of change ... are transforming the activity and scope of planning, across scales and across territories in varied ways and at varied times" (Hall and Tewdwr-Jones 2010, 268, emphasis added). Rather than "solution-thinking" that fosters simplifications, we need creative ideas that embrace complexities. The more options we have the more powerful our cities will become. But are we prepared for this? Do we have the necessary knowledge and tools? How are multiplicity and diversity managed? How are planetary and localized scales mediated and created?

Urban design practice has to become more flexible and cities thought of as "unfinished" frameworks that encourage individual creativity and ownership to authorship. As many examples of contemporary community-based initiatives prove, the challenge is chiefly procedural and not ideological. It is largely dependent on forging new approaches, with new methods, new behaviors, new schemes, new setups, new strategies... A long time ago, in the final chapter of *Cities and the Wealth of Nations*, Jane Jacobs advocated for *drift* – "a process of continually improvising" (1961, 221–222). And in the 1970s, Durth called for a transition towards an "aesthetics of improvisation" (1976, 194) in urban design education and practice accentuating the potentials of reuse, mixed use, programmatic design, and a public takeover of streets, plazas, and parks. Today, urban design practice has still not systematized this goal.

Nevertheless, new ideas regarding the practices of urban design and related fields are venturing into unfamiliar domains, calling for reforms, adaptations, and revolutions in the way cities are made. In order to navigate urban complexity and uncertainty, urban professionals need to not only understand the urban and its contextual conditions, but also to normalize engagement in envisioning urban tomorrows, and to assist in their re-grafting and remaking. The professional mastering of a wide range of methods and tools is of quintessential importance to urban design practice, which requires drawing on contexts encompassing multiple sets of (un)knowns, parameters, projections, and speculative designs. In the best-case scenario, imaginaries, anxieties, demands, and multiple perspectives on tomorrow's cities may be re-appropriated, amalgamated, and recombined innovatively into rooted, original hybrids. Insights from different domains (e.g. traditionally walled-in disciplines) prompt the conclusion that cities are able to develop not only one way or the other, but also into amalgams of formerly incompatible opposites.

As Mau phrases it, in these liquid times "the challenge of our era [is]: to synthesize incredibly complex inputs and reconcile those inputs into one coherent way of proceeding" (Mau in Hyde 2012, 30). With this in mind, the expectations of future urban professionals (of whatever disciplinary flavor and whether of theoretical or activist commitment) are high. Meanwhile, the expertise and experience necessary to catalyze urban change, weave together and amalgamate hybrid spaces, and navigate the multiplicity and plurality of urban tomorrows is not easily achieved.

Today, urban professionals need to comfort and reassure themselves with regard to their capabilities and options – including their methods and tools. What is necessary is a reconquering of the urban in terms of both discourses and physical manifestations; a fearlessness in attempting daring proposals for non-linear solutions that understand progress as the ability to simultaneously produce plural, creative, adaptable, and procedurally flexible flows of operations. On top of this, future urban professionals need to become better at understanding, communicating, and mediating different points of view. This relates to necessary new roles for urban professionals as curators, catalysts, and facilitators; roles that focus on implementing and nurturing elements that empower communities to forge and cater for liveable urbanities themselves. As Indy Johar puts it:

> This is a future in which architecture and our role as designers are changing; we are being invited to be protagonists, to be the change-makers and the propositioners. This is a future where we must become the makers of platforms – not the designers of containers for corporations. This is a future where, to evoke Cedric Price, we must be operational and innovative, and build social ecosystems. (2014, 204)

It is obvious that the education of future urbanists should be adapted to contemporary trends. Since everything is becoming more fluid and less permanent, and is in a state of constant adaptation, the education of urban professionals needs to follow suit – it must come out of the campus and into the urban. Knowledge concerning elasticity should become a core topic in academia, and methods of putting it into practice need to be developed and tested. Education needs to offer overviews of and training in the skills required for orientation, navigation, and pathfinding while accepting and employing complexity as a resource. We should be trained to ask divergent questions following dynamic inquiry methods that create variations, alternative answers, and scenarios for possible procedures rather than fixate on static knowledge for a "road map" or an "end product."

And even then we should not forget to constantly revise and reflect; even at times of accelerated speed, ultra-complexity, fast decision-making, and so on, we must carefully and continuously recalibrate what we do, learn, and teach – as well as the methods and tools we use.

Bauman, Z. Liquid Modernity. Cambridge: Polity Press, 2000.
Durth, W. "Zur gesellschaftlichen Funktion von Kritik und Theorie des Stadtgestaltung." PhD diss., Technische Hochschule Darmstadt, 1976.
Hall, P. and Tewdwr-Jones, M. **Urban and Regional Planning**. London: Routledge, 2010.
Hyde, R. **Future Practice. Conversations from the Edge of Architecture**. London: Routledge, 2012.
Jacobs, J. **The Death and Life of Great American Cities**. New York: Random House, 1961.
Johar, I. "Architecture of the Civic Economy." In **Make Shift City. Renegotiating the Urban Commons**, edited by Ferguson, F., 204–205. Berlin: Jovis, 2014.

Urban Design as an Interdisciplinary Inquiry

Emily Kelling

Urban and spatial studies are currently marked by recognizable gaps; firstly, between the different disciplines in the social sciences and humanities (Robinson 2002), and secondly, even more fundamentally, between the social sciences and the design disciplines (Fiori and Brandão 2010). The latter especially poses a challenge for urban design – at least if it is conceived of as sitting at this interface. However, urban design may also be predisposed to help with narrowing this gap. One avenue for doing so is to develop a research perspective for the spatial that recognizes the value of the knowledge-generating capacities of each discipline and the potential of their synergies. The premise is that both sides of the gap can benefit from the other, that urban dynamics can be understood better if both sides come together sensibly, and, finally, that such a perspective can contribute a new quality to the addressing of urban social problems.

This aim requires an in-depth engagement with the diverse methods of spatial analysis and knowledge generation. For one, design methods such as sketching need to be taken seriously for their knowledge-generating capacities. At the same time, the process of knowledge generation needs to be described so that its procedures and limitations, as well as its results and their specific context of emergence, can be discussed. This would eventually lift the meaning of the spatial understanding gained beyond the design itself. Similarly, the relevant methods from the social sciences and their methodological premises need to be made comprehensible on a level that makes them employable for design researchers without gross simplification. This would, first of all, provide a basis for the joint discussion of research results. Subsequently it may provide for the synthesis of diverse approaches into a joint perspective both for research and for the praxis of design and the politics of space.

When it comes to the ambition of bridging the interdisciplinary gap within urban design, the German academic system poses a somewhat peculiar complication. This is the rather rigid organization of the various traditional disciplines, which is also to be found at the Technische Universität Berlin. The Urban Design master's program is not offered by one institutionally identifiable entity within the organigram, but instead by a range of chairs from four significantly separated university departments who collaborate to offer the study program and to develop a joint Urban Design agenda. It is my impression that in the Anglophone realm – within urban studies but also beyond – it is more common than in Germany to approach academia from an interdisciplinary perspective. In this, interdisciplinarity itself has acquired a different meaning. The difference is one of a discipline-based versus a problem-based research approach. In the Anglophone realm, the traditional disciplines more commonly receive less emphasis than in Germany. This finds expression in the institutional set-up of universities, insofar as the differentiation of departments and study programs often follows a topic-based logic. It allows an approach to research and teaching that is based on a fusion of perspectives in which traditional disciplines cease to be of primary significance. In Germany, by contrast, disciplines remain the organizing principle in many cases, and interdisciplinarity usually means bringing together researchers with rather clear disciplinary positions, often confronting the individuals involved with the challenge of mutual incomprehensibility. Both modes have their advantages.

Looking in particular at the study of urban development and urban design, a discipline-based approach seems almost counterproductive in face of the complexity of cities and the historic evidence of the negative consequences of sector-based policies. Upon closer inspection, however, it turns out that the problem-based approach also takes its toll. Even if architects and designers have been among the driving forces of interdisciplinary Anglophone thinking in urban development, design, and environmental studies, this often seems to have been at the expense of their design skills. One can better grasp the meaning and implications of the "despatialization" of the debate (Fiori and Brandão 2010) when considering the potential that the German organizational set up – despite all its challenges – affords; that is, the collaboration between social scientists, architects, and planners who still consider themselves as such and who therefore have retained the specific qualities and capacities of their individual disciplines.

This dilemma has turned into an exciting task that we are addressing in the configuration of our program. In the sociology-based Introduction to Urban Design we draw on the sociology of space in order to develop the theoretical skills needed to read the social and spatial structures within which urban design interventions unfold. This includes a focus on social inequalities and their spatial (re)production. We use this perspective to reimagine the kind of impact an intervention can have, thus theorizing about the political potential of urban design. Moreover, in cross-disciplinary teaching and research projects, we have started bringing together the various relevant methods of the different disciplines and discussing them in a comparable format in order to develop a *shared language*. Indeed, I would argue that such a shared language is the core of any ambition to achieve the synergy of the disciplines. A shared and *non-hierarchical language* is the precondition for a true understanding of the others' work and aims. This, in turn, is key for the *recognition of the equal value* of the specialized skills and knowledge generated in the different disciplines. Only when all three conditions are achieved can the potential of mutual complementarity and synergy be understood and realized. This is a question of politics significant not only to the context of research, to which I refer primarily, but also to the praxis of design and the production of the city more generally.

Fiori, J. and Brandão, Z. "Spatial strategies and urban social policy. Urbanism and poverty reduction in the favelas of Rio de Janeiro." In **Rethinking the informal city: Critical perspectives from Latin America (Remapping Cultural History, Volume 11)**, edited by Hernández, F., Kellett, P., and Allen, L.K., 181–206. New York: Berghahn Books, 2010.
Robinson, J. "Global and World Cities. A view from off the Map." **International Journal of Urban and Regional Research** 26, issue 3 (September 2002): 531–554.

What Ever Happened to Landscape?

Making the Case for New Disciplinary and Material Intimacies

Xenia Kokoula

What ever happened to landscape?[1] The discipline of landscape architecture has long grappled with the dichotomy of nature and culture, which positioned the city firmly in the latter category. The last decades have brought a host of challenges, too numerous to discuss in full, that bring this core dichotomy into question. Theorists have pointed out that "nature cannot pre-exist its construction" (Haraway 1992, 296); as a result, we have become "excruciatingly conscious of nature's discursive constitution as 'other'" (Haraway 1992, 296). Human activities – both in their discursive dimension but primarily in their material impact – are understood as geological forces of planetary transformation, introducing the era of the Anthropocene (Renn and Scherer 2015). Global phenomena, such as conflict, migration, climate change, and natural disasters massively reshape territories. Their undeniable and forceful materiality makes clear that we lack adequate tools to debate and deal with them (Hekman 2010).

Recent developments in landscape architecture, such as landscape urbanism, ecological urbanism, and urban metabolism, can be understood within the context of the aforementioned challenges. Not all of them question, let alone effectively deconstruct, the separation between nature and culture. However, they have succeeded in expanding the disciplinary boundaries and generating an active debate with the potential to invigorate the disciplines that deal with the urban territory. These schools of thought share as a starting point the understanding that landscape, ecological, and metabolic processes are a driving force in urban transformation (Waldheim 2006).

Firstly, as *landscape urbanism* makes clear, we need to look beyond architectural objects as the single, human-made structural units that cumulatively shape our living environment (Waldheim 2006). Architecture and the city are just some of the building blocks that interact with natural phenomena and ecological processes to form larger systems. Accordingly, these systems are not limited to the traditionally dense urban settlements; they expand far beyond them to include rural spaces, as well as spaces that are not used as human settlements in the traditional sense, but are still intrinsically connected to them – such as infrastructure or bodies of water. Based on this understanding, *ecological urbanism* stands for a holistic, regional, and global approach to dealing with interrelated design problems including housing, environmental issues, access to food, water and energy, and other resources. These problems, however, cannot be resolved independently by the respective specialized subfields. *Urban metabolism* thus promotes a way of thinking in processes and flows, rather than in static spatial designs (Sijmons 2014). It seeks not only to reveal hidden or obscure spatial processes, but also to intervene in the natural and/or urban systems they sustain.

Even a very brief overview of landscape urbanism, ecological urbanism, and urban metabolism reveals two related points. On the one hand, urban and natural systems, the city, and the landscape cannot be explored separately but only through their multiple connections. As a consequence, disciplinary boundaries need to be questioned in practice and in academia, as we do in the Urban Design master's program. The focus on landscape does not seek to establish a new hierarchy or privilege one discipline over the others. The separate disciplines still serve an important role as repositories of specialized knowledge. At the same time, designers such as James Corner (2014) and Kate Orff (2012) are carving innovative cross-disciplinary methodological paths for engaging with urban and natural systems in the context of specific but complex problems: the urban metabolism in the harbor city of Rotterdam in the first case, and the petrochemical landscape of the Mississippi river in the second.

Following Timothy Morton and his consideration of *intimacy*, we understand our task as a radical search for integrating what at first seems incompatible; "an exercise in hubris" (2010, 273). Intimacy is understood in a material sense as the interdependence and inseparability of different materialities, life forms, and species. A further example of intimacy is the concept of *zero landscape*, which seeks to erase the outdated concept of an aesthetic distance between the human viewer and the surrounding landscape (Morton 2011). Last but not least, Morton is an advocate of a radical disciplinary intimacy, one that not only occasionally straddles boundaries but links disparate fields at their very foundations (Morton 2010).

Different forms of and platforms for such meetings across disciplines are currently being tested both in and outside of the academic world. The aim is to study and uncover the interaction of heterogeneous components in urban and natural systems, their human actors and the matter (food, water, energy etc.) that sustains them, along with other non-human forces as diverse as animals, affects[2], and technologies (Grusin 2015). The recent debates in landscape architecture have already succeeded in making such elements the focus of design, thus bringing the urban and natural sphere closer together. It is now time to fully acknowledge the functional and conceptual inseparability of urban and natural systems (Giseke 2018) in order to turn our imaginations to the challenges of the Anthropocene.

FABRIC and JCFO. "Project Atelier Rotterdam." In **IABR 2014 – Urban by Nature**, edited by Brugmans, G. and Stein, 164–179. Rotterdam: IABR, 2014.
Giseke, U. "The City in the Anthropocene—Multiple Porosities." In **Porous City. From Metaphor to Urban Agenda**, edited by Wolfrum, S. et al., 200–204. Basel: Birkhäuser, 2018.
Grusin, R. Introduction to **The Nonhuman Turn**, edited by Grusin, R., 7–29. Minneapolis: University of Minnesota Press, 2015.
Haraway, D. "The Promises of Monsters. A Regenerative Politics for Inappropriate/d Others." In **Cultural Studies**, edited by Grossberg, L.; Nelson, C.; Teichler, P., 295–336. New York: Routledge, 1992.
Hekman, S. J. **The material of knowledge. Feminist Disclosures**. Bloomington: Indiana University Press, 2010.
Koolhaas, R. "What Ever Happened to Urbanism?" In **S, M, L, XL**, edited by O.M.A., Koolhaas, R., and Mau, B., 959–971. New York: The Monicelli Press, 1995.
Misrach, R. and Orff, K. **Petrochemical America**. New York: Aperture, 2014.
Mostafavi, M. "Why Ecological Urbanism? Why Now?" In **Ecological Urbanism**, edited by Mostafavi, M. and Doherty, P., 12–53. Baden: Lars Müller Publishers, 2011.
Morton, T. "Queer Ecology." **Publications of the Modern Language Association of America** 125, no. 2, (2010): 273–282, https://doi.org/10.1632/pmla.2010.125.2.273
Morton, T. "Zero Landscapes in the Time of Hyperobjects." **GAM Graz Architecture Magazine** 07, (2011): 79–87.
Sijmons, D. "The Urban Metabolism. Introduction." In **IABR 2014 – Urban by Nature**, edited by Brugmans, G. and Stein, J, 120–122. Rotterdam, IABR, 2014.
Waldheim, C. (2006): "Introduction. A Reference Manifesto." In **The Landscape Urbanism Reader**, edited by Waldheim, C., 13–19. New York: Princeton Architectural Press, 2006.

Endnotes

1 This question paraphrases Rem Koolhaas, who a few decades ago called for a rethinking of urbanism in the face of global, unrestrained, and rapid urbanization (Koolhaas 1995). Arguably, landscape architecture is ready for a similar rethinking.

2 Unlike the more subject-oriented emotions, affects imply "an intensity moving through human and nonhuman bodies alike" (Grusin 2015)

The Turn of Theory: Urban Design at the University

Áine Ryan

Within the academic context, methods and their epistemological groundings define disciplines. In the practice context, corresponding professions are largely defined by the scope of their services. Urban design straddles these realms, albeit with an inherent bias towards "practice over theory" or "profession over discipline." It originated as a field of practice, but continually draws on theoretical positions from across the social, economic, and environmental sciences: mostly as an aid to understanding the urban condition, sometimes, perhaps, to bolster its legitimacy as a distinct field of activity or profession, and sometimes to advance the tools of its trade. The establishment of urban design as a stand-alone curriculum at universities over the past decade or so brings with it the opportunity for a more critical and consequential engagement with theory. Significant potential exists at universities such as TU Berlin, where the curriculum is delivered as a cross-faculty collaboration, simply because interdisciplinary conversation is conversation about methods.

Achieving such a conversation about "method" is not without significant challenges, especially for design disciplines. Design theory is comparatively scant; urban design theory is even more so. That said, a recent argument against the comparison of urban design with empirical sciences introduced a promising definition of urban design knowledge as "a particular form of diagrammatic socio-spatial knowledge that cannot be reduced to either words or numbers" (Dovey and Pafka 2015). This epistemological framing resonates with the design theory strand on "designerly ways of knowing" (Cross 1982) that sees design as "a third way" distinct from the humanities and social sciences (Nelson and Stolterman 2012).

To date, most reasearch on the methods and modes of design knowledge build upon Herbert Simon's examinations of the role of representation in design problem-solving from the late 1960s (Akin 2001). Rooted in the computational sciences, and typically framed as protocol studies of design exercises at the scale of architecture, this avenue of enquiry has articulated quite well how drawing and sketching cognitively assist designers in both grasping and solving complex problems: by abstracting and typifying information to trigger, order, develop, test, and refine ideas (Goldschmidt 1991). Yet despite this 'visual thinking' being the backbone of design theory to this day, designers themselves have scarcely contributed to this body of research. For example, little is empirically known about the types of information selected to solve specific design problems and how the substance of this information is changed in various stages of the design process, or about the typical types of judgements that underpin key decisions. This is probably because design is mainly learned implicitly "by doing," and without being taught about its scientific grounding or methods. Nevertheless, it is remarkable that fifty years after Simon began the design theory conversation, and twenty years after digital tools began to significantly alter the hand-to-head heuristics that underpin "visual thinking," even the field of design theory needed to be reminded that "design is not simply 'itself' but *is* the interplay (or in my language the mediation) *between* subjects and the substantive, real-world, essentially artificial, subject-matter with which it engages", and that knowledge of this mediation is still "in embryo" (Dilnot 2018, 145). This is the great opportunity for urban design at the university. By attempting to describe the "*situated negotiating of the incommensurables involved in moving from 'existing to preferred situation*'" (Dilnot 2018, 144), the urban design discipline could advance more robust epistemological underpinnings that contribute to the aforementioned critical areas of design theory and also inform approaches in urban design practice.

As in other design fields, "representation" is the main method of carrying out urban design, but it is next to impossible to "do" urban design in the intuitive and non-reflexive manner usual to "designing": sites must be "read" at many geographical scales; "solutions" must account for multiple sociopolitical aims concerning the environment, human well-being, and urban quality; the often conflicting agendas of numerous interest groups must be considered; delivery timeframes run into decades and must integrate with ongoing cultural, historical, economic, and ecological processes; and so on. "Negotiating" this degree of complexity forces more conscious thinking, as well as a retraceable decision-making sequence, and thus lends itself more easily to examination. Though the lens of "diagrammatic socio-spatial knowledge," such examinations may reveal the transformations made to the diverse types of qualitative and quantitative information selected, weighted, synthesized, and produced in the design process.

In this regard, the TU Berlin Master in Urban Design provides a seminal space for exploring urban design knowledge. The core Method and Tools module conditions students to critically compare methods across the "urban" disciplines. The Urban Design Studio module gives a first-hand introduction to thinking through "representation" and the "situated negotiations" that underpin the design process. The culture of openly questioning the role and tools of urban design, if explored through scientific research, could enable a truer synergy between theory and practice to emerge from this newest moment of urban design at the university.

Cross, N. "Designerly ways of knowing. Design discipline versus design science." **Design Issues** 17, no. 3 (Summer 2001): 49–55.
Dilnot, C. "Thinking design. A personal perspective on the development of the Design Research Society." **Design Studies** 54 (2018): 142–145.
Goldschmidt, G. "The Dialectics of Sketching." **Creativity Research Journal** 4, issue 2 (1991): 123–143.
Nelson, H. G. and Stolterman, E. **The Design Way. Intentional Change in an Unpredictable World**. Cambridge: MIT Press, 2012.
Dovey, K. and Pafka, E. "The Science of Urban Design?" **Urban Design International** 21, issue 1 (2016): 1–10.
Akin, Ö. "Simon Says. Design is Representation." Draft paper, School of Architecture, Carnegie Mellon University, 2001. http://users.metu.edu.tr/baykan/arch467/Readings/AradSimon.pdf Accessed March 28, 2018.

#A.3
external statements

Global urbanization is the key driver and geographical form of what has been called the Anthropocene, the proposed name for the era of human-induced transformation of the environment. Considering that urbanized and natural environments are irrevocably interwoven in deteriorating metabolic relationships, it might be more accurate to speak of what geographer Erik Swyngedouw has identified as the Urbicene, to implicate urbanization as the primary driver of anthropogenic climate change. However, additionally taking into consideration that urbanization processes are the prime expression of accelerated capitalist accumulation, circulation, and uneven development, other scholars – such as environmental historian and political economist Jason W. Moore – have been prompted to recast our common predicament with the more nuanced and connective concept of the Capitalocene. These three notions converge on the diagnosis that the world's environment, planetary urbanization, and globally integrated market capitalism are locked in an intimate symbiosis that is indeterminate and far from stable.

Marc Angelil and Cary Siress
Chair of Architecture and Design at the Institute for Urban Design at ETH Zurich; Senior Design Researcher at Future Cities Laboratory Singapore and at ETH Zurich

The complexity of urban challenges and the disciplines and practices that deal with them represent the paradoxical encounters between disciplinary knowledge, aesthetic regimes, spatial conditions, and a series of governmental forces. As such, the urban is shaped by certain material practices and normalized through design and the act of designing. This means that design and designing are separated neither from the politics they emerge from, nor from the politics they produce. As such, thinking about an urban design as the project for a city means thinking about it in a heterodox manner: not limited to the physical dimension, not exclusive to the activities of a professional-scientific elite that frames the space in which society is produced and reproduced. The concept of a plan itself, of design understood as a tool for imagining a future and as a path to achieving it, must be understood in relation to a global situation of inequality, social trauma, and environmental and social vulnerabilities of marginalization and exploitation. Imagining future urban possibilities must start by recognizing the greatness of the small gestures and efforts, the interstices and the potentialities, that collective actions have in thinking and modifying space and territory. The project here is not a master plan, but must be configured as an architecture of engagement: a form of situated, dialogic, relational process (where once we would have just talked about participation) that makes spatial practice and intervention in space both a criticism and a hope.

Camillo Boano
Professor of Architecture and Urban Design (Icar14), University of Turin

In practice, urban design deals with structural elements in the urban context. These organized elements are presented morphologically, encompassing political, economic, social, ethical, aesthetic, and technical features.

The operation can be understood at both two-dimensional and three-dimensional levels. Firstly, urban design sets up an overall urban structure at the two-dimensional level, in which all the significant urban elements – such as streets, squares, parks, and important buildings – can be integrated. Secondly, urban design defines the form of urban open space and buildings at the three-dimensional level. The typology of urban architecture is the decisive element in urban spatial quality, which is presented by the relations between the buildings.

In contrast to architectural design, urban design focuses on urban space, the invisible part of the urban texture.

Yongjie Cai
Chair of the Architectural Faculty, College of Architecture and Urban Planning (CAUP), Tongji University

When we observe a building, we observe it embedded in its local context. But we are aware of the fact that, down-scale, its details do not end with the doorknob; and that up-scale it is part of a quarter, a city, a region, the planet.

Good design reflects this parallel (in)finity: the relation between the scale of observation and the scale of the universe, and the relation between the detail and the overarching concept.

The awareness of this (in)finity may also be the reason that most successful urban projects are designed by (ex-)architects and landscape architects, and not by planners.

However, the traditional conflict between architects and planners regarding urban design disqualifies both. Urban design is the fusion of architectural design and the planning sciences. The urban designer combines creative disruption, evidence-based research, and communication skills from the perspective of design. The difference between an architect and an urban designer is that the architect works within the constraints of his own good taste, while the urban designer is the coordinator of the generic lack of taste. Contrary to the architect, the urban designer often does not survive the completion of his project. The urban designer needs to accumulate experience in order to develop robust structures that are resilient to different regimes, and in order to figure out where he has impact and where he does not.

Last but not least, a contemporary urban designer approaches construction from the inverse perspective. First, he determines what should stay, and then he allows certain development to take place: "urban design is about skiing; it's the art of braking elegantly."

Kees Christiaanse
Chair of Architecture and Urban Design at the Institute for Urban Design at ETH Zurich

The age-old discrepancy between the "civilized city" and the "backward country" has now all but disappeared. Today, there is little difference between how we live in towns and in the country. Despite this, the focus of the theory and practice of urban planning remains largely unchanged: towns and cities still dominate the agenda, while rural areas earn little more than a sideways glance. Economically, culturally, and politically, however, the continued growth of urban centers is as challenging as the ongoing decline of peripheral locations. Both have the potential to undermine social cohesion and democracy. The IBA Thüringen proposes the idea of StadtLand as a condition in which the urban and the rural are intertwined that requires greater recognition and definition. The form this recognition must take is more than a matter of urban design or socio-cultural settlement patterns: it must also take into account the land, its spaces, the landscape, and its resources. StadtLand represents a new social metabolism.

Marta Doehler-Behzadi
Managing Director of IBA Thüringen

Today I received a request from a farmer. He asked me to assist him with a letter on why a stable for horses was a valuable contribution to biodiversity. I thought, wow. Twenty-five years ago, when I began my studies as an urban planner, I would not have dreamed of being asked such a question. But that is the fascinating thing about our profession. Yesterday we were engaged in legal planning issues; today with the integration of immigrants, and tomorrow with how we might increase the number of bees in cities. To solve these broad questions, planners need something very simple: both openness to new topics and great curiosity. Due to the wide variety of issues one might encounter, it is not really possible to plan a career as a planner. Unexpected and random elements will cross your path. So, open your mind, no matter what crosses: a helpless bee, a stable owner, or an innovative authority.

Stephanie Haury
Researcher at the Department for Urban Development at the Federal Institute for Research on Building, Urban Affairs, and Spatial Development (BBSR)

The world is urban. And yet the most dramatic shifts from rural to urban are happening in poorly understood and under-researched regions such as sub-Saharan Africa. To act as an urban designer in this environment of rapid urbanization driven by poverty and environmental devastation is to do more than to navigate complexity, uncertainty, and unpredictability – it requires a new theory of urbanization based on knowledge produced locally through critically evaluated design approaches, careful observation, critical thinking, and the exploitation of lessons learned. This will need lead to a new interpretation of the field of urban design, to a new definition of the role of the urban designer, and hence to new schools of urban design. This will lead to more locally and regionally specific definitions of urbanity such as African urbanity,

Fabienne Hoelzel
Chair of Urban Design, Stuttgart State Academy of Art and Design

Over the last ten thousand years, we have developed remarkable forms and spaces for human habitation: cities. Urbanity has always sought a balance between an artificially-created modern utopia and the recognition that the natural and societal conditions and surroundings of urban areas are an undeniable influence on the environmental and social climate they create within the city. Those who have created cities have had to learn that a city is never a final product, but an undetermined process of continuous creation. These complex systems, which is what cities are, confront us with the insight that we have limited influence on the built environment that we shaped ourselves. Urban design can help us to think in process-oriented, strategic ways that can shape the way to a sustainable urban future.

Alexander Jachnow
Head of Urban Strategies and Planning at Institute for Housing and Urban Development Studies (IHS) of Erasmus University Rotterdam

The term and concept of Radical Urbanism is commonly used in fields such as planning, human geography, sociology, and critical theory to describe a politically engaged interpretation of the built environment that seeks to achieve social justice. With a few exceptions, this critical discourse is largely absent from the field of architecture and urban design. What is therefore missing is a strong analytical and propositional position that provides answers to the question of how social justice can be spatially and materially manifested in architecture and the built environment. It is for this task that urban design education should train engaged urban practitioners who are able to address such social and spatial justice in their future praxis.

Florian Kossak
Senior Lecturer in Urban History, Theory, and Design at the School of Architecture at the University of Sheffield

The complexity of today's urban landscapes requires design practices that are able to find their way through the entangled and shifting conditions of those landscapes. In this sense, designing in urban landscapes can be compared with risky navigating in unknown waters. The metaphorical comparison with navigation emphasizes a tactile kind of design approach that is exploratory and adaptive and responds to the given conditions of dynamic urban landscapes.

This navigational understanding of design provides room for experimentation; to try out, to search for possibilities within the pre-existing, to pick up existing threads, and to (re-)configure them. This step-by-step approach to developing suitable options requires a reflexive approach to designing in which the design idea, the context, the individual step, and the whole inform each another in a series of feedback loops. In this process of understanding, developing ideas and negotiating an explorative mapping – as a practice of reading, understanding, interpreting, and negotiating complex spatial relationships – offer great potential for designing.

Sigrun Langner
Junior Professor for Landscape Architecture and Landscape Planning at Bauhaus University Weimar

Urban designers are facing unprecedented challenges. One is the speed and magnitude of urbanization in the global south. This not only overwhelms local governments, but also the inhabitants – not yet citizens – who are not familiar with people-centered urban settings, and therefore have little if any capacity to articulate their aspirations concerning the design of a truly urban environment.

At the same time, urban designers are challenged by what seems to be a shift from an open society model of the city towards that of the so-called smart city, focusing on the functionality of a city and in doing so masking a growing trend towards authoritarian governance concepts.

Now more than ever, future urban designers need to be trained to analyze the political-societal context they are working in and to be aware of their own values as fundamentals for their future urban work.

Günter Meinert
Deutsche Gesellschaft für Internationale Zusammenarbeit (GIZ)

Cities are so much more than just a single spot on the globe – they are a whole universe of individual and collective perspectives and perceptions, of spaces and places, of memory and history, of action and lives. Is there a science to deal with this variety of human-to-space interaction? Urban design as an integrative approach, covering a range of spatial as well as socio-scientific disciplines and skills as taught at TU Berlin, seems to be the way forward. We need specialists trained to tackle problems on different scales, using multi-faceted approaches, tools, and methods, bringing in their profound knowledge and experience from cities all over the world. As the head of the urban planning department of a growing European metropolis, I can say that this is what we will increasingly need to govern urban settings and societies. This is what we expect from professionals in administration, architecture, and planning. This is how urban planning will be successful in providing environments and solutions for the future of urban life.

Elisabeth Merk
City Planning Councilor of Munich; President of the German Academy Städtebau und Landesplanung (DASL)

Today's challenges of urbanization are too complex to be adequately understood and addressed within the confines of traditionally bounded disciplines. They are also too important, too extensive, and too pressing to not take risks and challenge existing ways of doing things. In addition, it is time to do away with some inconvenient truths: this involves recognizing that we cannot simply design our way out of the world's current predicaments, and that urban design in practice, like all built environment professions, is often part of the problem rather than the solution. For this to change, we need to engage students to engage: to engage with the social purpose of urban design, as well as with the social context of its production and the roots of the problems it is trying to solve. Doing so won't guarantee that urban design's transformative potential is realized. But it ensures that students have the chance to make an informed choice on whether they wish to conform to or challenge the dominant logics of built-environment production.

Johannes Novy
Urbanist / Researcher at the School for Architecture and Cities at the University of Westminster

More than ever, urban and regional development are confronted with the consequences of worldwide changes. The planning disciplines are facing new challenges due to the increase of complexity while resources remain limited: how can we develop neighborhoods, cities, and regions in a spirit of collaboration? How should processes that connect spatial design to stakeholders' interests and their societal, economic, and environmental dynamics be designed? Which strategies and methods enable us to utilize the ideas and talents of many to design viable visions for the future? For too long, we counted on "genius" designs and an explicit authorship to reduce complexity and to create orientation in an unmanageable world only by "good composition."

Urban design is the key to an extended practice of space production, which includes the actors and driving forces in the designing of changing environments. Urban design does not attempt to domesticate complexity; it forms it into material for a new world.

Klaus Overmeyer
Chair for Landscape Architecture at the Bergische University in Wuppertal and Executive Partner at Urban Catalyst in Berlin

When more than half of the world's population lives in cities, a percentage that will increase to seventy percent by 2050, we can indeed state that the city is the locus of the biggest social and environmental challenges today. But also, I would say, of hope. Therefore, we need to recognize that the city is too important ontologically to be designed only by urban specialists and political decision-makers. It needs to be co-designed by those who live and work in it, as our common survival depends on the process of co-designing. The city has become the main site of social (re)production today and must recognized as such. The enormous social capital located in cities around the world needs to be activated, and the role of urban designers today is to enable this activation and to provide tools for it. Urban design should become design everyone can take part in: a field of co-produced experimentation and innovation that will help us to face the unpredictability of our future together.

Doina Petrescu
Chair of Architecture and Design Activism at the School of Architecture Sheffield University; Founding member of the planning network aaa: atelier d'architecture autogerée in Paris

How might the practice of urban design contribute to the proliferation of alternatives to current mainstream development paths? Urban design has the mission of advancing sustainable development; i.e. to envision, build, and transform cities and regions as resilient habitats for the future. Urban design also faces a dilemma; it necessarily complies with market forces, and often contributes to, rather than prevents, spatial and environmental injustice and uneven development.

Nevertheless, urban design is well-equipped to support an inclusive urbanism. As an inter- and transdisciplinary field combining experiential knowledge, generative design practice, and critical theoretical discourse, it may make education promoting sustainable development an important concern for a multitude of actors. For urban designers this requires the development of sustainable skill-sets based on intersectional perspectives of power analysis and an ethical orientation to practice that takes into account materialisms, situatedness, and civic organization as transforming agencies for an inclusive urban design practice.

Maike Schalk
Associate Professor of Urban Studies and Urban Theory at KTH School of Architecture and Head of Research Education at the School of Architecture

Complex urban challenges can only be addressed through integrated cross-disciplinary approaches. We may be sure of that!! But the tragic thing is that, as a result of our education, we are unconsciously inclined to a mostly technical or – at best – social framing of urban problems. But real, lasting solutions also need to occupy a central place within both planning teams and education in the life sciences. Landscape architects could fill this gap, and/or be intermediaries offering a bridge to this part of the scientific spectrum. Engineering needs to be redefined as working with natural processes to shape an urban environment that is not only nature-inclusive for educational purposes but is resilient to issues such as urban heat islands and flooding events. Broadly speaking, the regions of the planet where urbanization will be growing exponentially happen to coincide with the world's biodiversity hotspots. If this process is unmediated, it will lead to a head-on collision between the two.

Dirk Sijmons
Landscape Architect and Curator of IABR—2014—Urban-by-Nature

Urban design attempts to integrate the different scales of the built environment, considering the needs of the people, the individual buildings, the neighborhood, and the city in which these are situated. The heterogeneous complexity of resolving these elements demands a transdisciplinary approach that dissolves boundaries between the siloed professions and allows for genuine evolutionary co-production not only between members of the design team, but including the communities they are working with. Each design team should commit to a Hippocratic oath of doing no harm through their work. Understanding what is harmful and what is helpful requires not only new professional active listening skills to respond to the needs of communities and the environment, but also new professional values that are more ethical and more responsible. These new skills and values are best taught at the primary stage of professional education and honed through practice.

Fionn Stevenson
Chair of Sustainable Design at the School of Architecture at the University of Sheffield

We are leaving a period in which the state was responsible for most of what we call urban development. The next period may be one in which responsibility for the city is more decentralized. As such, planning processes will become more complex and confusing – however, I don't see that as a problem. It gives us the opportunity to shape these processes in a more open, less focused way, with more potential access for new actors.

If everyone can be a city-maker, the roles of urban designers, citizens, and businesspeople will become increasingly intertwined. This will require new skills of future urban planners: a post-heroic attitude, transversal thinking, an understanding of planning as non-planning, the ability to be surprised, to love the suboptimal, to live with the temporary...

I'm looking forward to seeing a new generation of urban designers!

Stephan Willinger
Researcher at Department for Urban Development at the Federal Institute for Research on Building, Urban Affairs, and Spatial Development (BBSR)

As cities are growing at a vertiginous pace, our urban world is becoming more and more multi-dimensional and interwoven. Many different dimensions interlace here, resulting in a sometimes-confusing composition of diverse issues to consider and complicated challenges to address. Hence, it sometimes might feel that it will take more than an urbanist's lifetime to fully understand these intricacies and to find appropriate responses to sustainable urban development that take into consideration all relevant sectorial issues and respective governance dimensions. However, this stands in extreme contrast to the urgency of many problems and the need of direct action. Consequently, urban designers and planners need to deal with this dilemma and find ways to handle both multi-dimensionality and urgency at the same time. University education related to urban development such as the master's program in Urban Design at TU Berlin has a crucial role in preparing future urban designers and planners for these challenges ahead by developing innovative skills to efficiently assess complex situations in order to quickly develop effective solutions. In this context, it is crucial to find a manageable balance between time-intensive comprehensiveness and pragmatic action in order to develop and maintain the ability to act in today's urban complexities.

Carsten Zehner
Urban and regional planner and consultant to international urban development organizations such as Deutsche Gesellschaft für Internationale Zusammenarbeit (GIZ)

To deal with the challenges associated with informatization and globalization over the past decades, urban design requires knowledge from across different disciplines and specializations in architecture, ecological environment, economic development, social equity, cultural diversity, historic continuity, and human experience. To this end, our urban design program must build on our existing strengths in physical design and planning, and include the following three critical aims:

Encourage interdisciplinary research as well as architecture practice in the field;

Design, build, and advocate for affordable, adaptive, and inclusive neighborhoods and social, sustainable cities;

Develop new modes of professional intervention – not only in spatial design, but also as a communication model and sharing paradigm.

Our moral vision is translated into professional education in a distinct way:

We do not expect students to absorb all urban knowledge, but instead emphasize training skills for independent analysis and problem solving;

We believe *People to People* is a positive approach to both urban design practice and education.

Li Zhenyu
Dean of the College of Architecture and Urban Planning (CAUP), Tongji University Shanghai

We need urban design studies! Many local and regional governments are pioneering integrated urban development, spearheading SDG implementation, and setting themselves ambitious targets for climate, mobility, inclusivity, and more. They need science and research to help them understand their challenges and opportunities for action, as well as how to deal with conflicting priorities and goals. They also need committed and well-educated young staff for whom urban sustainability is both a passion and a responsibility. As the roles and tasks of local governments evolve from implementing to forming, designing, and moderating, their employees' new skill sets are indispensable. Cooperation between people, departments, officials, and stakeholders, as well as integrated thinking and cross-cutting approaches to urban needs instead of single-theme policies, define the requirements of tomorrow.

Monika Zimmermann
Freelance expert, moderator, former Deputy Secretary General of ICLEI – Local Governments for Sustainability

#A.4

working across geographical boundaries: reflecting on sino-german cooperation in urban design

In 2018, the College of Architecture and Urban Planning (CAUP) at Tongji University and the Institute of Architecture at Technische Universität Berlin marked twelve years of close cooperation through the framework of the Urban Design Dual Degree program. Philipp Misselwitz (TU Berlin) asked four colleagues from CAUP – Professor Li Zhenyu (Dean), Professor Cai Yongjie (Head of the Architecture Faculty), Professor Yang Guiqing (Head of the Urban Planning Department) and Professor Han Feng (Head of Landscape Architecture) – to reflect on the program, on how it responds to changing urbanization contexts and challenges in China, and on what added value cooperation with Germany offers the College.

Philipp Misselwitz: What motivated you to set up the Urban Design Dual Degree program between TU Berlin and Tongji University?

Li Zhenyu: Germany is one of the birthplaces of modernist architecture, with a diverse and rich architectural culture. Especially when it comes to urban regeneration and high-quality living, as well as in the multi-use development of the city, there are many places worth learning from by China. China and Germany demonstrate both similar and different developments in architectural culture. Comparison and cooperation are particularly valuable. My first exposure to Germany was as a doctoral researcher at the Habitat Unit at TU Berlin between 1999 and 2001 under the supervision of Professor emeritus Dr. Peter Herrle. It was a great opportunity to revive the close link between Tongji University and TU Berlin, which dates back to the early twentieth century, and that's how the idea to build on this tradition and set up a Dual Degree program developed after I returned to China. We managed to obtain a generous starter grant from the DAAD and were able to admit the first cohort in 2006. The same year also marked the beginning of the Anting New Town project in Shanghai. Looking back now after twelve years, I think that German and Chinese design cooperation in practice benefitted hugely from a more structured cooperation between teaching institutions – and that perhaps some of the decisions made in Anting would now be made differently. In addition to offering design studios and master's thesis supervision, I myself have contributed to the curriculum by offering a course called Comparative Study of Architecture in Germany and China. The course is popular with Chinese international students, and thanks to the double-degree program, the discussions in class involve students from both countries and are therefore very interesting. I am proud to say that an entire generation of double-degree graduates can now demonstrate their abilities in various fields, especially in the areas of urban design, urban regeneration, and multi-innovation. To me, as well as to my Chinese and German colleagues, that is the most gratifying result.

Philipp Misselwitz: Today, more than twelve years after the program was established, China has changed dramatically. Can you describe the urbanization context then and now? From your professional perspective, what has changes in China in the last twelve years?

Li Zhenyu: When our Dual Degree program started in 2006, architecture and urban planning were already well-established programs in China. In the field of urban design, however, we were lacking in experience in research and practice. Since then, the urban design field has become more and more important and helps us on both sides –

in both China and Germany – to rethink how we transform our cities.

Cai Yongjie: The biggest change in the last years is a shift in focus: from the development of new greenfield sites to the regeneration of existing urban stock. The time of the massive construction of new towns and of reconstruction in old towns is over. Instead of "demolish, revise, and reserve," the new topic in urbanization is "reserve, revise, and demolish." We have to respond to these changing tasks and challenges through our teaching.

Philipp Misselwitz: How has the field of practice of architecture, urban planning, or landscape architecture changed in light of these new tasks?

Li Zhenyu: The practice of architecture and urban planning in China has clearly begun to embrace the new challenges of the transformation of existing Chinese cities. Over the last decade, professional practice, institutions, and firms have been gradually transferring from a "research for design" to a "research by design" approach – a new trend of "practice-driven research." Through this shift we can more deeply explore the architectural and urban problems of contemporary China.

Cai Yongjie: The tasks for architects and planners are clearly becoming much more comprehensive. Designers are now confronted with diverse new trends such as ecological and social challenges, questions of regional cultural identity, or the development of new technology related to digitalization or artificial intelligence. In the field of practice, the reuse of existing buildings and the regeneration of cities require a different kind of design knowledge. The big challenge for all participants is being prepared to change habits and learn new things.

Yang Guiqing: China's rapid urbanization and development process radically changed the urban and rural built environment. In particular, the construction of high-speed railways and highways has brought about convenient regional transportation links and the increased frequency of regional population movements, which has brought unprecedented development opportunities for the economic and social development of towns and villages in various regions of China. Changes in the socio-economic structure have, on the one hand, promoted the upgrading of urbanization in developed regions. On the other hand, the population loss in economically backward regions has been severe, leading to regional imbalances. The main challenges faced by urban planning practitioners are to construct systematic planning thinking, to understand and grasp the objective laws of their development as they apply to the ever-changing urban and rural environment, and to make their developments sustainable through appropriate planning interventions. At the moment, the main challenge is to reduce and eliminate regional development imbalances by treating cities and villages as an interrelated whole.

Han Feng: For landscape architecture, one of the most important tendencies has been the rise of landscape urbanism. The Chinese central government's "Eco-civilization Construction" and "Beautiful China" policies demanded new environmental ethics. Natural values, including associative spiritual and intrinsic values and environmental justice, are now to be considered in the urban environment after having been largely ignored during the fast-track urbanization of China over the past decades. The importance of a harmonious human-nature relationship will make landscape architecture play a much more important role in urbanization discourses in the future.

Philipp Misselwitz: How do you see the field for urban professionals evolving in China in the future? What are the key challenges to be addressed from now until 2030?

Li Zhenyu: In 2017, the State Council approved the "Shanghai Urban Master Plan (2017–2035)," which clarifies the overall goals, development models, spatial patterns, specific development tasks, and initiatives for Shanghai until 2035, as well as providing a long-term outlook towards 2050. By 2035, the resident population of Shanghai will be controlled at around 25 million, and the total scale of construction land will not exceed 3,200 square kilometers. Building targets should be in line with three aspects – "City of Innovation, City of Humanities, City of Ecology."

Cai Yongjie: There is still a lot to do. The urban development is far from being accomplished, especially in terms of an upgrade in quality. Redefining the urban quality could be one of the key points for the next years. Returning to the "Chineseness" of modern Chinese cities should be the common element throughout all such points.

Yang Guiqing: The urban and rural development environment facing China's urban planning professionals is complex and dependent on China's national conditions. Unbalanced and inadequate regional development requires us to adapt to the local conditions, combine theory with practice, and find and refine the urban and rural planning theories and methods with Chinese characteristics through practice. By 2030, urban planning will focus more on the quality of the built environment and more on the human scale. More attention will need to be given to urban planning from social, justice, humanistic, and local perspectives.

Han Feng: The human–nature relationship has been and always will be the central theme for landscape architecture. In the last decades, landscape architecture has been undervalued in urban planning and development in China. However, I believe this will dramatically change in the forthcoming decade, as restoration of the human–nature relationship is key for China. Meanwhile, however, great challenges remain for all of us. Firstly, we need to understand the importance of Chinese historical legacies, including traditional wisdom about the human–nature relationship. Then we need to apply this to create not only healthy environments, but also high-quality and poetic ones. Secondly, we need interdisciplinary knowledge to understand cultural, natural, social, environmental, and economic contexts and to work towards inclusive planning and design.

Philipp Misselwitz: In what way does the Urban Design Dual Degree program – an interdisciplinary course linking architecture, urban planning, landscape architecture, and urban-oriented social science – help to prepare young professionals for these challenges?

Li Zhenyu: In the twelve years of our Dual Degree program, 218 students have graduated with a double degree from Tongji and TU Berlin. This is a huge achievement. I would like to cite three aspects that help prepare our students. First of all, there is talent development. There are a lot of talented students who have graduated from the Tongji–TU Berlin program. Many of them already exert influence on urban design and architecture practice from within their jobs. For the Chinese students who graduate from our program, the overseas study experience has a great and positive influence. Secondly, career paths have changed and have become more varied. Our 218 alumni are now working in a changing and expanding field of practice, ranging from urban design to architectural practice. Thirdly, I would like to point out the reputation of the program, which is regularly considered to be the most popular program for students to apply to from within CAUP.

Cai Yongjie: One of the characteristics of our Dual Degree program is interdisciplinarity, which helps young professionals to understand urban complexities through different disciplinary lenses.

Yang Guiqing: The program provides students with a cross-cultural perspective, particularly through case studies and learning, and through providing an understanding of how to deal with urban and rural issues across different cultures, different systems, and different stages of development. This enables our students to have an international outlook, a sense of judgment during the economic and social development stages, and a clear understanding of the characteristics of each stage of development. In short, learning from vivid and excellent cases can develop our students' planning thinking.

Han Feng: The dual degree students have the advantage of investigating their research questions in different cultural, social, and economic contexts, and greatly benefit from comparative case studies. This also enables our students to respect other cultures and ethics, which I think is very important for them when stepping into society in the future.

Philipp Misselwitz: What are the potentials and limits of interdisciplinarity in education and practice?

Li Zhenyu: For students, different professional backgrounds both influence and restrict interdisciplinarity in education and practice. There are Tongji CAUP students from architecture, urban planning, and landscape architecture backgrounds, and even some TU-Berlin student with backgrounds in the social sciences. This helps to promote a stronger intersection of the disciplines in research and design.

Cai Yongjie: The potential is to cultivate a wide horizon, which is very important when facing our changing world and uncertain futures. The limits are present in our own program; there is a question of how to get the balance between skills training on the one hand, and expanding students' views on the other. That is a challenge.

Han Feng: I think working with an interdisciplinary team when designing or planning is the best way to expand our knowledge. There are a limited number of courses and credits and it is impossible to teach everything in our coursework. Letting students have the opportunity to work with the other disciplines, as well as the ability to bring in interdisciplinary knowledge and break barriers within the program, is extremely important.

Philipp Misselwitz: Chinese and German urbanization contexts are very different. In what way do you think students benefit from the exchange in the program?

Li Zhenyu: Exchanges between different cultures clearly open up students' horizons.

Cai Yongjie: Many years ago, when I still studied and worked in Germany, I noticed great similarity between the urban development of China and the Western world: the only difference is that Chinese urbanization came more than a century later. That means we can learn from international experience. But it is not easy. The challenge is to transform this experience into knowledge that can be absorbed by the Chinese context.

Yang Guiqing: China and Germany have different urbanization characteristics. Students can learn from the different urban and rural planning and construction approaches. There are two aspects to this: one involves learning methodology, research methods and planning methods, learning how to find, define, and solve problems, and learning how to propose targeted and creative solutions. The other is the study of operational methods, mainly based on the analysis of actual cases, to understand the entire process of planning, planning, design, implementation, and operation management for the project, including relevant government and legal support.

Han Feng: Because of such differences, there is both a great opportunity and a great need for research. Germany has been urbanized, and China is being urbanized as we speak. The two countries' urbanization processes have many things in common, but there are also differences. Comparative research will allow us to understand the context-based processes of urbanization and deduce appropriate solutions and policies for our own urbanization transition.

Philipp Misselwitz: What can Germany and Europe learn from Chinese architecture and urbanization processes? What can China learn from Germany?

Li Zhenyu: In the 1990s, there was a book published in China called *German Architecture Culture in China*.[1] There are many German architects working in China and many Chinese architects trying to practice in Europe. They definitely learn from each other and promote the transfer from both sides.

Cai Yongjie: In fact, we have already been learning from each other. The Chinese urbanization process could not be successful if we did not absorb experience from the West. Even the Chinese system of education for architecture came from the West. In the Dual Degree program, I observed an obvious difference between Chinese and German students. The Chinese students are diligent and solid, while the German students sometimes have a more critical perspective. We are different! That is why we can and need to cooperate. I believe we have benefited a lot from this cooperation over the past years. In general, I would like to say that China could learn the methodological skills needed for a careful urbanization process from Germany. Conversely, Germany could learn from some of China's flexibility and pragmatism.

Yang Guiqing: Europe and China are at different stages of urban and rural development and have different historical cultures and social systems.

Therefore, the difference between the two is relatively large. Perhaps the difference itself is the source of what we can learn. Seeking common ground while preserving differences, as well as the mutual exchange of technology and culture, should be the most immediate element of mutual learning.

Han Feng: First of all, we should understand each other. Both countries' management and legislative systems for urban processes are complex and require a sincere willingness and effort to understand. In the Dual Degree program, on-site observation and reflection often represent the best way to understand and exchange views and information. Only by making the effort to build a foundation of understanding will we discover what we can learn from each other.

Endnotes

1 Warner, Torten (1994) **Deutsche Architektur in China**. Ernst & Sohn

A profile page introduces each tool before its description and sources are presented. The upper part of this page is occupied by the title, subtitle, and a reference number, which helps you locate the paper within the publication.

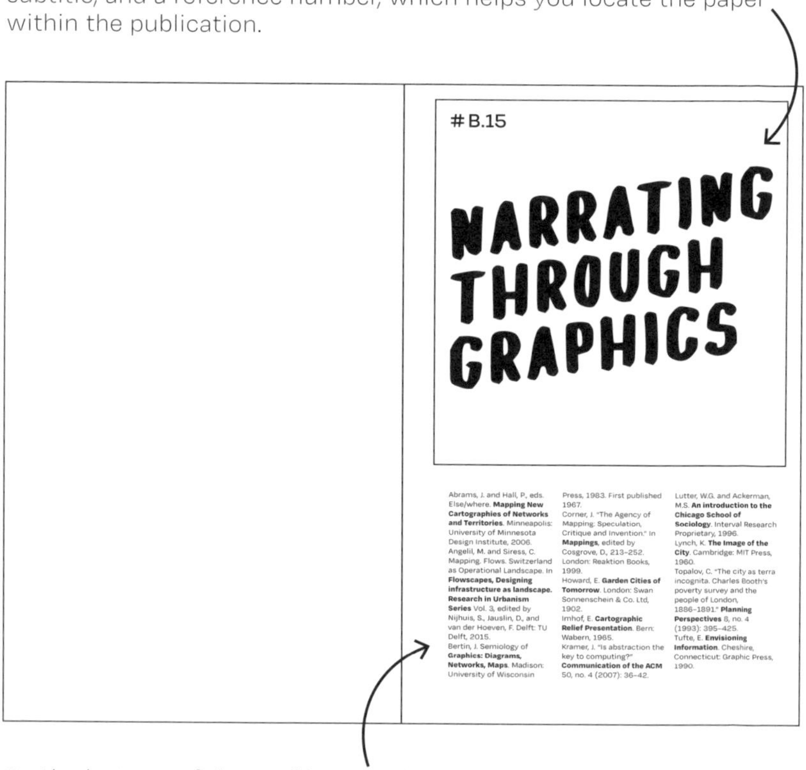

On the bottom of the profile page there are some recommended readings, which may be digital or analog in nature.

B.0

how to read this book

The tools are explained through a main text (top) and a reference text (bottom). At the top of the page, you will find more general information – such as the definition of the tool and its applications.

Narrative graphics are tools for visually communicating complex information, ideas, systems, and networks to an audience in a simplified, accessible, and attractive manner. The goal is not to present the raw data itself, but to gather, organize, and reduce the data in order to provide concise insight and information about the topic. As Edward Tufte put it, "to envision information – and what bright and splendid visions can result – is to work at the intersection of image, word, number, art" (Tufte 1990, 9). This section focuses on visual representations of space and time as maps and diagrams in the field of urban design. It is also informed by the evolution of narrative graphics in their application in a broad array of related fields throughout the twentieth century.

Following the revision of key literature and the review of reference projects (among others, Bertin 1983; Tufte 1990; Abrams and Hall 2006) alongside the definition of narrative graphics above, five possible but by no means exhaustive categories

London Poverty Maps, Charles Booth, 1902[1]
A social investigation initiated by Charles Booth in 1886 resulted in a series of maps visualizing the extent and spatial distribution of poverty amongst the approximately six million inhabitants of the ever-expanding metropolis. The London Poverty Maps were published in several editions – the last in 1903 – and used survey data along with ethnographic observation to create a potent and precise image of social inequality. A palette of colors ranging from black to yellow was used to distinguish the different social classes, which were in turn associated with other attributes such as income, criminality (for example, the lowest class in black is further described as "vicious, semi-criminal"), health, and so on, creating a compelling narrative.

Boston Cognitive Mapping, Kevin Lynch, 1960[2]
American planner Kevin Lynch's famous graphics were developed as part of his wide-ranging study of the perception of urban form. They are best known for visualizing the theory of the five basic elements (paths, edges, districts, nodes, landmarks) which, according to Lynch, help urban dwellers form mental maps of their environment. It is important to understand, however, that these maps were not simply derived from a theoretical argument but were based on extensive field research, including site visits and interviews as well as oral descriptions and sketches from the residents themselves. The evocative power of the cognitive maps, therefore, lies in the

Imhof, E. (1962–1976) Mount Everest Map. Printed map of Mount Everest 1:100 000. From a Swiss secondary-school atlas.

combination of a theoretical, academic perspective with the insights of the public.

Mount Everest, Eduard Imhof, 1962[3]
Eduard Imhof's hand-drawn maps of mountainous regions explore the potential of cartography to illustrate the third dimension through the use of color and shading. Also noteworthy are his theoretical contributions to the aesthetics of cartography and his use of scientific as well as artistic arguments to explain the working process of drawing a map.

Autobahnplanung Oranienplatz, Fotomontage, Kohlmaier and von Sartory, 1969[4]
The iconic collage by architect Georg Kohmeier and artist Barna von Sartory is a critical commentary on postwar urban planning in Berlin, and specifically the planning principles of the car-friendly city. The existing, dense, and compact urban fabric was being razed to make place for new developments with little, if any, consultation of the residents. This collage juxtaposes a Los Angeles highway with an aerial image of Oranienplatz in Kreuzberg in order to demonstrate the scale and extent of demolition that a new planned highway would necessitate.

Facemap Toronto, Julie Bogdanovicz, 2013[5]
This map of Toronto focuses on social inequality between the three clearly distinguished classes of poor, middle class, and wealthy. The "three cities of

The text at the bottom is more dense. This section is dedicated to gaining a deeper knowledge of the tool and includes all manner of references, from books to real, existing projects and related planning strategies.

B.1

UNDER-STANDING SPATIAL PRACTICES

Benze, A. **Alltagsorte in der Stadtregion. Atlas experimenteller Kartographie**. Berlin: Reimer, 2012.
Gehl, J. and Svarre, B. **How to Study Public Life**. Washington: Island Press, 2013.
Latour, B. and Hermant, E. **Paris: Invisible City**. [Online]. Available from http://bruno-latour.fr/virtual/EN/index.html. 2004. Accessed: July 5, 2015.
Marcus. C., and Francis, C. **People Places: Design Guidelines for Urban Open Space**. New York: John Wiley & Sons, 1998.
Paans, O and Pasel R. **Situational Urbanism. Directing Post-War Urbanity: An Adaptive Methodology for Urban Transformation**. Berlin: Jovis, 2014.
Read, S., ed. **Visualizing the Invisible: Towards an Urban Space**. Amsterdam: TechnePress, 2006.

Everyday reality and urban space intersect in spatial practice. Spatial practice both produces new space and is informed by the structure of existing space. An analysis of spatial practice entails investigating the movement patterns of everyday activities and their surrounding spatial and material conditions. The aim in doing this is to understand and represent everyday public life and people's everyday behavior. The analysis of spatial practices and everyday activities is mainly carried out when researching public space, everyday life, and their interrelations. This method aims to analyze people's practices in a specific location, excavating spatial, socioeconomic, and cultural dynamics with the goal of improving the environment for its users. Moreover, such an analysis helps designers improve their work and skills in general.

Spatial practice is applicable to different aspects of human life and is dependent on the spaces we act in, our individual experiences with space, and how we have learned to use it. Practices also differ and change depending on the people we share space with and the surrounding conditions. Different disciplines approach these aspects of spatial practice in various ways. In their project *Paris: Invisible City*, the French sociologists Bruno Latour and Emilie Hermant studied the social aspects of Paris in order to understand why a city cannot be captured at a glance (Latour and Hermant 2004). In the field of urban planning, Andrea Benze analyzed the structure and spatial situation of associations, their members, and their operations in urban regions in her book *Alltagsorte in der Stadtregion* (Benze 2012). In her public art project

Alltagsorte in der Stadtregion

For her dissertation *Alltagsorte in der Stadtregion*, Andrea Benze (2012) started with the general question of where people meet on an everyday basis in a metropolitan region – specifically, the urban region of Bitterfeld-Wolfen, Germany – and developed a detailed spatial practice analysis to answer it.
Benze used different methods to conduct and visualize her analysis: using interviews, photography, plans, mapping, pictograms, and drawings of details, she developed a cartographic atlas that illustrates characteristic situations, spaces, and objects, as well as intersections between physical space and social activity at various different scales.

How do pedestrians move at night?

This project focused on the question of how people move through urban space at night. The area around the Mehringplatz and the Hallesches Tor metro station in Kreuzberg, Berlin was used for the case study. The analysis was based on the assumption that people move differently at night than they do during the day. The analysis considered influencing factors such as illumination and boundaries and their effect on the movements of pedestrians. Over the course of an hour on a winter's evening, the movements of twenty randomly selected individuals were tracked on exiting from Hallesches Tor metro station. The analysis resulted in several maps that can be layered and

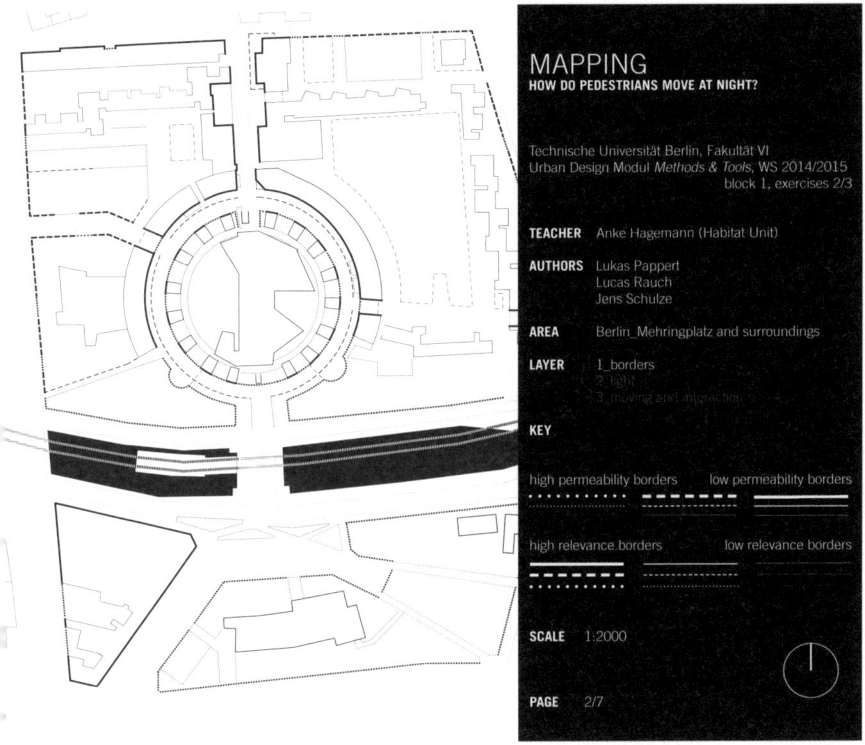

Lukas Pappert, Lucas Rauch, Jens Schulze (2015) **Mapping: How do pedestrians move at night?**

separately show the illumination, pedestrian movements, and boundaries of the case study area. A number of lines differentiated by intensity and style – continuous, dashed, and dotted – were used to represent pedestrian movements, simulating their speed and direction. Lines were further used to represent different boundaries (diffuse, strong, etc.). By contrast, illumination was visualized with solid dots indicating various intensities of light and dotted circles showing illuminated areas. The denser the dots appear on the map, the more illumination was present. The lines of movement are colored, with visualization of the other aspects shown in monochrome to direct attention to the key question.

Combining the layers delivers insights into movement patterns at a certain time of day. In this night-time case study, research has shown that the people observed took the shortest and most direct route. They preferred moving in illuminated areas close to shops, cafés, and lamps over dark areas. The darker and emptier the area, the faster pedestrians generally walked. The analysis seems to have identified two main aspects that play a considerable role in the way people move through urban spaces at night: on the one hand, "perceived safety" is a crucial determinant of movement. On the other hand, the usability of urban space in terms of functionality is evident (e.g., shortcuts are taken).

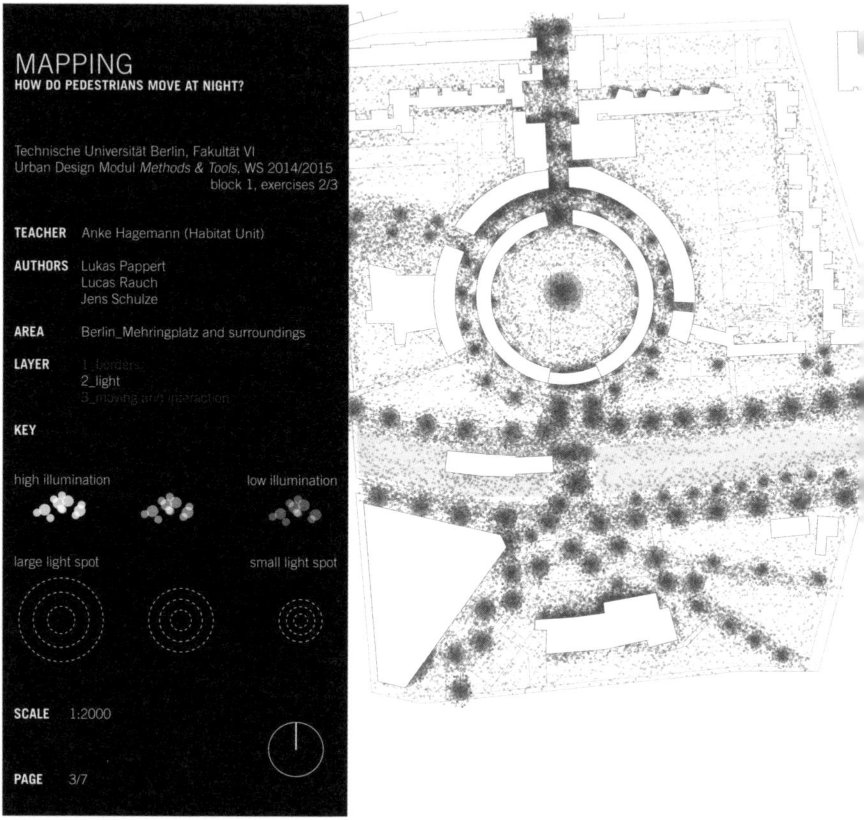

Lukas Pappert, Lucas Rauch, Jens Schulze (2015) **Mapping: How do pedestrians move at night?**

People Places

In the book *People Places: Design Guidelines for Urban Open Space*, the authors use observation to evaluate different public open spaces in the city, as Jan Gehl did in most of his case studies. Gehl examined activities on residential streets and plotted them according to type of activity, including exclusively social actions such as greeting others. Comparing a street with more dwellings and more clearly defined front yards with a street with fewer dwellings and open lawns clearly showed that more social activities took place on the street with front yards.

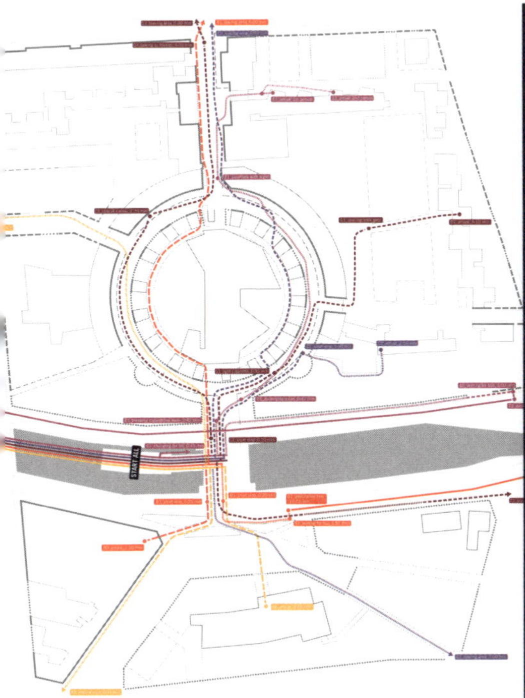

MAPPING
HOW DO PEDESTRIANS MOVE AT NIGHT?

Technische Universität Berlin, Fakultät VI
Urban Design Modul *Methods & Tools*, WS 2014/2015
block 1, exercises 2/3

TEACHER Anke Hagemann (Habitat Unit)

AUTHORS Lukas Pappert
Lucas Rauch
Jens Schulze

AREA Berlin_Mehringplatz and surroundings

LAYER 1_borders
2_light
3_moving and interaction

KEY

walking pace

slow
average
fast
public transportation

individuals (U1 arrival at station Hallesches Tor)

A_19:06
B_19:16
C_19:31
D_19:36
E_19:46

SCALE 1:2000

PAGE 4/7

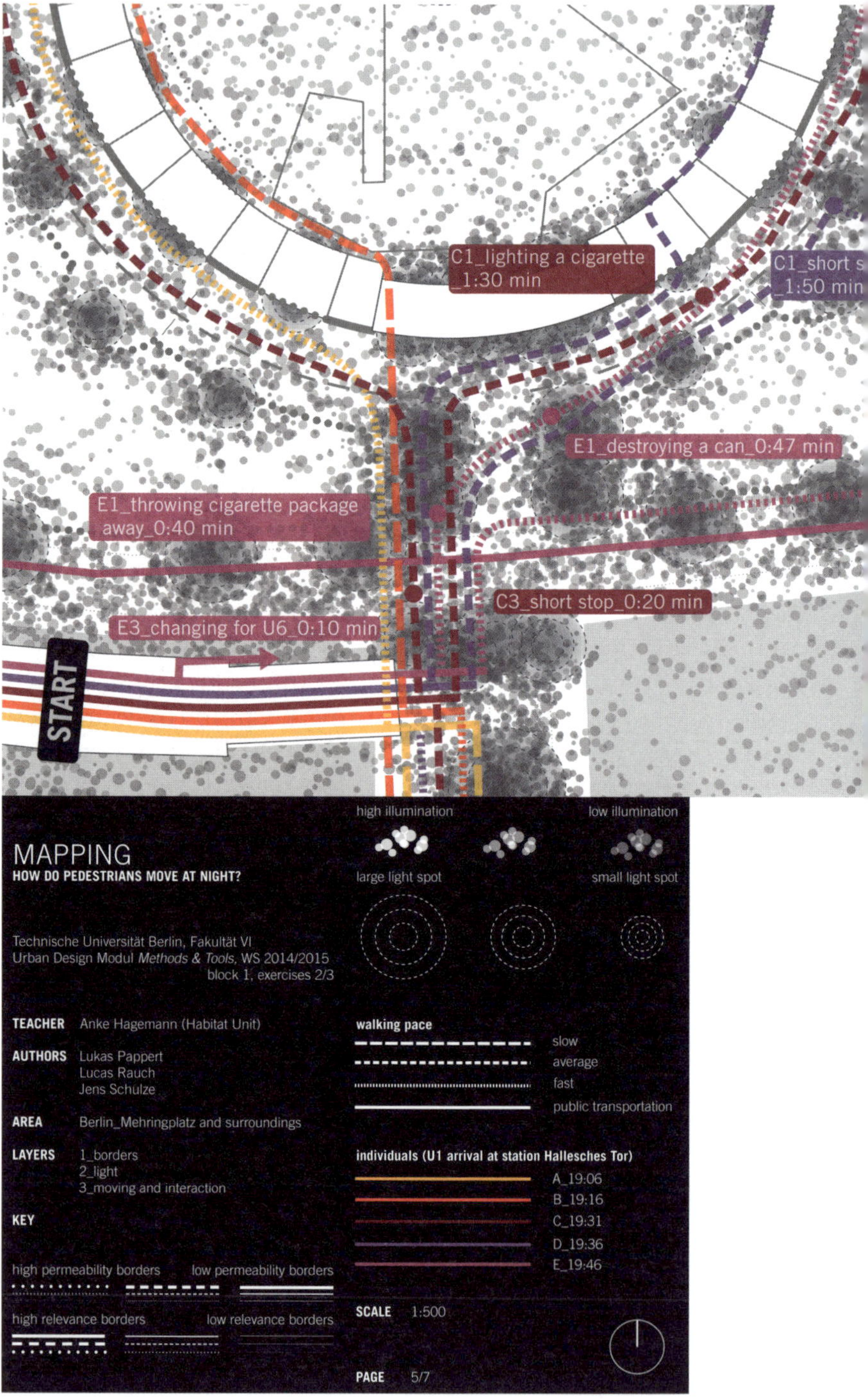

MAPPING

HOW DO PEDESTRIANS MOVE AT NIGHT?

Technische Universität Berlin, Fakultät VI
Urban Design Modul *Methods & Tools*, WS 2014/2015
block 1, exercises 2/3

TEACHER Anke Hagemann (Habitat Unit)

AUTHORS Lukas Pappert
Lucas Rauch
Jens Schulze

AREA Berlin_Mehringplatz and surroundings

LAYERS 1_borders
2_light
3_moving and interaction

KEY

high permeability borders — low permeability borders

high relevance borders — low relevance borders

high illumination — low illumination

large light spot — small light spot

walking pace

slow
average
fast
public transportation

individuals (U1 arrival at station Hallesches Tor)

A_19:06
B_19:16
C_19:31
D_19:36
E_19:46

SCALE 1:500

PAGE 5/7

Mapping Manhattan (2013), Becky Cooper asked New Yorkers to map their memories related to Manhattan on maps she had prepared.

These different approaches to spatial practice analysis focus on different aspects of human and social behavior. Andrea Benze (2012) looked for the everyday places where people meet in urban regions in order to disprove the perception of urban regions as being faceless and empty. By contrast, Bruno Latour and Emilie Hermant examined "the nature of the social link and the very particular ways in which society remains elusive" (Latour and Hermant 2004). Becky Cooper searched for a way to make invisible cities visible and to preserve the lives that have been lived in a city through an artistic approach. Numerous other approaches are possible: for example, investigating the acceptance of design in daily use or the functionality of certain spaces.

Various approaches to analyzing spatial practice have been used for different studies. The choice of methods is based on the topic of investigation and the author's skills and background, and may include methods such as observation, tracking movements, looking for traces of use, field mapping, interviews, photography, counting people, video/audio recording, keeping a diary, and test walks. To study people's activities, we may choose interviews and observation. To find out how people use a place, we may choose to combine multiple methods, such as video or audio recording and counting visitors to the location. At different stages of the spatial analysis, different methods may be used. The process

Lukas Pappert, Lucas Rauch, Jens Schulze (2015) **Mapping: How do pedestrians move at night?**

usually begins with identifying the field research methods that are key to the analysis of spatial practice (Gehl 2013). This can be carried out in different ways. Field research can be done merely through observation, but it is helpful to use simple tools – such as, for example, a pen and a notebook or a camera. The aim is to explore human behavior, interactions, or movements as they pertain to the observed space. External circumstances such as the time of day, weather, and so on should always be noted. After collecting the data, the findings are analyzed. Here, the method of space syntax is helpful in doing this (Read 2006). Furthermore, field mappings are helpful to show the space's structure. In their book *Situational Urbanism* (Paans and Pasel 2014), the authors used different master mappings to show different layers in public space.

The strength of this methodology is the analysis of the close relationship of people's everyday life and activities to a certain place. The results are useful for developing an environment based on human needs: a vivid and dynamic public space. However, there are also limitations: Firstly, field research usually requires a lot of time and labor. Secondly, the data is easily affected by factors such as weather conditions or special events.

This text is based on the writing of Pauline Bruckner and Ying Li and was edited by Anke Hagemann and Christian Haid.

#B.2

DIA-GRAMMATIC SKETCHING

Do, E.Y.-L. "Computability of Design Diagrams. An Empirical Study of Diagram Conventions in Design." In **CAADFutures 1997. Proceedings of the 7th International Conference on Computer Aided Architectural Design Futures**, 171–176. Dordrecht: Kluwer Academic Publishers, 1997.

Do, E.Y.-L. and Gross, M.D. "Thinking with Diagrams in Architectural Design." **Artificial Intelligence Review** 15 (2001): 135–149.

Dovey, K. and Pafka, E. "The Science of Urban Design?" **Urban Design International** 21 (2016): 1–10.

Gänshirt, C. **Tools for Ideas. An Introduction to Architectural Design**. Basel: Birkhäuser, 2007.

Goldschmidt, G. "The Dialectics of Sketching." **Creative Research Journal** 4 (1991): 123–143.

Kazmierczak, E.T. "Design as Meaning Making. From Making Things to the Design of Thinking." **Design Issues** 19, issue 2 (2003): 45–59.

Laseau, P. **Graphic Thinking for Architects and Designers**. Hoboken: John Wiley & Sons, 2001.

Pyo, M. **Architectural Diagrams 1. Construction and Design Manual**. Berlin: DOM Publishers, 2015.

Schön, D.A. "Designing. Rules, Types and Words." **Design Studies** 9 (1988): 181–190.

Tversky, B. "Visualizing Thought." **Topics in Cognitive Science** 3 (2011): 499–535.

Diagrammatic sketching is a common design tool in architecture and urban design, and is most often applied at the very beginning of the design process. Done by freehand drawing and using geometric elements, lines, and labels to abstractly describe phenomena as well as spatial relationships and flows (Do and Gross 2001, 3), it helps the the designer approach a spatial and programmatic task. This type of sketch "is made of symbols and is about concepts" (Do and Gross 2001, 3) and is not the same as the architectural sketch employed to generate a three-dimensional form. The latter "is about spatial form. It is executed with a finer resolution that indicates attributes of shape. A sketch (architectural) often comprises repetitive, overtraced lines made to explore precise shape, rather than the intentionally abstract shapes of a diagram, and it uses graphic modifiers such as tone and hatching to convey additional information," (Do and Gross 2001, 3–4).

The use of abstract, detail-omitting graphical elements assists the designer not only in solving spatial problems but also maybe even more importantly, to break down the complexity of the problem in order to grasp it. As Pyo explains, the complexity architects and urban designers face grows with the "increase in information and desires of the city, where architecture is the design subject" (2015, 10). As a visual thinking aid, diagrammatic sketching allows a number of ideas and thoughts to exist simultaneously and visually, and diagrammatic sketches are most often employed by architects as "early efforts to explore and resolve spatial layout concerns" (Do and Gross 2001, 2) – distinct from

Computability of Design Diagrams, Ellen Yi-Luen Do, 1997
Computability of Design Diagrams. An Empirical Study of Diagram Conventions in Design
Project Type 04: Scientific Study
Format: Experiment and Paper
Author: Ellen Yi-Luen Do
Year: 1997
Institution: College of Architecture, Georgia Institute of Technology, Atlanta

An empirical study about whether designers use shared drawing conventions when designing was conducted by Ellen Yi-Luen Do in 1997. In one part of the study, three designers (one instructor and two students) were asked to design an architect's office with a range of functions – workspace, CAD operations room, meeting room, bathroom, etc. This was broken down into four subtasks with distinct emphases: first planning the spatial layout, followed by addressing lighting concerns, then tackling visual access and privacy issues, and finally fitting a large meeting table into a conference room.
The experiment identified that designers shared universal graphic symbols and drawing conventions when designing (lines, arrows, simple geometric shapes, keywords for understanding the design), and that they preferred to use certain "views," such as plans and sections.

Impromptu Design Exercise at the Ernst-Reuter-Platz, Katrin Beyer and Timo Hartmann, 2016
Testing the Universality of Graphic Language of

descriptive sketches of existing or proposed building forms. Additionally, diagrammatic sketches "facilitate the designer's reflection, dialogue, and self-critique" (Do and Gross 2001, 8) through the designer's interaction with the drawings, thus also influencing their response to the spatial problem and design.

Diagrammatic Sketching as a Language

Diagrammatic sketching can be understood as a type of language, as it is used by designers to communicate ideas with others and to visually examine problems themselves. Inherent to it are fundamental elements equivalent to the vocabulary, grammar, and sentence structure of spoken language, and like the formation of meaningful sentences, diagramming takes place "on a mental plane of thought-shaping, and on the material plane of its sensory (external) counterpart," (Kazmierczak 2003, 51).

In several empirical studies, Schön (1988), Goldschmidt (1991), and Do (1997) refer to diagrammatic sketching as an interactive and complex act. Schön (1988) describes the design process as alternating between "seeing" and "moving," which can be related to Goldschmidt's (1991) approach of "oscillating arguments" in a rhythm of "seeing as" and "seeing that" which moves the design process forward, similar to the rules of a verbal discussion. "Design brings into existence mental diagrams of our conceptualizations about objects and events" (Kazmierczak 2003, 51). However, compared to the sequential structure of verbal language, graphic language contains simultaneity, which is an

Diagrammatic Sketching. Impromptu Design Exercise at Ernst-Reuter-Platz.
Project Type 04: Repetition of Scientific Experiment
Format: Design Exercise
Author: Katrin Beyer and Timo Hartmann
Year: 2016
Institution: Technical University Berlin

To test for themselves whether the graphic language employed in diagrammatic sketching is universal, a short design exercise was undertaken by two urban design students with undergraduate backgrounds in architecture (Kathrin Bayer) and urban and regional planning (Timo Hartmann). The design task they devised for participants was to plan a creative hot-spot for students and lecturers at the Ernst-Reuter-Platz roundabout, assuming that the site could be accessed freely (everyday access is currently difficult because of traffic), and stipulating that it should contain a materials shop, workshops, ateliers, reading rooms, restaurants, and a public square.

Following the structure of Do's study, different steps and sub-tasks were given that related to various issues in conceptual schematic design. Task 1 allowed the designer ten minutes to develop a conceptual spatial arrangement for the overall site. Task 2 allowed five minutes to focus on the lighting for the public square. Task 3 allowed five minutes to prepare a schematic proposal for a large temporary event structure on the site. The three sketches were drawn on separate sheets of paper.

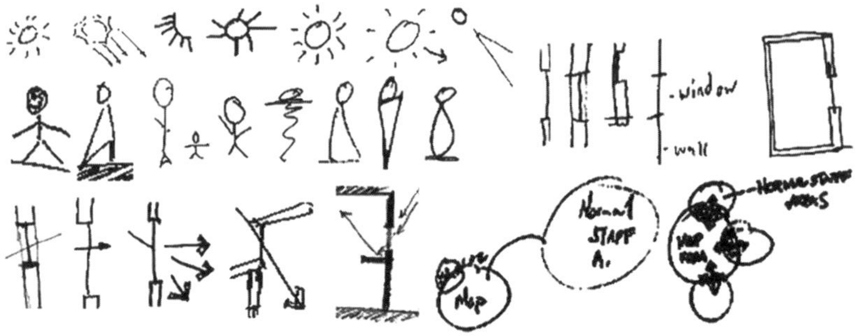

Do, E.Y.-L. and Gross, M.D. (2001) **Graphic Lexicon**. From a 1997 protocol study examining graphic symbols and notations in architectural design by E.Y-L. Do.

advantage when handling multi-layered problems. As Laseau points out, the "simultaneity and complex interrelationships of reality accounts for the special strength of graphic language," (2001, 55).

Laseau also argues that "graphic language ... has grammatical rules comparable to those of verbal language" (2001, 56). Do (1997) found that diagrammatic sketches by architects are based on a fairly standard lexicon of graphical symbols. This "vocabulary" of a graphic language employs "a full range of graphical indicators: ... typology, shape, size, position, and direction" (Do and Gross 2001, 2) to represent certain characteristics or forces, including intangible aspects like wind and sunlight. To result in a clear outcome understandable by others, this lexicon is, or

Despite their different disciplinary backgrounds, the students used a similar and understandable lexicon of graphic elements, including arrows, symbols, labels, and hatching to indicate buildings. Furthermore, the elements were often used in the same context or with the same intention. However, it was also apparent that the diagrams from the student with an architectural background were presented in more detail and looked at more aspects. For example, in the second task focusing on the lighting, a diagrammatic section was prepared in addition to a plan.

The experiment raised questions for the students as to whether graphic language is also universal to people from disciplines with no visual focus (e.g. sociology), and for other geographic regions or cultural contexts.

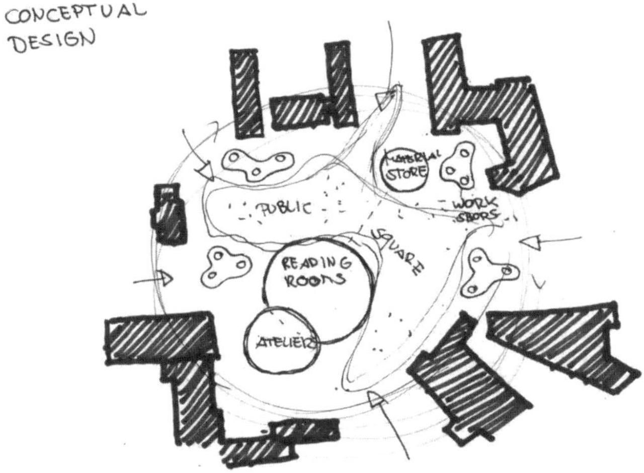

Beyer, K. and Hartmann, T. (2017) **Conceptual Diagram 1**. Output of Task 1 – Conceptual and spatial arrangement by student with background in urban and regional planning.

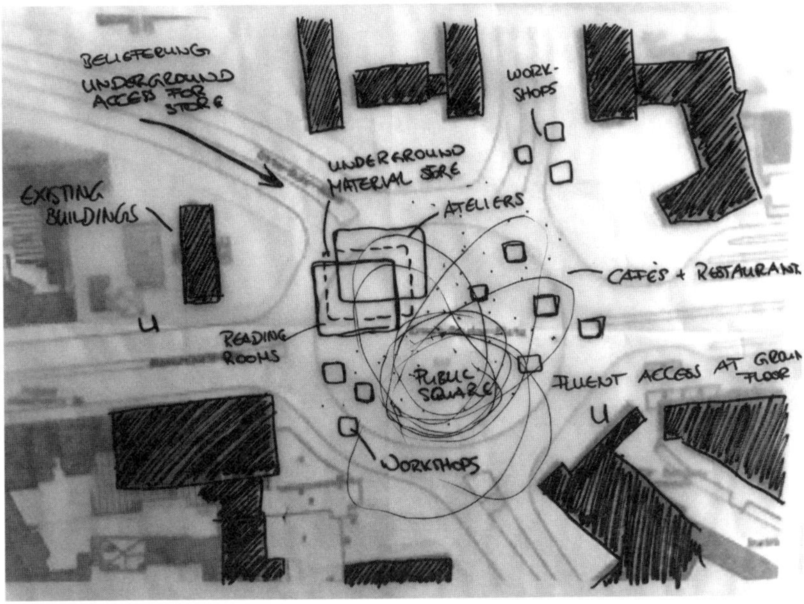

Beyer, K. and Hartmann, T. (2017). **Conceptual Diagram 2**. Output of Task 1 – Conceptual and spatial arrangement by student with background in architecture.

should be, "shared" (Laseau 2001: 59), "conventional and consistent" (Do and Gross 2001, 10), and have a "rational foundation" (Kazmierczak 2003, 53).

Further parallels with language include the use of annotation or text labels to introduce information that might be impossible to translate into a graphic abstraction and to facilitate the reading and understanding of the diagrammatic, and the "use of properties of the page (e.g., proximity and place: center, edges, horizontal/up–down, vertical/left–right) ... to convey meanings" (Tversky 2001, 499), explaining how "the effects of reading order on judgements of agency, where figures on the left are seen as more powerful, seem to derive from language syntax, where the actor is typically earlier in the sentence than the recipient of action" (Tversky 2001, 512).

Standard Types of Diagrammatic Sketches

Typically, three types of diagrammatic sketch guide the design process. The bubble diagram is "probably the most broad-based, versatile grammar" (Laseau 2001, 53) in the graphic language. Architects use this "to explore relationships among the sizes, adjacencies, and approximate shapes of the spaces needed for various activities" (Do and Gross 2001, 12). The second type includes some additional graphic elements, such as lines and arrows, to add detail pertaining to constraints to be applied to the emerging design – factors concerning the surroundings, that enable the architect to "read off visually whether the design in its current state satisfies a certain predicate" (Do and Gross 2001, 14). In the third type of diagram, the design proposal is semi-complete. It has assumed a loose spatial form, but contains many "abstractions for details that are to be filled in later" (Do and Gross 2001, 14). As a set, they demonstrate how the design process is one of "incremental formulation." However, "an important design skill is matching the level of detail of a diagram to the level of decision-making" (Do and Gross 2001, 14).

The Further Importance Sketching has for Designers

There is little scientific research or explanation from architects and other designers regarding their use and experiences of sketching. Their writings on drawing and sketching tend to be emotional and vague, do not distinguish between diagrammatic and form-generating sketches, and mostly reinforce aspects of sketching that empirical research has already highlighted. Additional perspectives on the potential influences of professional, personal, or environmental factors are lacking. Christian Gänshirt has compiled some observations in this regard. The act of sketching is "rapid, imprecise, open, and direct"; due to the closeness of the developed idea to the original idea, the value of a sketch for the architect is often immense; sketching is a mode for switching between logical-verbal and intuitive-pictorial thinking, accomplished by the interaction between the descriptive sketching of something given, and prescriptive sketching representing something new; and the sketch works as a type of meta-layer that unifies all other information layers – conversation, texts and even calculations (Gänshirt 2007).

Conclusion

Urban design is about "drawing interconnections between the materials of urban space and the socialities of urban life" (Dovey and Pafka 2016, 10). Without a profound understanding of the design problem and its context, there is a risk of reducing the city, as well as the emerging design, to measurable components and illustrative representations. At this junction, Dovey and Pafka propose "approaches that cut across dichotomies between objective and subjective, between materialities and representations, between science and humanities" (Dovey and Pafka 2016, 10) in order to handle the complexity of a city and society. Good graphic language skills are by no means a guarantee of a good outcome, but they do provide a resilient tool with which to grasp the complexity of a spatial problem. It is therefore all the more critical for the field of urban design, where we focus on an interdisciplinary exchange between science and design, to strengthen this tool in its entirety. The professional and personal relevance of sketching for the designer must be stressed and highlighted more in the scientific world.

This text is based on the writing of Katrin Beyer and Timo Hartmann, Wang Yueqi and Li Ziyue, and Michael Fay and Phillipa Weyers, and was edited by Áine Ryan.

#B.3

UNPACKING DISCOURSES

Bardici, V., M. "A Discourse Analysis of Eco-City in the Swedish Urban Context-Construction, Cultural Bias, Selectivity, Framing, and Political Action." Master's thesis, Malmö högskola/ Kultur och samhälle, 2014.

Dovey, K. **Urban Design Thinking. A Conceptual Toolkit**. London: Bloomsbury, 2016.

Fairclough, N. **Media Discourse**. London: Edward Arnold, 1995.

Fairclough, N. **Analysing Discourse: Textual Analysis for Social Research**. London: Routledge, 2003.

Foucault, M. **The Archaeology of Knowledge**. London: Routledge, 2002.

Foucault, M. **The Discourse on Language.** New York: Pantheon, 1972.

Gee, J., P. **An Introduction to Discourse Analysis: Theory and Method**. 4th ed. New York: Routledge, 2014.

Goodchild, B. "Triadic classifications and triangular thinking. Their use in urban planning and urban design." **People, Place & Policy Online** 2 (2008): 122–131.

Hajer, M. (1993): "Discourse Coalitions and the Institutionalization of Practice. The Case of Acid Rain in Great Britain." In **The Argumentative Turn in Policy Analysis and Planning**, edited by Fischer, F. and Forester, J., 43–76. Durham-London: Duke University Press,1993.

Jacobs, K. (2006): "Discourse Analysis and its Utility for Urban Policy Research." **Urban Policy and Research** 24, issue 1, 39–52. Available at https://www.researchgate.net/publication/ 228633 40 5_Discourse_Analysis_and_its_Utility_for_Urban_Policy_Research. Accessed August 3, 2016.

Jäger, S. **Kritische Diskursanalyse. Eine Einführung**. Münster: Unrast, 2004.

Jensen, O.B. "Discourse Analysis & Socio-Spatial Transformation Processes. A Theoretical Framework for Analysing Spatial Planning." Working paper series 61. Newcastle: University of Newcastle-upon-Tyne Department of Town and Country Planning, 1997.

Rogers, R. **An Introduction to Critical Discourse Analysis in Education**. 2nd edition. New York: Routledge, 2011.

Discourse analysis is used as an umbrella term for a set of different theoretical approaches to and methods for analyzing language use and hence the construction of knowledge and what one generally refers to as *the truth*. The aim of discourse analysis is to unveil the patterns in which topics are constructed, manifested, and reproduced in social practices (Bardici 2014, 4). Use of vocal, written, and sign language is considered to be a fundamental of social discourse. Discourse analysis tries to describe the way in which language use has social implications (Bardici 2014, 4). Discourse should be understood as a social practice.

In urban design, discourse analysis has been a widely used and described means of analyzing policies and decision making in the planning process (Goodchild 2008, 122). Urban design and planning can be considered a form of social discourse, in which urban imaginaries and conflicts are constructed and translated into institutionalizations and economic/political structures (Bardici 2014, 5).

There is no generally agreed-upon methodology for conducting a discourse analysis, but there is a series of different theories and methods. Stemming from different disciplines, each approach has its own distinct character and objectives, which should be considered when choosing between them. In contextualizing and situating some of the most influential approaches, two major movements can be distinguished (Jacobs 2006, 40):

Political economy-informed analysis, known as *critical discourse analysis*, which is associated with Norman Fairclough (1995

A Discourse Analysis of the Eco-City in the Swedish Urban Context, Vera Minavere Bardici, 2014
This master's thesis analyzes how the discourse around the eco-city as a sustainable urban model has gained increasing importance and developed into an urban discourse. The eco-city is perceived as a vision of transformation for the future, and has been translated into concrete projects, strategies, and policies, mainstreaming urban sustainability and being replicated and expanded upon across the world. In doing so, Bardici (2014, see above) uses six analytical phases of discourse analysis, focusing on definitional and thematic issues, cultural bias, selectivity, framing, and political action.

An Investigation of the Processes of Urban Image Construction in Dublin, Ireland, Ruth Comerford-Morris, 2015[1]
This paper researches what urban images are produced of Dublin in the course of place-making, marketing, and branding. In the past decade, cities have become increasingly competitive regarding investments in an attempt to attract foreign capital and investors. The promotion of urban images has been instrumental to city branding as well as to the process of shaping the city landscape. Comerford-Morris (2015) uses discourse analysis and the evaluation of promotional pictures of Dublin to reveal the actors who are producing various different images of Dublin.

and 2003), and the *discourse coalitions* model, which is associated with Maarten Hajer (1993).

This manual will mainly draw on the works of Michel Foucault to describe discourse analysis and its utility for urban design. The French philosopher and psychologist Michel Foucault was one of the key actors in this field in Europe, developing the concept of discourse analysis in the early 1970s in his books *The Archaeology of Knowledge* (1973) and *The Discourse on Language* (1972). His work has had a big impact, especially on the social sciences, and has led to a great diversity of approaches. Cultural geographers introduced the term and methods to the field of urban planning through their work (Jacobs 2006, 40). Foucault's discourse analysis can be contextualized in the field of poststructuralist and postmodernist schools of thought, both of which question the relationship between language and social reality. Goodchild (2008, 122) describes discourse analysis as a "key element of postmodern research methodologies," and "the means through which interpretation is taken." In terms of urban design and planning, discourse analysis can help to understand how the "social construction of urban problems" takes place and how key actors produce and reproduce urban issues (Bardici 2014, 5). It has been used, for example, in housing policy and housing studies, in urban and regional planning, and in environmental policy (Goodchild 2008, 122).

Foucauldian approaches pay attention to the recursive relationship between power and language. According to Jäger

DEMO:POLIS – The Universal Declaration of Urban Rights, Zuloark, Julia Förster, and Andreas Krüger, 2015[2]
In five parliamentarian working sessions that were open to the public, an "Urban Rights Charta" was developed for Berlin (UR_BER). Each working session had a different topic, and accordingly different guests from initiatives and experts were invited to discuss a specific question and have a debate. The aim of the working session was to develop a new approach to dealing with Berlin's public spaces, as well as its implementation in politics. The discourse concerning current urban policies was rethought, and in the last working session the UR_BER was handed to the Senate of Berlin – the local government – with a list of precise demands and requirements.

The Ideal Urban Soundscape: Investigating the Sound Quality of French Cities, Catherine Guastavino, 2006[3]
This paper focuses on the ideal urban soundscapes of several French cities, and was researched by evaluating questionnaires with discourse analysis. Participants (seventy-seven in total) answered a free-response-format questionnaire, in which they were asked to describe familiar urban soundscapes. The results were analyzed using a psycholinguistic approach to spontaneous verbal descriptions, identifying a variety of different sound quality criteria for urban soundscapes.

DEMO:POLIS (2016) **Universal Declaration of Urban Rights.** Graphical representation of the process of developing the Universal Declaration of Urban Rights for Berlin.

(2004), the following sequence can be useful for a simple discourse analysis inspired by Foucault:

- Definition of the research question and the discourse in which this question shall be researched.
- A short characterization of the discourse material, such as online media or print, movies, written texts and architecture magazines, and so on.
- Preparation and access to the material to be researched, and the creation of a reader.

Endnotes

1 Comerford-Morris, R. "An Investigation of the Processes of Urban Image Construction in Dublin, Ireland." In **Addressing complex urban challenges: Social, economic and cultural transformations in the city (Young Scholars Book 4: Geography)**, edited by Moore-Cherry, N., and Piñeira-Mantiñan, M.-J., 97–110. Santiago de Compostela: Nino-Centro de Impresión Digital, 2015. Available at https://www.unil.ch/igu-urban/files/live/sites/igu-urban/files/Young%20Scholar_2015/Moore-Pineira_4.pdf#page=97

2 Zuloark. **Urban Rights** Project. [Online]. n.d. Available at http://berlin.urbanrights.org/ Political project. Concept by Zuloark. Berlin edition by Julia Förster, with support by Andreas Krüger, shown at the exhibition DEMO:POLIS 2015.

3 Guastavino, C. "The Ideal Urban Soundscape. Investigating the Sound Quality of French Cities." **Acta Acustica** 92 (2006), 945-951.

DEMO:POLIS (2016) **Session in the Urban Parliament.**

Second Stadtforum Berlin (2015) **Cityforum Berlin: Who does the public space belong to?**

- An evaluation of the material used for the discourse analysis.
- A detailed analysis of one typical discourse fragment (a text fragment) of the material (for example, one newspaper)
- An overall analysis of the discourse in the section in the relevant material (for example, newspaper). All information shall be reflected and combined for a general statement about the section of discourse and the relevant material.

Some studies claiming to use discourse analysis as a means of investigation fail to actually do so, ending up with a historical description of events and developments rather than an unveiling of power mechanisms and the patterns that (re)produce them (Jacobs 2006, 45). Often, discourse analysis is accused of "privileging individual agency and in particular subjectivity over structural factors arising from institutional practices and economic inequalities" (Jacobs 2006, 46).

On the other hand, discourse analysis has been decisive in understanding how – and which – language is used in urban planning policies, their implementation, and the representation of those policies. Jacobs (2006, 46) states that discourse analysis has made an important contribution to an increase in public awareness about the marketing of policies and the importance of their presentation.

This text is based on the writing of Jennifer Gehring and was edited by Martina Löw.

#B.4

EXPERIMENTING

Eiffler, S. "Experiment." In **Handbuch der empirischen Sozialforschung**, edited by Baur, N. and Blasius, J., 195–209. Wiesbaden: Springer, 2014.

Kromrey, H. **Empirische Sozialforschung. 12th edition.** Stuttgart: Lucius und Lucius Verlagsgesellschaft, 2009.

Leibniz-Institut für Wissensmedien. **Was ist ein Experiment?** [Online]. Available at https://www.e-teaching.org/didaktik/qualitaet/experiment. 2016. Accessed 27.06.2016.

Shadish et al. **Experimental and Quasi-Experimental Designs for Generalized Causal Inference.** Boston: Houghton Mifflin Company, 2002.

Wundt, W. "Über Ausfragemethoden und über die Methoden zur Psychologie des Denkens." **Psychologische Studien** 3 (1907): 301–360.

The origin of experiments lies in the human need to gain new knowledge about certain causes and effects. The classical definition of an experiment goes back to Wundt (1907), who was the founder of the first institute of experimental psychology. In his general rules he tries to sum up the experimental method: the process to be studied has to be consciously initiated by the researcher; the conditions that might lead to a certain effect have to be varied in a planned manner; and, finally, the experiment has to be repeatable at any time, and has to be recordable.

According to Kromrey (2009), the experiment is a form of empirical research that addresses the question of causal analysis. It can be distinguished from a regular observation because the researcher actively changes and controls the conditions. Eiffler (2014) also stresses that the control a researcher has over various factors in an experiment is very crucial. The factors that have to be controlled for might point to alternative explanations or other potential causes.

Shadish et al. (2002) discuss the nineteenth-century philosopher John Stuart Mill in order to define an experiment. Three necessary conditions for proving the causal relationship between a hypothetical cause and a hypothetical effect are mentioned:

1. The hypothetical cause must be manipulated and the results need to be observed.
2. The variation of the cause and the variation of the effect must be analyzed in relation to each other. Alternative explanations for the relationship between cause and effect must be excluded.

The Drawing Power of Crowds, S. Milgram, L. Bickmann, and L. Berkowitz, 1969[1]

This experiment was based on the personal observations of Milgram, Bickman, and Berkowitz (1969). They noticed that many random passers-by would stop when they saw a crowd of people looking at a specific point. In their experiment they wanted to find out how many people would stop in a busy street if there was group of people looking up at the sixth floor of an office block where nothing was actually happening.
In the end, 4% of passers-by stopped to join a single person gazing up, and 40% stopped in the case of fifteen people looking up. The experiment shows the significant magnetic effect that crowds have, which we also experienced in our own experiment project, *Urbanhafen*, described below.

The Shadow[2]

Sophie Calle is an artist known for taking a detective-like approach to strangers. For her experiment *The Shadow*, her mother hired a detective to follow Calle at her own request in order to report on her daily activities and to provide photographic evidence of what happened. In a second phase of the project, she hired another person to follow the detective and to take pictures of him as well. Here, the detective is the observer and at the same time becomes the observed. For a whole day, Calle, the detective, and his observer walked around the city of Paris. The photo

3. Finally, the aim of the experiment must be "to gain knowledge about cause-effect-relationships and to use this as a basis for explaining social phenomena" (see also Eifler 2014, 195).

The most common fields of application for this method are the natural sciences, the social sciences, sociology, and psychology (Leibniz-Institut für Wissensmedien 2016), but we can easily adapt this method to urban design issues. Therefore, it is important to differentiate between two approaches to applying the method. Kromrey (2009) makes a distinction between laboratory experiments and field experiments.

The laboratory experiment takes place in an artificially constructed situation. The experimental stimulus can be controlled. All other factors are excluded. The laboratory experiment is very appropriate for research questions in which only one variable has to be examined in an ideal-typical situation.

In field experiments, the researcher can capture processes and structures in real-life situations. Nevertheless, the researcher tries to consciously control the conditions and manipulate the variables of the experiment. In this way, the logic of a classical experiment is transferred to the social field. A research question must be defined and a suitable design for the experiment chosen. The researcher needs to make a choice about what their experimental group (and control group) will look like. The variables must be defined, measurements taken, notes made, evaluations undertaken, and an interpretation provided. Is the result replicable at any time?

reports, in combination with the detective's description of the artist's activities, are useful tools for confronting one's subjective experience through an objective observation.

Urbanhafen[3]
For this social experiment we decided to focus on how citizens react to top-down planning. To do this, we wanted to confront people with a planning concept for expensive housing units to be built at a popular and intensively used public space. Due to the fact that discussion of top-down planning has been very critical in Berlin in the past, we expected that people would reject the construction plans. The planning of offices on the piece of land known as the Cuvry Brache and the closing of the Tempelhofer Feld, for example, were not supported by the general public. In our second step, we wanted to see how citizens reacquire space once it had been taken away from them.
We created an on-site construction sign that depicted expensive-looking townhouses at the Urbanhafen in Kreuzberg. We also added a telephone number to be called for information and comments. We chose the open space in front of the Klinikum am Urbanhafen, directly on the waterfront, as the setting. We put up the construction sign on a sunny Saturday afternoon. We then sat beside the sign, had a drink in the sun, and observed the reactions unobtrusively. We took notes of the comments we heard and photographs of people's reactions. Following this, we put up

Brennauer, J.; Reifferscheid, J. and Binz, S. (2015) **Experiment at Urbanhafen**.

warning tape to create a blocked-off area and in doing so added another dimension to the experiment.

Two of us created the setting while a third person documented the activities. Immediately after putting up the construction sign the first subjects began to take an interest in it. Shortly after this we received a phone call from a man who wanted to buy an apartment. Our observations lasted until early morning. In the night, two drunk teenagers knocked over the sign and tried to throw it into the water.

During the day the kinds of reactions we observed varied a great deal. There were positive reactions as well as rejections of the project, although the negative reactions were quite mild and restrained. One possible reason for this could be that most of the citizens appeared alone or as part of a couple. At this point we began to consider the above reference project The Drawing Power of Crowds. The more people in front of the sign, the more people joined the crowd. And yet it was rare to have large groups looking at the sign at one time. The conditions for group dynamics were almost nonexistent. While rejection was expressed verbally during the day, a physical intervention occurred during the night. Nevertheless, there was some level of awareness of the option of a public petition, probably through pilot projects like the one at the Tempelhofer Feld. Surprisingly, everyone accepted the barrier in the form of warning tape. As soon as the warning tape

Milgram et al. (1969) **The Drawing Power of Crowds**. Students from UEL take part in a recreation of Milgram's Manhattan Experiment. Picture by Jeff Ellis, published in Tony D Sampson (2012) Virality: Contagion Theory in the Age of Networks.

According to Kromrey (2009), the limitations of a laboratory experiment are the lack of contact with reality and the artificial character of the situation produced by the researcher. It is therefore hard to come to conclusions, especially about complex social phenomena. However, due to its isolation from other factors, the laboratory experiment has a great amount of internal validity.

was implemented, most people thought that the project was real. This shows the necessity of a setting that is close to reality and not too temporary.

Endnotes

1 Milgram, S., Bickmann, L. and Berkowitz, L. "Note on the drawing power of crowds of different size." **Journal of Personality and Social Psychology** 13, no. 2 (1969): 79–82.

2 Artistic experiment by Calle, S. "The Shadow." [Online]. http://medienkunstnetz.de/werke/the-shadow/ Accessed 11.12.2018.

3 Experiment by Julia Brennauer, Jim Reifferscheid and Svenja Binz, published in a 2015 term paper. (Seminar Methods and Tools in Urban Design, TU Berlin)

On the other hand, Kromrey (2009) claims that it is difficult to isolate the research from other influencing variables in field experiments. The researcher also has to act very passively and is not allowed to interfere directly in the experiment. However, the results in field experiments can be close to reality and therefore have a high degree of external validity. This is why scientists normally tend to choose field research: in order to achieve results which are as closely connected to reality as possible.

Generally, one needs to keep in mind that the test persons or subjects must not be deceived, manipulated, or harmed in any way. All in all, the experiment is considered to be a very helpful tool for explaining (social) phenomena by gaining knowledge about cause-effect relationships.

This text is based on the writing of Julia Brennauer, Jim Reifferscheid, and Svenja Binz and was edited by Martina Löw.

#B.5

INTER-VIEWING EXPERTS

Bogner, A., Littig, B., and Menz, W., eds. **Interviewing Experts**. Basingstoke: Palgrave Macmillan, 2009.

Flick, U., von Kardorff, E., and Steinke, I., eds. **Qualitative Forschung. Ein Handbuch**. Reinbek bei Hamburg: Rowohlt, 2000.

Gläser, J. and Grit, L. **Experteninterviews und qualitative Inhaltsanalyse als Instrumente rekonstruierender Untersuchungen**. Wiesbaden: VS Verlag für Sozialwissenschaften, 2010.

Lamnek, S. and Krell, C. **Qualitative Sozialforschung**. Weinheim, Basel: Beltz, 2010.

Meuser, M. and Nagel, U. "ExpertInneninterviews – vielfach erprobt, wenig bedacht. Ein Beitrag zur qualitativen Methodendiskussion." In **Qualitativ-empirische Sozialforschung. Konzepte, Methoden, Analysen**, edited by Garz, D. and Klaus Kraimer, 441–471. Opladen: West German Edition, 1991.

Expert interviews are qualitative interviews with a specific target group: experts. There is no universal definition of what constitutes an expert (Lamnek and Krell 2010, 655). We can use this method when a research project focuses not on personal orientations and attitudes in the context of an individual life (Meuser and Nagel 1991, 442 onwards), but on a clearly defined part of this individual's reality. This reality may be, for example, his or her function as a representative of an organization or institution (Meuser and Nagel 1991, 442). The decision concerning who is considered an expert assigns a relative status and depends on the research interest under consideration (Meuser and Nagel 1991, 443).

The expert is always part of a research field (Meuser and Nagel 1991, 443). If his or her knowledge is accepted as the truth, the expert can significantly influence the actions other actors take (Lamnek and Krell 2010, 656). The value of expert interviews lies in understanding the knowledge and experience that experts gain from their tasks, activities, and responsibilities in their functional context.

Expert interviews are applied in a variety of fields. For example, top managers in the fields of politics, economics, justice, and science, as well as planners and architects, teachers and social workers, and so forth, are considered to be experts in their disciplines. One possible application of expert interviews is to use them as contextual knowledge within a range of methods; for example, in research about social problems and inequality.

Urban Interspaces[1]
The location of the project was the area surrounding the Ostbahnhof in Berlin. The aim was to develop concepts and designs for new interspaces within the area. The first step of the project was to do basic research on the area. In addition to groups that carried out research on planning and development concepts, history and urban structures, socio-demographic structures, traffic and mobility, and public space, one group focused on local actors. This group did ethnographic field research that included participatory observation (dérive, mental mapping, and so on), questionnaires, systematic analyses, media image analyses, and expert interviews. As such, the expert interview method was applied in the context of various research methods, with the aim of gaining contextual knowledge about this specific neighborhood. The research question revolved around the question of what the character of the area around the Ostbahnhof in Berlin was: was it really a *Kiez*, a defined neighborhood?
1) First, Sabrina Hövener and Farina Runge specified a research question, developed an interview guide, and contacted a variety of actors.
2) They set up different tasks for the implementation of the interviews: one researcher guided the interview while the other one wrote down important facts and information. Additionally, they recorded every interview.
3) Afterwards, they transcribed each interview. In some interviews they

Another possibility is to use interviews as an independent method in order to generate basic knowledge – for example, in research about elites, urban conflicts, the sociology of planning, or in implementation and professionalization research.

Expert interviews are very popular, but have not been very well researched as of yet. A special investigation of the subject began in the 1990s, leading to Bogner, Littig, and Menz (2005) distinguishing between three different types of expert interviews according to their specific goals (Lamnek and Krell 2010, 656):

The systematizing expert interview, which focuses on the practical knowledge of the interviewee with regard to his or her experiences and actions;

The theory-generating expert interview, which takes an interest in an expert's subjective orientations and indirect decision models;

The explorative expert interview, which is part of a multi-methodological design: its aim is to structure a field of research by gaining additional information in the form of background knowledge and eyewitness reports.

The aims of a research project basically define the category of interviews. For example, there may be an objective to gain basic knowledge about an expert's field of activity. In this category, experts are part of the research's target group (Meuser and Nagel 1991, 445). The aim is to generate social and spatial theory, and so hypotheses are developed with which the theories are tested.

only transcribed those parts which dealt with the research question directly as their objective was to gain context knowledge.
4) In the next step they paraphrased the interviews.
5) In order to densify the content, they developed headlines. They ordered the paraphrases with regard to the headlines.
6) Afterwards, they identified the different topics and fields that were discussed in the interview and interpreted the results with regard to one specific statement.
The interview provided useful information for the whole research project. As a result of the interviews, the researchers were able to show that experts have a greater impact on the development of the Ostbahnhof location than they expected. This led to the hypothesis that stakeholders can influence the character of the neighborhood, and that professional urban development can therefore influence civil structures.

Star Architecture and its Role in Repositioning Small and Medium-Sized Cities[2]
This research project was conducted by a research team of sociologists, architects, and economists. Nowadays, flagship buildings are purposefully constructed not only in metropolitan areas but also in small cities whose authorities deem them crucial for increasing recognition and inclusion in global cultural circuits. In order to achieve the desired resonance and its putative urban benefits, such projects are

Alternatively, expert interviews can be used to gain contextual knowledge. Even though experts are not part of the target group in this case, they can provide information about the context in which the target group acts (Meuser and Nagel 1991, 445). The interviews are considered a source of information in addition to other sources. They are not appropriate for testing the validity of theories about a situation (Meuser and Nagel 1991, 446 onwards).

It is important to distinguish between the categories and to define the objective of the interviews at the start. The category regulates the level of depth of the analysis and interpretation of the data. In order to have a better understanding of the various steps involved, we have separated the instructions for carrying out expert interviews into instructions for the implementation of the interview and instructions for the analysis of the transcript.

First, the research issue as well as the role of the interview should be determined. That means the researchers have to reflect on whether they want to address basic or context-related knowledge with the interview. Next, an interview guide should be developed in order to structure the conversation and set thematic emphases (Meuser and Nagel 1991, 454). Once the expert has been contacted, the interview can take place. We highly recommend recording the interview if the interviewee consents to this request. This recording should then be transcribed.

On the basis of this transcript, an analysis of the content can be made. The different paragraphs should therefore be summed up and paraphrased in the researcher's own words (Meuser and

generously funded and star architects commissioned to carry them out. The goal is to endow a given city with an urban attraction capable of giving distinctive local expression to a global trend, through which the city's profile and visitor-friendly infrastructure are taken to a new level. The research project asked if urban strategies implemented in one medium-sized city can be directly grafted onto comparable ones elsewhere. To gauge and categorize the implications of star architecture in specific non-metropolitan settings, a series of expert interviews was conducted in three German-speaking cities across three countries: Wolfsburg (Germany), Graz (Austria), and Lucerne (Switzerland). Each of these cities has constructed its own iconic buildings in the twenty-first century. The research combined the method of expert interviews with ethnography, media analysis mapping, and economic analysis. The research findings indicate that in small and medium-sized cities in particular, the construction of flagship buildings fills many with pride, and that collective representations change. The more uncertain the position of a small or medium-sized city is, the greater the potential effect of implementing a flagship building project will be on the development of municipal agency. Morphological effects are less disputed than economic or socio-cultural effects.

Stollmann, J. (2018) **Martina Löw und Seonju Kim at an expert interview**. IFEZ control center, Seoul, South Korea.

Nagel 1991, 456). Afterwards, this information will be condensed into headlines that represent the content (Meuser and Nagel 1991, 459). In a thematic comparison, the information from different interviews can then be compared. In this step, the language used in the headlines of the different interviews is unified, thus reducing the amount of terminology (Meuser and Nagel 1991, 461).

Endnotes

1 Expert interviews and analysis by Sabrina Hövener and Farina Runge in a term paper for the seminar Methods and tools in urban design and the Design Studio: *Urban Interspaces* hosted by the Institute of City and Regional Planning, TU Berlin, 2016

2 Research project funded by the German Research Foundation, TU Berlin/TU Munich/HCU Hamburg 2015–17. See e.g. Alaily-Mattar, N., Dominik Bartmanski, Johannes Dreher, Michael Koch, Martina Löw, Timothy Pape and Alain Thierstein. "Situating Architectural Performance: 'Star Architecture' and its Roles in Repositioning the Cities of Graz, Lucerne and Wolfsburg." **European Planning Studies** 26, issue 9 (2018): 1874–1900.

A very important step of interpretation – sociological conceptualization – then follows, in which an abstraction in the form of an empirical generalization is created. The task is to search for similarities among the different interviews and then to create (sociological) categories on this basis (Meuser and Nagel 1991, 463). As a last step, a theoretical generalization follows. Here, the previously generalized facts will be interpreted in the context of sociological concepts and terms (Meuser and Nagel 1991, 465).

Of course, expert interviews also have their strengths and limitations. First of all, the biggest challenge in the use of expert interviews is defining who is an expert for the purposes of your research question. Since there is no theory underlying this, it is a subjective decision by the researcher. This problem leads us to the next point, which is the lack of methodological reflection (Meuser and Nagel 1991, 41). The act of carrying out of an interview, its analysis and interpretation still rely on a researcher's knowledge and decision-making. Moreover, there are several possibilities for failure in implementation and analysis. An interview may be considered of no use if the interviewee refuses to answer, has no knowledge of the topic, or switches between the roles of a private person and that of a representative. An additional indication of failure is when experts put the researcher into the role of a confidant when talking about sensitive data. The outcome is always dependent on the willingness of the experts to engage. Additionally, factors such as age, sex, prejudice, sympathy, and antipathy can influence the course of a conversation. Besides this, errors can occur in paraphrasing, there can be a lack of comprehension in the analysis, and interpretations can be misunderstood.

Despite all of these limitations, the method has many strengths that should be highlighted. Firstly, the method provides fast and easy access to a research field, as well as to situations which would be difficult or impossible for researchers to gain access to themselves. Every interview also generates unique content and has a unique form. Furthermore, insight into different approaches to the field of research facilitates a wide range of information.

This text is based on the writing of Sabrina Hövener and Farina Runge and was edited by Martina Löw.

#B.6

MAPPING SPATIAL SYSTEMS

Corner, J. "**The Agency of Mapping. Speculation, Critique and Invention.**" In **Mappings**, edited by Cosgrove, D., 213–252. London: Reaktion Books, 1999.

DeLanda, M. **A New Philosophy of Society. Assemblage Theory and Social Complexity.** London, New York: Continuum, 2006.

Fryszer, A. and Schwing, R. **Systematisches Handwerk. Werkzeug für die Praxis.** Göttingen: Vandenhoeck & Ruprecht, 2013.

Karvounis, A. (2015): "**Urban Metabolism.**" In **Understanding Urban Metabolism. A Tool for Urban Planning**, edited by Anselmo de Castro, E., Chrysoulakis, N. and Moors, E.J., 3–11. London, New York, Routledge.

Misrach, R. and Orff, K. **Petrochemical America.** New York, Aperture, 2012.

Tonkiss, F. **Cities by Design. The Social Life of Urban Form**. Cambridge: Polity Press, 2013.

Sedlacek, K. et al. **Emergenz. Strukturen der Selbstorganisation in Natur und Technik.** Norderstedt: Books on Demand, 2010.

Swyngedouw, E. "**Metabolic urbanization: the making of cyborg cities.**" In **The Nature of Cities. Urban political ecology and the politics of urban metabolism**, edited by Heynen, N., Kaika, M. and Swyngedouw, E., 20–39. London: Routledge, 2006.

Walloth, C. "Emergence in Complex Urban Systems. Blessing or Curse of Planning Efforts?" In **Understanding Complex Urban Systems. Multidisciplinary Approaches to Modelling**, edited by Walloth,C., Gurr, J.M., and Schmidt, J.A., 121–132. Cham: Springer, 2014.

Mapping visually displays and construes existing structures, spatial knowledge, and power relations, while at the same time revealing new insights about known realities (Corner 1999, 213). It is therefore not only a reflecting but also a creative instrument for reinterpreting space on different scales and discovering hidden opportunities and interconnections. The more complex and interwoven space becomes, the more important it is to expand the scope of mapping from the sole representation of physical objects to a more dynamic visualization of political, natural, and social processes and interrelations (Corner 1999, 225–228).

A system consists of a set of related elements (components and subsystems) that interact towards a common purpose, thus forming a functional unit that can be clearly distinguished from its surroundings (Sedlacek et al. 2010, 20). The definition, description, and demarcation of a system and its specific components increases abstraction and reduces complexity to a practicable working model (Fryszer and Schwing 2013, 22). The focus, boundaries, and selection of components according to the field of interest thereby represent strategic decisions that can still be readjusted if circumstances change over time (Sedlacek et al. 2010, 22). Therefore, systems do not represent static entities, nor are the processes that occur temporally or spatially restricted.

Above all, a system is more than the sum of its components, since new functions arise from their interplay. These so-called emergences cannot be predicted or explained through the characteristics of the isolated elements, but are spontaneous, unplanned

Petrochemical America[1]
Richard Misrach and Kate Orff's study investigates the area known as Cancer Alley – the chemical corridor along the Mississippi River – through a series of maps, narrative diagrams, and atmospheric images. It illustrates the region's history of transformation due to the arrival of the oil and petrochemical industry, connecting industrial processes with urban and natural systems, physical space, and landscape production.

The collision of human-made interventions with the fragile landscape has fundamentally changed the area's appearance and structure and resulted in a patchwork of natural and artificial elements. Large agricultural plantations, farms, small towns, and cities exist right next to the petrochemical industry, with its factories, oil pipelines, and transportation infrastructure, as well as next to the remaining wetlands and swamps.

Kate Orff's analytical tools, multi-scalar spatial mapping, and explanatory diagrams, in combination with Richard Misrach's atmospheric photographs, form a powerful narrative of landscape transformation, thus increasing awareness of the interconnection of seemingly separate processes. The two highlight how this industrial landscape was created; not through a deliberate planning process but through a spatial overlapping of diverse practices that has left permanent traces and structures in this space.

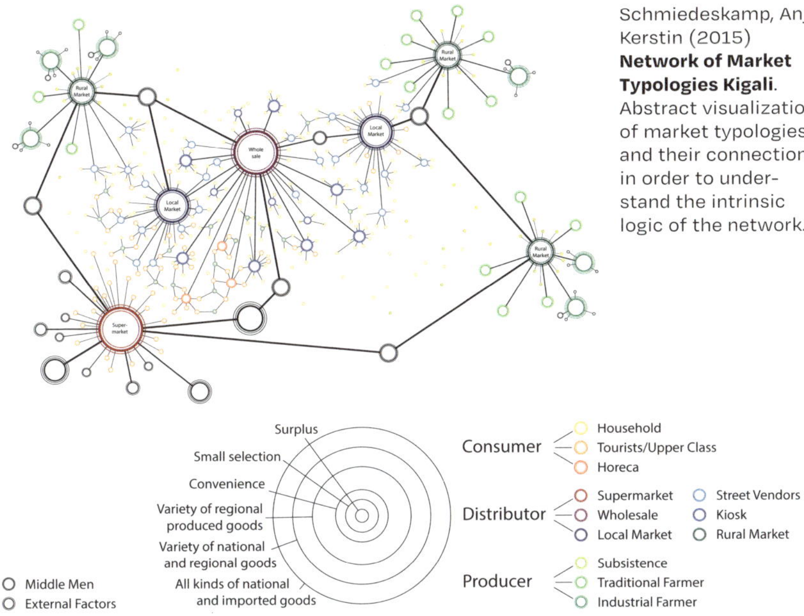

Schmiedeskamp, Anja Kerstin (2015) **Network of Market Typologies Kigali**. Abstract visualization of market typologies and their connections in order to understand the intrinsic logic of the network.

phenomena and can be positively or negatively perceived (Sedlacek et al. 2010, 44; Walloth 2014). In systemic thinking and design, cause and effect do not represent a linear process and wicked problems can arise from the interplay of different systems (Misrach and Orff, 2012). An abstract approach enables an understanding of the context and the processes generating these highly complex issues. It also leads to the identification of possible points

Waste Flows, Backflows, and Reflows of the Maas-Rhine River Delta[2]
This study of the port of Rotterdam by Pierre Belanger with OPSYS combines different types of information and different temporal scales in order to show the interaction between the infrastructural system of the port and the natural and urban systems along the river delta. Firstly, the graphic shows the historical process of the expansion of the port of Rotterdam and the resulting transformation of the river delta. Additionally, it visualizes the massive scale of material flows passing through the region. These flows include both resources, such as fossil fuels and other goods transported through the port, and waste, such as carbon emissions and solid waste. Understanding waste as an integral flow of the infrastructural and natural systems enables a look into the secondary backflows or reflows, which usually remain hidden in the capitalist economy.

Urban Food System Kigali[3]
The design studio *Tasty Kigali: designing interactive urban food systems* focused on the importance of acknowledging food as an omnipresent element of urban infrastructure interwoven in various socio-cultural, economic, ecological, and spatial processes. After an analysis of the general components of the food system, such as production, processing, distribution, access, consumption, and reuse, a focus was placed on the subsystem of food markets as a key point for

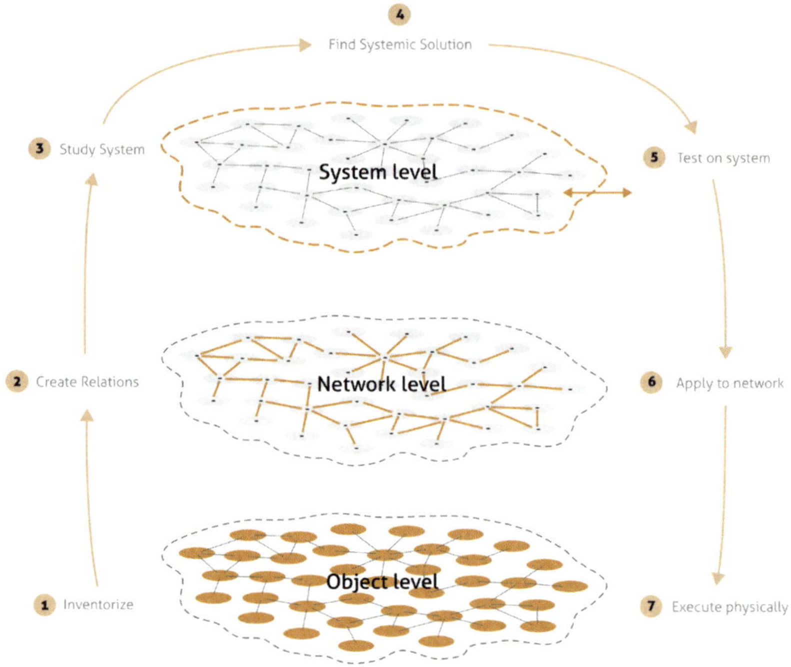

Bosschaert, Tom (2009) **Symbiosis in Development (SID)**. Hierarchic Layer Structure.

systemic analysis and intervention. The aim of the subsequent design was to improve the urban food system by implementing and adapting market elements and creating interconnections, making it more resilient for future challenges related to ongoing rapid urbanization.

The systemic analysis of the urban food and market systems within the specific context of the rapidly growing city provided a thorough understanding of interconnections and dependencies. These are determined by the typology of the market and its location in relation to production and consumption sites, as well as the products on offer. In total, the transportation routes of four staple foodstuffs (beef, coffee, potatoes, and rice) were analyzed, and six spatial typologies of urban, peri-urban, and rural markets were identified. If the physical and socio-economic aspects of the market had been considered separately and not as parts of a system, it would not have been possible to understand the market's multiple functions within the city.

Furthermore, small-scale, catalytic interventions were designed which, together, led to an improvement of the overall system. Their objective was to promote the role of markets as social facilities and to improve the distribution and (re)use of resources as well as the links between the rural and urban production and consumption sites. This appears to be a more holistic and promising approach to the challenges for catalytic interventions, where the manipulation of strategic elements triggers far-reaching alterations in the overall system.

In the context of urban landscapes, a core challenge in design is understanding the multifaceted interactions between the urban and natural systems. The urban landscape is complex and multilayered; it consists of more than its physical appearance, and thus the simple reduction to built forms cannot explain its ambiguous logic, its specific character, or the various dimensions that constitute it (Tonkiss 2013, 24). In addition, the analysis of isolated sites cannot decipher the socio-environmental dependencies of the sometimes-apparent, but mostly concealed, processes of production of space (Karvounis 2015, 4). A fundamental shift is thus required when dealing with the urban landscape. Systemic thinking, spatial mapping, and the analysis of the various layers of the urban realm lead to a better understanding of the multidimensionality of spatial practices and their inseparable connections.

With the arrival of the urban millennium and continuing rapid urbanization, cities are becoming increasingly reliant on global dependencies while at the same time becoming unintelligible. The coexistence of global, regional, and local networks and the overlapping of multiple systems all contribute to the production of a multilayered space. A comprehensive understanding of urban and natural processes, infrastructures, resources, and flows is imperative (Swyngedouw 2006, 20). Through the analysis of systems and components, what appears chaotic at first

of rapid urbanization than the official top-down planning strategy, which already struggles to meet the needs of the citizens.

Endnotes

1 Misrach, R. and Orff, K. **Petrochemical America.** New York: Aperture, 2012

2 OPSYS & Bélanger, P. **Waste Flows, Backflows, and Reflows Maas-Rhine River Delta**, 2009, digital image.

3 TUB Students. "TASTY KIGALI - designing interactive urban food systems". Design studio for the Master in Landscape Architecture / Urban Design at Technische Universität Berlin, supervised by Kasper, C. and Agudelo Ganem, M., 2015

sight becomes more accessible and the various socio-ecological interactions become visible. The systemic approach to urban landscapes creates a framework for more resilient, open-ended, and process-oriented design solutions, taking global and local consequences into account (Karvounis 2015, 11).

While mapping and system analysis are common tools for dealing with complex situations in various fields, the spatial and multi-scalar approach is especially important in space-related disciplines. In order to come up with design solutions, a thorough understanding of both the overall system and the concrete spatial consequences is needed, which in turn requires connecting and continuously switching between multiple hierarchically structured levels and scales (Swyngedouw 2006, 35). When working at different scales simultaneously, it is possible to examine each scale as a separate analytical unit with its own specific properties and temporal and spatial dynamics. However, it then needs to be reinserted into the multi-scalar context so as to assess the impact and feedback loops beyond the single level of analysis (DeLanda 2006, 118–119).

In order to lay bare the complexity of space, the first step is making an inventory of relevant system components. An overall system is thus defined, which serves as a guide through the design process. However, this is an abstract and selective definition that depends on the research focus, system boundaries, and choice of components. Through the analysis of the components' properties and their location in space, first indications of interrelations and linkages can be identified, which then lead to an analysis of processes of interaction. The identified relations, dependencies, and synergies are then visualized in a diagrammatic way as well as located on the map. A reflection on the overall system and the processes of production of space within it is already intrinsic to the graphic work of visualization and mapping. The decoding of the system's rules and logic helps to identify problems, potentials, and points for subsequent design intervention, and to lay out a strategic course of action.

A systemic analysis is not a linear, but rather a recursive, process. New findings on additional system components can alter prior strategic decisions, calling for a constant back-and-forth between the steps recounted above. Thus, boundaries and component selections can be expanded or reduced depending on growing knowledge and/or changing design conditions. All the relevant steps have to be carried out as abstract and spatial mappings simultaneously and on multiple scales in order to understand the full impact of the intended interventions and strategies on the mechanisms of spatial production.

Spatial systems are endeavors to understand the complexity of the urban realm through reduction and abstraction that reveal the messy and interwoven reality; a reality that, however, resists this abstraction. The initially set focus, system boundaries, and definition of the components are based on subjective interests and strategic decisions that could be manipulated. What seems an improvement within a chosen system may have negative consequences for excluded aspects, which is why a recursive working process is necessary. Further caution is required as mapping not only displays real conditions but can also distort them. Maps are graphic representations of knowledge; they usually follow a set of universally accepted rules and may inadvertently create a notion of homogeneous space. The contextualization of any systemic interventions and design solutions in the specific environment is fundamental, as these are locally anchored and not globally reproducible.

Systemic description through mapping enables designers to achieve a thorough understanding of processes of production of space, and can make hidden dependencies among practices assumed to be unconnected visible. This can help to identify interfaces for future intervention that possess the ability to change the urban landscape. The modification of single components on such an interface acts as a catalyst with far-reaching consequences, creating synergies between spatially overlapping networks and thus achieving improvements in the overall system. The still-flexible construct of the defined system can adapt to changed conditions over time, and can therefore be used to design for future uncertainties. Additionally, maps as a visualization technique enhances communication, as images and graphics tend to be more easily legible and can be understood by different actors.

This text is based on the writing of Anja Kerstin Schmiedeskamp and was edited by Xenia Kokoula.

Andrienko, G., Gunopulos, D., Ioannidis, Y., and Verscheure, O. "Mining Urban Data (Part B)." **Journal of Information Systems** 57 (April 2016): 75–76. Available from: https://www.researchgate.net/publication/293016564_Mining_Urban_Data_Part_B (2017-07-18).

Andrienko, Gennady, Dimitrios Gunopulos, Yannis Ioannidis, Vana Kalogeraki, Ioannis Katakis, Katharina Morik, und Olivier Verscheure. "Mining Urban Data (Part C)." **Information Systems** 64 (März 2017): 219–20. https://doi.org/10.1016/j.is.2016.09.003.

Behnisch M. "Urban data mining. Operationalisierung der Strukturerkennung und Strukturbildung von Ähnlichkeitsmustern über die gebaute Umwelt." Dissertation, Universität Karlsruhe, 2008. Available from https://www.ksp.kit.edu/9783866442498 Accessed July 17, 2017

Panagiotou, N., Boutsis, I., Gunopulos, D., Kalogeraki, V., Katakis, I., Lynch, S., O'Brien, B., Zacheilas, N., Zygouras, N., "Intelligent Urban Data Monitoring for Smart Cities." In **Machine Learning and Knowledge Discovery in Databases. ECML PKDD 2016. Lecture Notes in Computer Science, vol 9853**. Cham: Springer, 2016. Available from: http://www.katakis.eu/wp-content/uploads/2013/07/ECML2016i.pdf Accessed July 18, 2017.

Cleve, J. and Lämmel, U. **Data Mining**. München: Oldenburg, 2014.

Dürr, H. "Anwendungen des Data Mining in der Praxis." Seminar work for Data Mining seminar, Universität Ulm, 2004. Available from: http://www.mathematik.uni-ulm.de/sai/ws03/dm/arbeit/duerr.pdf Accessed

#B.7

URBAN DATA MINING

July 15, 2017.

Fayyad, U., Piatetsky-Shapiro, G., and Smyth, P. **Advances in Knowledge Discovery and Data Mining**. Menlo Park: American Association for Artificial Intelligence, 1996.

Fayyad, U., Piatetsky-Shapiro, G., Smyth, P. "From data mining to knowledge discovery in databases." **AI Magazine** 17, issue 3, (1996): 37–54. Available from: http://www.kdnuggets.com/gpspubs/aimag-kdd-overview-1996-Fayyad.pdf Accessed July 16, 2017.

Lämmel, P., Schieferdecker, I., and Tcholtchev, N. "Urban Data Platforms – An Overview." [Online]. 2016. Available from: http://www.opensym.org/os2016/proceedings-files/c304-schieferdecker.pdf Accessed July 16, 2017.

Malerba, D., Lisi, F.A., Appice, A., and Sblendorio, F. "Mining Census and Geographic Data in Urban Planning Environments." [Online]. Bari: Università degli Studi di Bari, Dipartimento di Informatica, 2003. Available from: http://www.di.uniba.it/~malerba/publications/input03.pdf Accessed July 18, 2017.

Sumathi, S. and Sivanandam, S.N. **Introduction to data mining and its applications**. Berlin/Heidelberg: Springer Verlag, 2006.

VaVeL, w.Y., **Urban Data Challenges**. Available from: http://www.vavel-project.eu/blog/urban-data-challenges Accessed July 18, 2017.

Zimmermann, A. "The Data Problem in Data Mining." **ACM SIGKDD Explorations Newsletter** 16, no. 2 (2015): 38–45. Available from: https://www.researchgate.net/publication/277943896_The_Data_Problem_in_Data_Mining Accessed July 18, 2017.

Data mining describes an interdisciplinary field in which potentially useful, valid, and not-yet-understood information is discovered in a non-trivial way within an existing dataset. This is achieved via a combination of statistical, machine learning, and artificial intelligence methods. Stored data is used and re-evaluated and useful information is extracted (Sumathi and Sivanandam 2006, 8). The aim is to generate further knowledge by identifying patterns, exceptions, and anomalies in the data, and based on that to discover trends and new relationships (Sumathi and Sivanandam 2006, 5). Due to the large amount of data mined, the process of analyzing and managing unfiltered data is mostly computer-based (Sumathi and Sivanandam 2006, 16) Data mining is generally considered a part of Knowledge Discovery in Databases (KDD). KDD is defined as the whole process of discovering data, including the preparation and interpretation of extracted data (Fayyad et al. 1996, 16). Although KDD and data mining are often used simultaneously and synonymously, data mining refers specifically to the process of extraction (Sumathi and Sivanandam 2006, 187 onwards).

Fields of Application

Even though data mining is not specific to any one industry (Sumathi and Sivanandam 2006, 8), it is mainly used to extract market advantage and is as such largely used in fields such as marketing, fraud detection, manufacturing, telecommunications, and so on (Fayyad et al. 1996, 38). The aim is "(a) to improve business

Airbnb vs. Berlin[1]
Airbnb vs. Berlin is a data journalism project and website application that uses data mining with an urban focus. The project aims to visualize the impact of Airbnb on Berlin by turning urban data points into easily readable and useful information for the public. It serves as a tool for harvesting data points from various sources, primarily the Airbnb.com API (Airbnb vs. Berlin, 2016). Only publicly available and anonymized data points are used, generated, and spatially and statistically visualized.

Smart Citizen Kit[2]
Developed in Barcelona in 2013, the Smart Citizen Kit is a tool for urban data mining. The Smart Citizen Kit functions not as a tool to harvest, analyze, or visualize data, but instead represents a participatory process to collect data points in real time. Packed into the Smart Citizen Kit are sensors that measure temperature, humidity, light, sound, carbon monoxide, nitrogen dioxide, and light levels. Every Smart Citizen Kit is wirelessly connected to the API and aims to foster collective and co-productive ways of constructing cities based on residents' needs.

Treepedia (MIT SENSEable City Lab)[3]
Treepedia is an application developed by the MIT Senseable City Lab under Carlo Ratti that mines data in over thirty cities around the world. It is designed to measure data that aids in our understanding of the cities' tree canopies. By gathering, analyzing, and interpreting the data on tree canopies, the tool aims to understand and

and services and (b) to help develop new techniques and products" (Sumathi and Sivanandam 2006, 6). Potential uses are therefore in different fields of knowledge and applications such as market segmentation, trend analysis, forecasting defaults, etc. (Sumathi and Sivanandam 2006, 16). Regardless of industry, the main differences in application are related to the diverse data used, the models and parameterizations applied, the aims or problems researched, and so on (Sumathi and Sivanandam 2006, 52). Due to the growth in data created in urban settings by users of digital gadgets, data mining is increasingly used to analyze and understand complex urban systems. Such explorations are becoming relevant to municipalities, industries, and others considering multiple aspects of the city. As a result, urban data mining is now used in areas such as infrastructure, traffic, energy, and similar sectors (Andrienko et al. 2017). The aim is to better understand cities and ultimately to make systems more efficient, or to use the gained knowledge to further develop urban environments and improve the daily life of their populations. See the reference projects for examples of this.

Different approaches

As data mining is used for diverse tasks, there are a variety of different algorithmic approaches for extracting useful information from databases. Their use depends on the kind of problem to be solved. The most common analyses are as follows:

promote urban tree coverage. The data is collected through publicly available satellite images, Google Street View, and open maps. The data then is analyzed and interpreted, and as a result not only visualizes urban tree canopy percentages but also calculates a Green View Index (GVI) that can be used to evaluate and compare canopy cover in urban areas around the world (Treepedia, 2017). This application illustrates the main principles of urban data mining perfectly: it harnesses publicly available data, layers different sources of data, analyses and visualizes the data points, and creates visual information that can be used to quantitatively compare urban areas.

Illicit Housing Rentals in Socially Protected Areas (Berlin/Bologna)
In 2017, a project at the ISR at TU Berlin used urban data mining to generate data on illicit property procedures in socially protected (*Milieuschutz*) areas in Berlin. Over the course of six months, different stages of urban data mining were carried out and are explained in detail in the following sections.

Different Sets of Data:
In an initial step, different sets of data were considered (Airbnb, Inside Airbnb, Booking.com, Berlin vs Airbnb, and so on) to accumulate information on what data points were freely available and potentially useful. The different data sets were all incomplete (as in most cases), and as a consequence using multiple sets

Association analysis is used to explore correlations between variables and to recognize patterns in doing so. It is often used in shopping-basket analyses, which aim to obtain knowledge about items bought by customers in order to identify patterns (for example, which products are usually bought together). These analyses can be extended into sequence analyses, which discover behavioral frequencies over time to identify trends (Sumathi and Sivanandam 2006, 52).

Clustering involves splitting objects of interest into homogeneous clusters by considering different attributes. The objects within one cluster should possess similar attributes and differ from those in the other clusters. By doing this, a model of clusters is built that arranges objects of interest and additional objects into categories (Cleve and Lämmel 2014, 57).

Classification analysis involves digging for patterns by using existing data, which is organized to create a classification model. This is then used to forecast new variables and rank them using the created classifications (Cleve and Lämmel 2014, 59 onwards). For example, safe areas are classified by choosing specific attributes that classify an area as safe. Afterwards, the shown areas can be classified as more or less safe based on that model. Additionally, probability calculations and prognoses can be made (Cleve and Lämmel 2014, 59 onwards).

Estimation aims to estimate the values of future data via an approximation function. In this way, data is used to calculate, extrapolate, and estimate future data (such as tem-

of data points was the most generative option. The websites *Inside Airbnb* and *Airbnb vs Berlin* (see example) generated, when combined, a useful and in most cases complete database. Both these applications use data scraping in an urban context to make private corporate data public and freely available.

Data Messiness:
A common difficulty in urban data mining is the messiness of the available date. This means that in most cases – and this one in particular – the datasets include messy, incomplete, duplicate, and out-of-date data points. Thus, the second step in urban data mining procedures is a cleaning process that aims to eliminate all irrelevant data points. In this project, all data points were managed using a massive Excel file.

Generating and Communicating Information:
Once the appropriate data was identified, mined, and treated for errors, it was possible to start transforming the data points into viable urban information. In this case, adding a time factor to the date and then visualizing the data both quantitatively and spatially was deemed appropriate.

Generation of New Data:
However, once the data was transformed into visual information, it became apparent that the data points were incomplete. In addition to communicating the information well, visualizing the generated urban data in this case helped identify shortcomings in the data. To resolve this,

peratures or weather conditions) (Cleve and Lämmel 2014, 61 onwards).

Instructions for Application

The main steps of mining data are to select, explore, transform, mine, interpret, and visualize the data. It is an iterative process where the outcome of each step is validated and used for the next step (Behnisch 2007, 21). Selecting data means deciding which data should be used to complete the task (Sumathi and Sivanandam 2006, 43). In addition to the basic dataset, external data can be used. Available data is therefore scanned to determine whether it is useful to the task at hand (Cleve and Lämmel 2014, 9). This leads to a transformation of the data. To do this, the data is organized by aggregating data, cleaning the dataset of useless attributes or null values (Sumathi and Sivanandam 2006, 43), removing outliers, converting unsuitable entries into numerical values, and so on. In the end, a useful dataset is produced that allows the data to be mined. The data can be mined using the different techniques mentioned above. The best-fitting method is chosen for the intended task. Following this, the dataset is transformed for use with the chosen method and searched for interesting patterns. In this way, a data mining model is generated that can be used for the chosen dataset and tested by integrating external data (Cleve and Lämmel 2014, 9 et. seq.). As one of the last steps, findings are interpreted with regard to the original research question (Sumathi and Sivanandam 2006, 733) by evaluating the

further mapping in the actual area of study had to be done. This, of course, is only possible when area of study can be accessed.

Outcomes:
While it would go beyond the scope of this report to explain the findings concerning illicit housing rentals in Berlin in full, a few things are worth noting for future urban data mining projects. Before starting any mining process, it is useful to investigate a variety of potential sources – even private sources – to see whether the data points can be made available through any kind of layering or scraping. The more potential data one can acquire, the more complete the information generated will be. Next, it is necessary to identify a way of sifting out non-useful data to avoid outdated or incorrect data skewing the information generated. While this removes most bad data points, it recommended that this only be done after the initial data visualization. When it comes to visualizing the data, it is important to do so in a way that provides an answer to your research question. Doing this can involve editing and visualizing the data in various ways – for example sequentially across different time periods, spatially, quantitatively, or any number of other ways.
Overall, however, there does not appear to be "one right way" of conducting urban data mining. In this case, clear research questions guided the data-mining process and indicated that using multiple sources was

findings with respect to validity, novelty, utility, and perceivability (Cleve and Lämmel 2014, 11). Findings can ultimately be visualized via graphics, tables, maps, and so on (Sumathi and Sivanandam 2006, 40) to make the findings directly understandable to third parties (Cleve and Lämmel 2014, 15).

Strengths and Limitations

Data mining can have a positive impact and be conducive to understanding big data and identifying undiscovered patterns and trends. This is thanks to the possibility of creating models and algorithms that allow us to categorize new variables and approximate behaviors. Furthermore, mining urban data can improve the efficiency of urban systems (such as infrastructures) and benefit the citizens' quality of life. By discovering new relations and identifying new aspects of knowledge, a diverse set of urban issues (such as traffic, energy, security, health, building design, civic protection, the environment, and social issues) can be improved (Panagiotou et al. 2016, 1; Andrienko et al. 2016, 2). In order for this to work, data from multiple sources is needed; not only governmental data, but "data from public, industrial, scientific or private sources" (Lämmel et al. 2016, 1).

Limitations result from a lack of data, meaning that patterns can only be discovered from small number of variables. This leads to non-representative evaluations if the dataset is not enhanced with additional data (Zimmermann 2015, 3). A lack of data may be caused by a lack of access to the necessary datasets or

beneficial. However, many different factors affect the suitability of any given method, and are therefore worth noting before any urban data mining endeavor.

Endnotes

1 Airbnb vs Berlin. [Online]. Available at http://airbnbvsberlin.com/ Accessed April 21, 2020.

2 Smart Citizen Kit. [Online]. Available at https://smartcitizen.me/ Accessed April 21, 2020.

3 MIT SENSEable City Lab. **Treepedia.** [Online]. Available http://senseable.mit.edu/treepedia Accessed April 21, 2020.

by technology restrictions such as the incompatibility of data formats. On top of this, there are technological and methodological restrictions and problems that might lead to the inaccuracy of the data, resulting in errors in exploring patterns and trends (Cleve and Lämmel 2014, 9). As such, systematic errors may arise during the data mining process. Additionally, the potential of low data quality – such as "noisy" data or data that is not labelled – must be taken into account, as this leads to low reliability in the information obtained (Panagiotou et al. 2016, 2; VaVeL, w.Y.). Moreover, privacy concerns with regard to available data may pose an issue when the data used reveals confidential information.

This text is based on the writing of Nanuk Rennert and Vera Fabinyi and was edited by Andreas Brück.

B.8

ANALYZING PICTURES

Breckner, R. **Sozialtheorie des Bildes.** Bielefeld: Transcript Verlag, 2010.
Langer, S. **Philosophie auf neuem Wege. Das Symbol im Denken, im Ritus und in der Kunst,** Frankfurt: Suhrkamp, 1979.

The segment analysis method is used to analyze all kind of images. This term was first introduced by Roswitha Breckner. In her book *Sozialtheorie des Bildes*, Breckner describes the subdivision of images and photographs into segments and their subsequent analysis. She divides the process of segment analysis into four distinct steps:

1. Documentation of the viewer's initial reception of the image
2. Formal description of the image
3. Creation of segments
4. Analysis of segments and their context

Breckner develops a toolkit with which to carve out symbolism and layers of meaning in images and contextualizes them to the sociological and societal fabric. Photographs especially obtain their own potential for symbolism through the pragmatics of their social use. Breckner enables the viewer to consciously examine his or her own initial reception of the image and why it evokes a distinct type of emotional reaction "as a culture-specific coherence of family life, success, wealth, and political power is staged in the symbolic presentation alongside texts" (Breckner 2010, 16, translation by the author).

Breckner introduces Susanne Langer's (1965/1979) term *Sinngewebe* (web of meaning), which interrelates with the terms *Bedeutungsfunktion* (function of meaning), *Form der Symbolisierung* (form of symbolism), *Bedeutungstypus* (type of meaning), and *Erfahrungstypus* (type of experience).

Bilder in sozialen Welten
In her postdoctoral habilitation, Roswitha Breckner applies her method to a photograph with text from the Austrian magazine *Trend*, to a photograph by Helmut Newton, and to a family's private photo album.[1] In her analysis of the photograph by Helmut Newton, Breckner follows the previsouly described procedure by first of all documenting her reception process. Her gaze rested initially on the standing naked woman, but at nearly the same time it landed on the man wearing a suit and sitting on a bed. Following this, she looked at the room's interior (bed, lamp) and finally at the wallpaper in the background. Breckner then continues with the formal description of the image. She delineates the composition area of the image and identifies a spatial perspective and vanishing point. The man is identified as the image's iconographic center, with the strongest visual impact in terms of both contrast and lighting.
Breckner further recognizes the tension between the male-dominated composition area and the female-dominated spatial perspective. The next aspect of her analysis is the separation of the image into segments. These segments include the figures of the man and the woman, as well as the space between them containing the lamp. Finally, Breckner arrives at the meaning of the image by using the allegory of the Madonna/whore: the man desires the naked woman but is overwhelmed by her beauty and does not dare to become involved with her.

"With the analysis of important types and the emblematic fabric that arises through their linkages, according to Langer, historical and cultural aspects beyond epistemological and anthropological questions can be examined," (Breckner 2010, 49, translation by the author). Breckner points out that these dimensions of meaning cannot be separated empirically but create a combined denotation. The separation into segments, however, offers an analytical method to understand the background context of the motif.

Segment analysis can be applied to any given image. As it is a tool for understanding an underlying pattern, it makes the producer's intention obvious. In the advertisement industry, for example, images in magazines or on billboards are meant to convey emotion and to convince the viewer of the value of the product shown. By enabling viewers to understand their emotional response, however, viewers become less vulnerable to succumbing to the advertised product.

In the first step, the documentation of the reception process, users of segment analysis are required to pay attention to their own process of observation while looking at the image. They are asked to formulate their approach to the image; to ask where they look first, second, third, and so on.

The second step is the formal description of the image. This is meant to yield a listing of the image's content: *what do I see?* The beholder is asked to formally describe the picture's elements, their relationship to each other, their colors and proportions. The findings of the second step need to be available in order to apply

A segment analysis of an image of the Warsaw Spire[2]
When I first look at the picture, my focus is on the structure right in the middle. It is framed by two adjacent buildings, which help guide my gaze to the middle of the picture. I next focus on the crowd of people in the courtyard. In particular, I look at the left-hand side, where most of the pedestrians gather. Afterwards, I distinguish between the built structures and the open spaces and have a closer look at the arrangement of the vegetation, trees, and walkways.
A formal description of the image is as follows:
There are three buildings to be seen in the image. There is one tower in the middle of the picture with buildings with curved facades to either side of it. All of them are cut by the frame of the picture.
A cloudless sky can be seen between the buildings. In the foreground and in front of and between the buildings we can see an open square divided by pathways and patches of lawn. The green patches are designed in geometric forms (triangle, circle) and filled with green, closely mown grass. Some trees are planted alongside the pathways. Some small fountains emerge from water basins in front of the buildings. An additional large fountain emerges from a circular water basin situated in the middle of the courtyard. The overall colors in this part of the image are green and grey.
The image is arranged in a way that emphasizes the central tower building.
When I highlight the directions given by the buildings to the left and to the right of the tower, they

Jonas Dimter (2015) **Warsaw Spire: Dekomposition der Visualisierung und Auswertung der Einzelelemente**.

the third step. The description of the image and its elements gives users a general idea of what the important elements of the image might be and of what the producers intended to be the focus.

In the third step, users are asked to subdivide the image into segments. The number of segments depends on the num-

all meet at the main building. The viewer's attention is clearly being directed there.
When the image is divided horizontally into four parts of equal size, the upper three parts are exclusively occupied by the buildings and the sky. The lower quarter depicts the scenery (square, pedestrians, vegetation). The vanishing lines converge on the building in the middle, right above the lower quarter occupied by the public space. In other words, the upper three quarters are private while the lower quarter is open to the public. The open space between the buildings is filled with pedestrians. Some of the figures are seated in the bars or cafés right next to the buildings on the right and left sides. The colors of the peoples' clothes are muted and mostly dark. The main source of light is from the sun, which has to be situated behind the viewer. The following is an analysis of the segments and their context:

Segment 1: The buildings. It is worth mentioning that the buildings reference themselves; that is, the reflecting glass facades mirror the neighboring buildings. No other buildings can be seen in the picture. Despite the developers' efforts to create an open and public atmosphere, the self-referencing provides a hint of their true intentions: to shape their development in their own interest, and to create a secluded space for their commercial interests in terms of content.

ber of important picture elements. It is essential that the whole image is subdivided without any parts being omitted. Although reassembling all the segments should once again create the initial image, it is possible to use the same part of the picture in different segments.

The fourth step requires an exact analysis of each of the segments. This step contains not only a thorough description of each segment but also characterizes the arrangement of the elements in relation to each other. This step reveals information about the social relationship between the different elements of the picture and provides a conclusion about the background of the images.

Breckner applies her method to images and photographs, but segment analysis can also be used for movies, visualizations, paintings, drawings and collages.

This text is based on the writing of Jonas Dimter and was edited by Martina Löw.

Segment 2: The sky. The shiny glass facades of the buildings are in different shades of blue. The sky consists of a light blue while some fountains in the middle of the square and next to the building on the left feature a deeper blue. Blue suggests seriousness, business, and modernity. The sky serves as a connecting element between the buildings. The color coding has been chosen to highlight the construction by providing a uniform background.

Segment 3: The scenery. In general, an atmosphere of openness, accessibility, and transparency is intended to be implied. The notion of a balance between the built and the natural environment is established; for example, the tree on the far left is reflected in the glass facade of the building on the left, transferring the perception of nature to the human-made construction. The color green is exclusively used for nature, i.e. for grass and trees.
The parasols on the lower left side stretch across the water basin next to the building and extend the ground floor into the "public" space of the courtyard. The public space aims to have a park-like quality and thus be human-friendly (water basins, fountains, grass, trees, clean air). The overall impression is that of a publicly accessible square with a publicly accessible ground floor (bar, art gallery).
The waving flags in the background on the right convey a feeling of lightness and celebration and visually connect the background with the

foreground. The color red is used for the flags and for the signage of the bar on the left. The water basins surrounding the buildings are intended to connect the square with the buildings. The predefined pathways (bridges) aim to give a sense of a smooth and pleasant transition from the outside to the inside. However, they could potentially be understood as implying access control and exclusive restrictions. The exclusivity of the buildings may be intended but does not fit with the analysis of segment 4.

Segment 4: People. The investor is eager to present his project as being as compatible with public accessibility as possible. However, no people can be seen on the office floors of any of the three buildings. Only on the inside of the ground floors are a few humans observable. The people visually connect the outside space (solar panels, tables, and chairs) with the ground floor's inner space and function (gastronomy). All the chairs are occupied, underlining the overall imagery of public and social acceptance.
As established in the investor's advertising slogan, the intention is to associate this project with local character ("The heart of Warsaw"), with making a contribution to the common good ("The perfect place to meet for business and leisure") and with regard for the residents ("You deserve it"). For this reason, the overall feeling of the picture created by its contents, perspective and color coding is pleasant.
After a thorough analysis of the image, however, it becomes obvious that the investor's interests are not accessibility or the common good. Despite the efforts made to use connecting elements, the built structure remains lifeless and is clearly separated from the public. Symptomatic of Warsaw's present development in the construction sector, the municipal administration provides international investors with great freedom and few restrictions. The result is investor-driven development with a focus on economic elements rather than on social needs and requirements. Provided with this information, the investor's claim of offering "A truly inspiring partnership" has a different ring to it.

Endnotes

1 Breckner, Roswitha. "Bilder in sozialen Welten. Eine sozialwissenschaftliche Methodologie und Methode zur interpretativen Analyse von Bildern." Habilitation, University of Vienna/Austria, 2010.

2 Analysis by Jonas Dimter in a term paper for the seminar Methods and Tools in Urban Design at TU Berlin.

B.9

USING QUESTIONNAIRES

del Rio, V. and Levi, D. (2009): "Internet-based surveys and urban design education. A community outreach graduate project in Redding, CA." **Urban Design** 14, no. 4 (2009): 192–206.

Diekmann, A. **Empirische Sozialforschung. Grundlagen, Methoden, Anwendungen**. Reinbek bei Hamburg: Rowohlt Taschenbuch Verlag, 2007.

Hewson, C. et al. **Internet Research Methods. A Practical Guide for the Social and Behavioural Sciences.** Los Angeles: SAGE Publications, 2003.

Merriam-Webster. **Merriam-Webster Learner's Dictionary**. [Online]. 2015. http://www.merriam-webster.com/dictionary/survey Accessed June 27, 2016.

Reinecke, J. (2014). "Grundlagen der standardisierten Befragung." In **Handbuch Methoden der empirischen Sozialforschung**, edited by Baur, N. and Blasius, J., 601–617. Wiesbaden: Springer Fachmedien.

The survey is the classical instrument of data collection for empirically oriented disciplines like the social and economic sciences (Reinecke 2014, 601). To conduct a survey means "to ask (many people) a question or a series of questions in order to gather information about what most people do or think about something" (Merriam-Webster 2015). Surveys gather information from a population of interest. The size of the sample depends on the purpose of the study.

In urban-design-related contexts, surveys usually aim either to find out more about certain target groups or about a defined space. Surveys may be used for the following purposes:

1. For research in an academic context; to prove or disprove a hypothesis from a well-known research field in urban design.
2. To find out about the satisfaction, wishes, needs, and suggestions of urban dwellers regarding the spatial qualities of their city, for example concerning green public space or the use of public transportation.
3. To find out about the satisfaction, wishes, needs, and suggestions of urban dwellers regarding the services on offer from their city's public administration or other city-related institutions; for example, whether vacancies are filled properly in order to provide good public service, or whether there are enough employees.
4. To find out about perceptions of, attitudes to, and expectations concerning a city or a project area, and to examine design alternatives (del Rio and Levi 2009).

The Local Conventions of Hairdressing: The Intrinsic Logic of Cities and Economics of Convention[1]

This research project was conducted by a research team of German sociologists led by Nina Baur and Martina Löw. The project sought to combine the concept of an *intrinsic logic of cities* with the *economics of conventions*. Using the hairdressing industry as case study, the project investigated whether and how economic sectors are structured by (the logic of) a particular city. The project examined the various ways in which economic actions and processes are organized according to local conventions.

During the first two years of this project, the research group used ethnographic research to explore which economic practices were specific to each city, systematized these across cities, and developed hypotheses based on their analyses. In the third year, they tested their hypotheses using cross-sectional survey data based on responses from the whole population of the four cities' hairdressing businesses.

The research group showed that (irrespective of the market segment they belong to) each city's hairdressers share (1) beliefs in what constitutes economic rationality, i.e. what must be done in order to be economically successful. These doctrines reproduce path-dependently and result in typical local (2) conventions – that is, ways of solving problems, especially in organizing the salon and everyday working

5. As political surveys designed to find out more about the attitudes, opinions, and suggestions supporters and opponents have during a political campaign. Political surveys are usually limited to a certain area or region.

To conduct a survey with a questionnaire, the following steps need to be followed:

At the very beginning, a central research question must be developed. This should be put into one single, precise sentence. After that, several hypotheses should be developed based on this research question. Proving or disproving these hypotheses should be highly relevant to answering the research question. A hypothesis can be defined as an assumption about a defined issue or an assertion about the correlation of two or more variables (Diekmann 2007).

From these hypotheses, several questions for the questionnaire must be developed. The answers to these questions in the survey should prove or disprove the initial hypotheses. It is important to ensure that the questions are framed in an appropriate manner and to choose an appropriate number of questions. One rule of thumb is that there should be no more than twenty questions in a survey in order to avoid people not answering all the questions.

Following this, researchers need to consider the following factors, which are often needed for analysis in an urban context:

1. What is the percentage breakdown of the participants by age group?

life; (3) forms of communication and interaction with customers and colleagues; and (4) time and space arrangements.

Endnotes

1 Research project funded by the German Research Foundation, TU Berlin and TU Darmstadt, 2011–14. See e.g. Baur, N., Hering, L., Löw, M. and Raschke, A.-L. "Tradition, Zukunft und Tempo im Friseursalon." In **Städte unterscheiden lernen**, edited by Frank, S., Gehring, P., Griem, J. and Haus, M., 97–124. Frankfurt am Main: Campus, 2014

2. What was the gender breakdown within these age groups?
3. What percentage of those who answered had children living at home?
4. If you conducted the survey in different cities, it is important to find out how many respondents are residents of the city in which the survey was conducted.
5. Did you make any hypotheses about potential planning conflicts? It might be interesting to find out about whether they exist through the survey, and about what interests and needs there are behind them.

After developing a set of questions, several preliminary assessments should be made to check whether the survey and its diction are clear to other people in order to avoid mistakes. Finally, it is important to decide how the survey will be conducted – online, by telephone, by (e-)mail, or on paper. In an urban design context, surveys are usually conducted using a web-based format. Sending out a paper version of the survey is usually too expensive for municipalities. However, there is a risk that a certain part of the population – especially the elderly population – may not be reached through online questions. Online surveys do not fully comply with the criteria of representativeness. The aim of web-based surveys, therefore, is to obtain the highest possible amount of feedback in order to create a basis for further actions and decisions. Nevertheless, all members of the target population should have the same opportunity to take the survey.

If the main aim of those creating a survey is to find out about the needs and wishes of a target group (or about their social constructions of reality), the option of carrying out a lower number of well-chosen interviews, rather than conducting a survey with many participants, should be considered. Usually, the relevant information needed in this type of research is not explicitly stated and needs to be asked for individually. A survey can fulfil this objective only in a very limited fashion – and a survey should not serve as a simple checklist for the planner's wishes!

There is a high chance of distortion when using surveys. They should be developed so as to minimize factors that may cause distortion as much as possible in order to get a useful result. The following are examples of factors that may cause distortion during polling and analysis:

- The way the questions are phrased in the questionnaire. Take a closer look at the phrasing of sensitive and personal questions. Phrase the questions as precisely as possible.
- The traits of the interrogated person (answering behavior). People have a tendency to react to personal questions by giving answers that are (socially) expected, rather than answers that express their personal opinion (Reinecke 2014, 603).
- The way the answers are presented. For example, it is not useful to visualize pie diagrams in 3D, as this distorts the relationships of the percentage shares through optic contraction.

If the objective is to find out about a change over time, conducting the survey several times at different points in time should be considered.

This text is based on the writing of Hilde Rosenboom and Finya Eichhorst and was edited by Martina Löw.

B.10

APPLYING ANT

Hasbun Chavarria, Y. and Stollmann, J. "Städtischen Akteur-Netzwerken folgen: Praktische, auf ANT basierende Werkzeuge." In **Das Kotti-Prinzip. Komplizenschaft zwischen Raum, Mensch, Zeit, Wissen und Dingen**, edited by Bock, C., Pappenberger, U., and Stollmann, J. Berlin: Ruby Press, 2018

Callon, M. and Latour, B. "Unscrewing the Big Leviathan; or How Actors Macrostructure Reality, and How Sociologists Help Them To Do So?" In **Advances in Social Theory and Methodology**, edited by Knorr, K. and Cicourel, A., 277–303. Routledge & Kegan Paul: London, 1981.

Callon, M. "Some elements of a sociology of translation: domestication of the scallops and the fishermen of St Brieuc Bay." In **Power, action and belief: a new sociology of knowledge?** edited by Law, J., 196–223. London: Routledge, 1986.

Callon, M. "Can methods for analysing large numbers organize a productive dialogue with the actors they study?" **European Management Review** 3, no. 1 (2006): 7–16.

Farias, I. and Bender, T., eds. **Urban Assemblages. How Actor-Network Theory changes urban studies**. London: Routledge, 2010.

Additional Reading:

Kurath, S. **Stadtlandschaften Entwerfen? Grenzen und Chancen der Planung im Spiegel der städtebaulichen Praxis**. Bielefeld: transcript Verlag, 2011.

Latour, B. **Reassembling the Social: An Introduction to Actor-Network-Theory**. Oxford: Oxford University Press, 2005.

Law, J. "Notes on the Theory of the Actor-Network Ordering, strategy and heterogeneity." **Systems Practice** 5, no. 4 (1992): 397–393.

Murdoch, J. and Marsden, T. "The Spatialization of politics: local and national actor-spaces in environmental conflict." **Transactions of the Institute of British Geographers**, 20, no. 3 (1995): 368–380.

Yaneva, Alberta. **The making of a building: a pragmatic approach to architecture**. Oxford: Lang, 2009.

Science and Technology Studies (STS) and Actor-Network Theory (ANT) have always had a close affinity with subjects in the fields of engineering and design. Today, they have become favored approaches for architects and urban designers reflecting on their practice and on the production of space in general. There may be two major reasons for this. The first of these is the growing acknowledgement that urban environments and buildings are performatively co-produced over time by a huge number of actors, professionals, laypeople, and users; the second is a new awareness concerning the role of both non-human nature and non-human actors such as technical devices and buildings. ANT attributes agency to non-human actors and assemblages of humans and non-humans as well as to individuals. ANT's concept of distributed agency resonates strongly with a contemporary sensitivity within the profession. It draws the attention from the architect personally (as the main creator) towards their embeddedness or entanglement in more complex networks of co-production. While the field of urban studies has embraced ANT (Farias and Bender 2010), it may still be difficult for designers and planners to understand how ANT, as a methodology, operates – and how one can apply it either in designer practice or for critically discussing the co-production of our built environment and the designer's role within it. It seems that "there is a widely shared feeling that ANT is a difficult thing to grasp because it is either 'too philosophical / too complicated,' or, on the contrary, 'too simple / too obvious.'" (Hasbun and Stollmann 2018, 46, translated by the authors).

ANT + Kotti&Co – a scenario including the non-human perspective[1]
Kotti&Co, a collective of tenants based around Kottbusser Tor in Berlin's Kreuzberg district, is an urban activist movement that has become influential in the current discourse concerning affordable housing in the city. The group of designers, activists, and residents of the housing estates at Kottbusser Tor in Berlin first joined forces in 2012 to develop strategies demonstrating that their calls for affordable housing were legitimate and to enlist local politicians in the campaign. Following the analytical sensitivities of ANT, these participants are here referred to as the human-actors.
"On an October afternoon at the Gecekondu, the newly and collectively erected headquarters of Kotti&Co, the human-actors are exchanging their diverse opinions using spoken words and physical gestures. The human-actors make use of the modest sitting facilities and tables available inside the Gecekondu. Suddenly, a group of neighbors offers all the human-actors present a cup of tea and a slice of homemade cake. After several hours of discussions, the human-actors find consensuses around a list of arguments that they all agree on. A smaller group of the human-actors make use of a megaphone to read their list of arguments out loud. At the same time, another group of human-actors makes use of a portable computer and software to design a flyer and a sticker that condenses this list of arguments into short

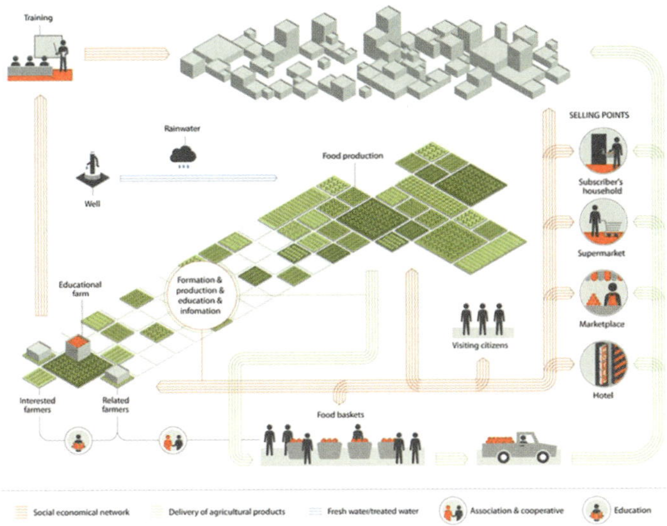

UAC Projekt led by Undine Giseke, TU Berlin (2015)
Multidimensional processes and actors in Pilot Project 4: Urban agriculture and healthy food production.

There are a number of reasons for this resistance. Firstly, practicing designers are irritated by the way that ANT conceives of realities as socially constructed and doubts the pre-existence of most phenomena they see as factual, such as nature and society. Instead, ANT contends that such phenomena are the local effects of social interactions between designers and material objects. In ANT, after all, the network is best understood as a method,

punchlines. These two newly designed products are then reproduced using a laser printer, a photocopier, paper, and ink. Once printed, the human-actors split the total amount of flyers and stickers into equal parts and proceed to hand them out to passing pedestrians as well as placing the stickers on traffic signs, light posts, bus stops, public bathrooms, trains, and railway stations. This scenario brings a wider variety of actors into play – namely the non-human actors. By enlisting more heterogeneous actors, the durability, range, scale, and overall strength of the network increases." (Bock, Pappenberger and Stollmann 2018, 49–50, translated by the authors)[2]

The Food Basket: Connecting urban and rural spheres in Casablanca – the healthy food production project[3]

The pilot project *Urban Agriculture and Healthy Food Production* aims to develop organic food production in cooperation with the agricultural-ecological pedagogical farm at Dar Bouazza. The organic products produced as part of the project are identified with a local quality label and distributed through "food baskets" – a veg box subscription scheme. They enable the building of direct relationships between the producers and the consumers supporting the local production of food. The pilot project is aimed at producers and consumers in Dar Bouazza and Casablanca. It encourages peri- urban farmers to try out organic agricultural activity for the sake of a healthy life and

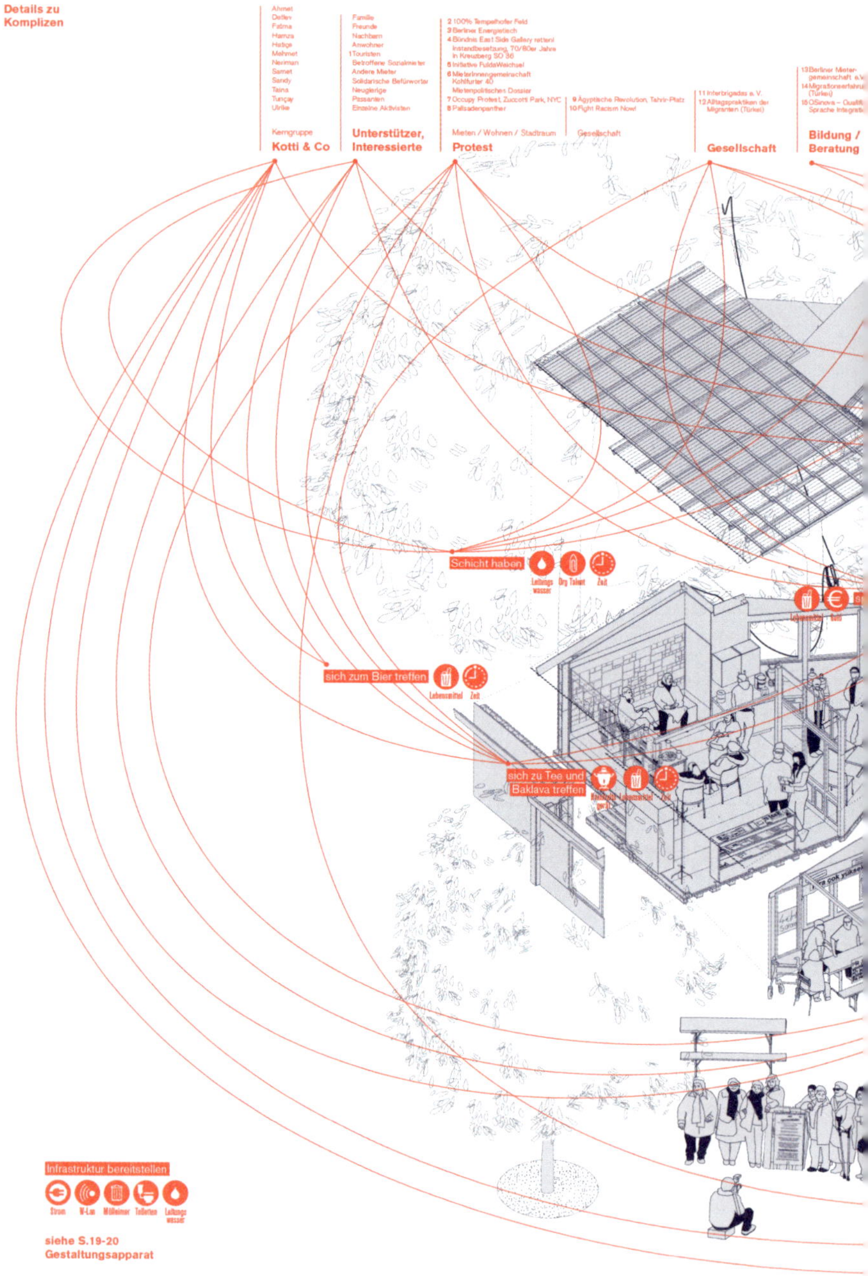

CC BY NC SA 4.0 International/Christine Bock and Ulrich Pappenberger (2018) **Das Kotti-Prinzip: Tenant initiative Kotti&Co's protest house "Gecekondo" at Kottbusser Tor and everyday assemblages of human and non-human actors**.

r Rockstar)
Theater
rer
20 Café Morgenstern
21 Copystudio am Kotti
22 Studierende (Urban Design, TU Berlin)
23 Studierende (Ethnologie, EUV Frankfurt/Oder)
Stadt
Kultur / Soziales
24 Ephraim Gothe (Staatssekretär, Berlin)
25 Oliver Hoefinghof (Piratenpartei, Berlin)
26 Katrin Lompscher (Die Linke, Berlin)
27 Cem Özdemir (Bündnis 90/Die Grünen, Bundesvorstand)
28 Katrin Schmidberger (Bündnis 90/Die Grünen, Berlin)
29 Franz Schulz (Bezirksbürgermeister, Friedrichshain-Kreuzberg)
Kottiundco.net
Facebook.com/kottiundco
Arte
Focushaber (Türkei)
Hürriyet (Türkei)
Märkische Oderzeitung
TAZ
TV Berlin
ar
Gewerbe
Wissenschaft
Politik / Verwaltung
Medien
Gecekondu aufräumen
Org.Talent
Zeit
(sich) informieren
Infomaterial
Fachwissen
Erfahrung
Zeit
sich austauschen
Fachwissen
Zeit
Interview führen
techn.Gerät
Fachwissen
Erfahrung

van Duivenbode, Ossip (2014) **Luchtsingel**. Top view of the roundabout.

rather than something "out there" waiting to be discovered (Latour 2005). Secondly, architecture and urban design researchers might find it unsurprising that networks are important, particularly as approaches to network-thinking have dominated planning theory since the mid-twentieth century. Hasbun and Stollmann propose a position between these two critical attitudes that could still be productive. They suggest that ANT "could usefully be understood as a loose compendium of analytical principles and instruments that are nevertheless based on very

as a source of income. The food baskets function as an active connecting actor within the regional producer-consumer network that has been built up through the subscription system. The baskets are an active, maintaining component within the business model, constituting a regular and continuous interaction between producers and consumers.

Luchtsingel Project Rotterdam[4]

The Luchtsingel is a 390-meter-long pedestrian bridge connecting three districts in the center of Rotterdam. The project was initiated and designed by the Rotterdam-based architects ZUS. A starting point for the project was a former office building, the *Schieblock*, which had been standing empty for years. It was transformed to develop a "city laboratory" acting as an important incubator for young entrepreneurs. New design, financing, and planning instruments were developed to make the Luchtsingel a reality. The *I Make Rotterdam* crowdfunding campaign was started to finance the project; for €25 anyone could buy a board inscribed with their name, which would be used in the construction of the Luchtsingel. Over 8000 boards were sold. The Luchtsingel thus became an innovative piece of public infrastructure accomplished mostly through crowdfunding. The bright yellow wooden structure is raised to the level of a story above ground, creating an uninterrupted pedestrian pathway that connects the recently renovated

van Duivenbode, Ossip (2014) **Luchtsingel**. Bird's eye view.

van Duivenbode, Ossip (2014) **Luchtsingel**. Perspective shot of the bridge.

specific philosophical grounds. The purpose of this application of ANT is to empower designers facing and acting in politically contested controversies in urban development." (Hasbun and Stollmann 2018, 46, translated by the authors).

An ANT approach can help designers to critically reflect on and better understand their own biases, positions, and particular conditions of power within the network of people, industries, materials, and knowledges that co-produce a project. This can lead to a more powerful self-positioning, but most importantly might prevent designers from "reproducing existing power constellations unknowingly" (Hasbun and Stollmann 2018, 46, translated by the authors). Designers will also become more open to and understanding of the knowledge cultures of citizens, non-professionals, and even their antagonists, and of how to navigate through, rather than in spite of, the heterogeneity of worldviews. Even though an ANT analysis can result in an analysis of power structures, the approach is based on the assumption that power is not an inherent condition of any given actor or entity, but that it is collectively given – even if not intentionally (Callon and Latour 1981).

Three simple principles proposed by Michel Callon (1986) will be introduced in order to explain the specificity of an ANT approach to urban phenomena and processes: free association, generalized agnosticism, and generalized symmetry. Rather than being a theory in and of itself, ANT is a way of looking at and understanding how a particular actor-network operates. Thus,

Rotterdam Centraal station with the historic Laurens-kwartier district. From an ANT perspective, the physical intervention itself, its marking in yellow, and its financing campaign are just a few components of the human-non-human actant assemblage that contributed to building and maintaining the network as a whole.

Endnotes

1 Bock, C., Pappenberger, U. and Stollmann, J., eds. **Das Kotti-Prinzip. Komplizenschaft zwischen Raum, Mensch, Zeit, Wissen und Dingen**. Berlin: Ruby Press, 2018.

2 Bock, Pappenberger, **Das Kotti-Prinzip.**

3 Giseke, U. et al. "Urban Agriculture for Growing City Regions. Connecting Urban-Rural Spheres in Casablanca, Routledge" [Online]. 2015. Available at http://uac-m.freiraum.tu-berlin.de/de/pilot-projects/pilot-project-4/index.html

4 archdaily.com. **The Luchtsingel / ZUS.** [Online]. 2015. Available at https://www.archdaily.com/770488/the-luchtsingel-zus and https://zus.cc/projects/luchtsingel-rotterdam

as a principle, free association means that the observer must abandon all a priori distinctions between polarities – such as left/right, powerful/weak, urban/rural – which are organized as "binary oppositions" that sustain a series of imaginary "invisible structures" believed to order all scales of society and natural science. Instead, the researcher should be aware that they cannot know beforehand how a certain actor will act, and should therefore follow them closely as they act. The principle of generalized agnosticism means that the observer/researcher should not judge or censor the actors and not assign them to pre-defined roles (such as "victim" or "offender"). Categories of actors are established only after the analysis (Callon 2006). Thirdly, generalized symmetry demands that the observer/researcher applies the same analytical principles to all actors that have agency in the network, whether they are human, machines, objects, plants, or building codes. As such, this principle also implies that the observer must use the same vocabulary and critical lenses to see and talk about all the actors being followed. These actors assemble into hybrid actants; for example, man-machine actants composed of technology and users acting together.

Applying ANT to the analysis (more usually called "tracing" in ANT) of urban development and design processes demands a fairly in-depth follow-up of the actors, making use of observations, interviews, and/or the study of sources like legal documents of protocols. However, a basic understanding of ANT and the agency of non-humans also allows for a way of seeing that empowers the designer to attribute value to the spatial, aesthetic, and performative qualities of objects, architecture, and urban spaces, thus adding value to the products of their own practice.

This text is loosely based on an essay by Ari Maximiliano Rizian and Rocio Garcia Gravino and was edited by Undine Giseke, Jörg Stollmann, and Yamil Hasbun Chavarria.

Benevolo, L. **Die Geschichte der Stadt.** Frankfurt/Main: Campus Verlag, 1980.

Conzen, M.R.G. **Thinking about Urban Form. Papers on Urban Morphology, 1932-1998**. Bern: Peter Lang, 2004.

Curdes, G. **Stadtstruktur und Stadtgestaltung.** Stuttgart: Kohlhammer, 1997.

Curdes, G. **Stadtstrukturelles Entwerfen.** Stuttgart: Kohlhammer, 1995.

Çalişkan, O. and Marshall, S. "Urban Morphology and Design: Introduction." **Built Environment** 37, no. 4 (2011): 381–392.

Dempsey, N., Brown, C., Raman, S., Porta, S., Jenks, M., Jones, C., and Bramley, G. "Elements of urban form." In **Dimensions of the Sustainable City**, edited by Jenks, M. and Jones, C., 21–51. Dordrecht, Heidelberg, London and New York: Springer, 2010)

Gauthiez, B. "The history of urban morphology." **Urban Morphology** 8, no. 2 (2004): 71–89.

Humpert, Klaus: **Einführung in den Städtebau**. Stuttgart, Berlin and Cologne: Kohlhammer, 1997.

Humpert, K., Brenner, K., and Becker, S. **Fundamental principles of urban growth**. Wuppertal: Müller + Busmann, 2002.

Koolhaas, R. and Mau, B. **S, M, L, XL.** New York: Monacelli Press, 1997.

Krier, R. **Town Spaces. Contemporary Interpretations in Traditional Urbanism**. Basel: Birkhäuser, 2006.

Krier, R. **Urban Space**. London: Academy Editions, 1979.

Kropf, Karl **The handling characteristics of urban form**. Urban Design 93 (2005): 17–18.

Kropf, Karl "Morphological Investigations: Cutting into the Substance of Urban Form." **Built Environment** 37, no. 4 (2011): 393–408.

Lampugnani, V.M., Albrecht, K., Bihlmaier, H., and Zurfluh,

B.11

UNDERSTANDING TYPOLOGIES AND MORPHOLOGIES

L., eds. **Manuale zum Städtebau. Die Systematisierung des Wissens von Stadt 1870–1950**. Berlin: Dom Publishers, 2017.
Lang, J. **Urban Design: A Typology of Procedures and Products**. Oxford: Architectural Press, 2005.
Larkham, P. "Understanding Urban Form?" Urban Design 93, (2005): 22–24.
Lee, C.C.M. **Working in Series: Towards an Operative Theory of Type**. London: AA Publications, 2010.
Moudon, A. V. "Urban morphology as an emerging interdisciplinary field." **Urban Morphology** 1, (1997): 3–10.
Quatremère de Quincy, A.-C. "Type." First published in 1825 in **Encyclopédie Méthodique**, vol. 3, trans. Samir Younés. Reprinted in **The Historical Dictionary of Architecture of Quatremère de Quincy.** London: Papadakis Publisher, 2000.
Raith, E. **Stadtmorphologie. Annäherungen, Umsetzungen, Aussichten**. Wien: Springer, 2000.
Rowe, C. and Koetter, F. **Collage City**. Basel: Birkhäuser, 1984.
Sharr, A. **Thinkers for Architects. Heidegger for Architects**. London. Routledge, 2007.
Sitte, C. **Der Städtebau nach seinen künstlerischen Grundsätzen**. Basel: Birkhäuser, 1889.
Streich, B. **Stadtplanung in der Wissensgesellschaft**. Wiesbaden: Springer, 2011.
Stojanovski, T. and Axelsson, Ö. "Typo-morphology and environmental perception of urban space." Conference paper presented at ISUF 2018 XXV International Conference on Urban Form and Social Context, Krasnoyarsk, 2018.
Stübben, Joseph: **Der Städtebau**. Darmstadt: n.p., 1890.
Syahidah, M., Nor Zalina, H., and Alias, A. "Typo-Morphology as an Approach for the Conservation of the Early Malay Towns." **Asian Journal of Environment, History and Heritage** 1, no. 2 (2017)

Designing a city requires knowledge of inherent spatial principles and interdependencies. As such, the analysis of spatial structures in the urban fabric is a fundamental tool for architects, planners, and urban designers. In design practice, the complexity of the urban form is conceived of as the development of physical elements according to formal or informal rule systems over time (Conzen 2004, Gauthiez 2004, Raith 2000, Koolhaas and Mau 1997, Krier 1979 and 2006). To facilitate the analysis, "the urban spatial structure is understood as a quasi-composed whole of layers" (Streich 2011, 351). However, the identification and selection of different layers relates to the specific design task or research question. The methods applied should, therefore, not be understood as a predefined sequence of analytical steps, but rather as partly parallel and interlocking lines of investigation blending the identification of morphological principles, key elements, and organizational units.

Since their appearance, morphological and typological analysis have served as catalysts for theoretical turns in urban design theory. They are also closely related to professional and societal discourses on the urban and how it should be conceived and transformed. Tracing back the literal meaning of the term *morphology* leads us to the Ancient Greek words *morphé* (form, shape) and *lógos* (word, reason, principle). The Greek *typos* refers to the study and theory of types and classification systems (Lang 2005, 43). Architectural perspectives on these terms in particular tend to assume universal ruling forces governing the generation

Nolli Map
The Nolli Map is one of the most-cited plans in architectural history. Drawn by the Italian architect and cartographer Giovanni Battista Nolli in 1748, it was originally named "Nuova Topografia di Roma." The plan represents the city of Rome in the eighteenth century in an unusual way. Not only is the external appearance of the urban morphology shown, but it is overlaid with another layer showing the public accessibility of buildings. By showing the ground-floor plans of all buildings accessible to the public, the ordinary figure-ground diagram becomes more complex. The Nolli Map thus extends the notion of urban morphology beyond a simple analysis of spatial volumetric elements by identifying spaces in which social interaction can take place – both outside and inside buildings.

Chicago School
Emerging in the 1920s and 1930s, the Chicago School was the first major research group to focus on urban sociology. It conducted intensive studies on the relation between the urban environment and the social and ethnic patterns within it. Research by the School's members combined grounded theory with profound ethnographic fieldwork carried out within the urban morphology of the city of Chicago. The results were mapped on various diagrams, which were then placed on top of a basic morphological map. By superimposing the layers, the notion of urban morphology was expanded with the inclusion of social

of spatial and material forms. This is the case, for example, in classification systems based on the works of nineteenth-century architects Jean-Nicolas-Louis Durand and Gottfried Semper (Sharr 2007, Lee 2010). As such, morphological analysis as a scientific method consists of the profound study of the shape of objects, whereas typology is a creative approach to emulation. In his *Dictionnaire historique d'architecture* (1825), Quatremère de Quincy pointed out that "the word 'type' presents less the image of a thing to copy or imitate completely than the idea of an element which ought itself to serve as a rule for the model" (1825/2000, 175). This analytical approach summarizes the characteristics of streets, squares, buildings, and monuments represented by structural elements in order to reveal and render legible planning and urban development history, as well as collective memories – and, in doing so, a city's inherent formal logic.

The first urban planning manuals were published in reaction to nineteenth-century urban expansions in order to categorize and illustrate exemplary urban spaces and design principles (Lampugnani, 2017). In particular, the textbook collections by Sitte (1889) and Stübben (1890) effected the establishment of urban design as an independent discipline. Initially focused on the two- and three-dimensional shape of the city, morphology now takes into account the forms of the city's constantly developing networks, blocks, and buildings, as well as the integration of other space-generating factors such as transport and industrial infrastructure facilities, vegetation, and systems of open space

patterns, and underlying relations and structures between the social and the spatial elements could be interpreted.

Typological Bombardment

In the winter semester of 2014, the urban design studio at the Chair for Urban Design and Urbanization at TU Berlin focused on the Dragoner Areal (today known as the Rathausblock), Berlin's second-largest inner-city property. The studio developed two scenarios for future development based on two different operating models in dialogue with the citizens' initiative Stadt von Unten (City from Below) and a consortium made up of a public housing corporation and the Mietshäuser-syndikat (a network supporting resident ownership in self-governed apartment houses). Earlier in 2014, both the citizen's initiative and the consortium had applied for the site as project developers in a public bidding process. To start the design studio, thirty urban morphologies – abstracted from historic urban design projects and existing urban models (with associative names such as 'Residential Classic', 'Generic City Fabric', and 'Accidental Bastard') – were projected onto the site. The complex site, characterized by heritage buildings and deep plots, was tested on its capacity for densification. The projected urban morphologies, too, were tested for their spatial qualities as they related to the site. The process of projection also required adapting the morphologies to the site without losing

Martin Murrenhoff (2014–15) **"Generic City Fabric" typological bombardment category, Freie Universität, Berlin**. Architects: Candilis, Josic, Schiedhelm, Woods, 1973.

(Benevolo 1980). Topography is also an integral element, representing one of the material physical layers in morphological analysis. In short, morphological analysis serves as a basic research tool; as an "approach to conceptualising the complexity of physical form" (Larkham 2005, 22). A thorough understanding of the internal structural conditions of the physical fabric is essential to understanding urban development processes and to successfully "manipulating" and designing the urban.

their specific characteristics. The resulting outcomes were then examined for suitability to be adapted to the programmatic requirements of the two scenarios. The most suitable and promising proposals were selected and developed further. In contrast to deductively developing a design concept from the programmatic requirements, this non-linear process permits intuitive design discoveries.[1]

Endnotes

1 Murrenhoff, M., Stollmann, J. and Chair for Urban Design TU Berlin. "Urban design studio Dragoner-Areal Berlin." Design studio at Technische Universität Berlin, 2014/2015. In 2020, the publication **Neue Kreuzberger Mischung** will be published by the TU Berlin University Press.

Martin Murrenhof (2014–15) **"Residential Classic" typological bombardment category, Interbau, Berlin**. Architects: Bakema, Baldessari, Niemeyer et al., 1957.

During the 1970s, the functionalist approach to urban design that had characterized post-war planning was increasingly criticized. Architects and urban designers turned to the rich historical repository of urban forms and thus rediscovered the formal analysis of building types and urban morphology as an inspiration for designs. Such reading of the built environment became internationally established in typo-morphological approaches. *Collage City* (Koetter and Rowe 1979) was a seminal, groundbreaking work on the comprehensive analysis of the contemporary urban form as an assemblage of different and equally valid morphologies and types. The publication prompted architects and planners to re-examine the subject of their work in structural and aesthetic terms, providing tools for analysis and design – although it did not yet provide urban researchers with a scientific method to apply to their work. Nevertheless, *Collage City* was echoing theories of urban planning and design of the time that influenced spatial sciences worldwide. One of these theories held that urban forms can be characterized via specific, recognizable elements and their relationships at different scales (Humpert 1997, Kropf 2005 and 2011, Moudon 1997, Dempsey et al. 2010). On the basis of this approach, Aldo Rossi and Rob and Leon Krier advocated the rediscovery of archetypical typologies from the history archives, as well as urban design favoring the "reconstruction" or continuation of the urban fabric over demolition. This framework of urban analysis has characterized a substantial portion of contemporary design practices through to the present day (Caliskan and Marshall 2011, Syahidah Amni et al. 2017, Stojanovski and Axelsson 2018).

In German-speaking countries, morphological layering in analysis and design is based primarily on the findings of the first academic studies carried out in the 1980s. Gerhard Curdes and Klaus Humpert contributed significantly to the development of morphological theory, identifying three basic forms for urban structures (line, area, and point) based on anthropological research. The point elements (building, city center), linear elements (traffic lines, networks), and area elements (land plots, area units) form the compositional basis for the formation of urban units organized using basic principles and logics (Curdes 1995 and 1997, Humpert 1997, Humpert et al. 2002). This structural approach is then combined with stratification into discrete layers (built mass, open space, public transport, etc.) related to the analysis or design objectives. Curdes's and Humpert's approach is based not only on their own research but also on the contributions and findings of the architects Gerd Albers (1919–2015) and Oswald Matthias Ungers (1926–2007).

Morphological and typological analysis is based on abstraction. Complex forms must be reduced to their essential characteristics in order to be categorized. This reduction of the complexity of the city has also generated criticism (cf. Albers 2000, 27; Kropf 2005). While the generic layout of infrastructure networks, blocks, and buildings remains fairly consistent across different planning approaches, the structural layers are always the result of social and cultural processes. Here, only a more detailed analysis can reveal the great diversity of spatial production within different social habitats. As such, scaling and defining the degree of abstraction is part of the individual analysis process. Additionally, the formal analysis should be complemented by social, ecological, or economic data with the help of the layers approach.

Morphological and typological analysis is used both for research and as a tool to generate and test new design proposals.

Firstly, the analysis of historical time periods can serve as an archive of knowledge for new design solutions. Secondly, a design proposal can be tested in terms of its impact and integration into its typo-morphological context. This is an integrative method that does not follow a set, predetermined procedure. The main principle is an abstraction of urban complexity to support a particular argument by highlighting specific elements of the city's spatial appearance. Through the decomposition and decoding of space, specific composition contexts can be described, examined, and evaluated by adding and removing layers. The analysis starts by defining the main focus of interest in order to reduce information, both in terms of removing elements in order to focus the analysis and by reducing elements to their basic characteristics. Based on this definition, specific urban elements are selected for mapping. The resulting maps should make it possible to assess specific formal and spatial qualities. This not only enables spatial information such as patterns of arrangement or the characteristics of connecting lines and surfaces to be read, but also allows abstract planning concepts and processes to be reconstructed. By adding new layers, logics of interaction and relationships between different spatial elements or periods can be visualized and recognized. The basis onto which these additions are mapped is always an analysis plan that is as single-layered as possible.

This text is based on the writing of Frederik Springer, Anne Gunia, Samuel Barben, and Xianglin Zhang and was edited by Felix Bentlin and Jörg Stollmann.

B.12

VIEWING THE URBAN THROUGH AN ETHNOGRAPHIC LENS

Geertz, C. **The interpretation of cultures. Selected essays**. New York: Basic Books, 1973.

Malinowski, B. **Argonauts of the Western Pacific. An Account of Native Enterprise and Adventure in the Archipelagoes of Melanesian New Guinea**. London: Routledge and Kegan Paul, 1922.

Moore, J. D. **Visions of Culture**. Lanham, New York, Toronto, and Plymouth: Altamira Press, 2009.

Schensul S.L., Schensul J.J., and LeCompte, M., eds. **Initiating Ethnographic Research. A Mixed Method Approach**. Lanham, New York, Toronto, and Plymouth: Altamira Press, 2012.

Wacquant, L. "Habitus as Topic and Tool. Reflections on Becoming a Prizefighter." **Qualitative Research in Psychology** 8 (2011): 81–92.

The word *ethnography* is made up of the following roots: *ethno*, referring to specific cultures, and *graphy*, referring to writing and theorizing.

Ethnography involves the study of cultures that are unfamiliar and the writing of field notes supported by theory.

Ethnographic research is largely understood as the process of observing and studying a group of people, institutions, or places/spaces in order to systematize the findings and from there deduce phenomena, social structures, or cultural patterns specific to the given group, groups, or area.

In the fields of anthropology and sociology, ethnographic research entails spending an extended time with the given group or in the area and, during this time period, interviewing informants, observing rituals, eliciting kin terms, making a linguistic analysis, collecting and systematizing totems and artefacts, tracing property lines, taking a census of households, and/or keeping a journal.

Ethnographic research mostly concludes with the production of a monograph: the ethnography. This monograph is the work produced through the analysis and evaluation of all material and knowledge gathered through the ethnographic research. Ethnography always includes self-reflection. While Bronislaw Malinowski claimed to take "the native point of view" in 1922, Clifford Geertz had taken the individual influence of the ethnographer into account by 1973 and spoke of "thick descriptions."

Ethnographic research is seen as a key to understanding a particular culture or social setting. The method is used to inves-

Amazing Grace[1]
In this book, Jonathan Kozol portrays the realities of young people's lives in the South Bronx in New York City. He describes children who live among poverty, but who cling to hope and love for survival. Presenting his findings through a report of his own experiences and observations, he blurs the line between being a distant observer and a concerned speaker in discussing the situations examined. Beyond an exact and captivating description of the circumstances he observed, he looked for explanations – such as segregated communities or the social system as a whole – on a larger scale.

Patterns of Culture[2]
This work, published in 1934, is one of the important works by American anthropologist Ruth Benedict. The work's most important assumption was that human behavior is mainly learned and not innate, and that cultures therefore develop lasting social patterns. The basis for her work was a study of three tribal cultures: the indigenous people of Vancouver Island, referred to by anthropologists as the Kwakiutl, the Zuni in New Mexico, and the people of Dobu Island in Melanesia. The ethnography on the Dobu Islanders in particular demonstrates that Western ethics are not the only possible basis for a functioning civilization, as theft was identified as the highest virtue on Dobu.

tigate the meaning of social life from an everyday perspective. Ethnographic techniques have spilled over into other disciplines, such as urban studies, heritage studies, and planning, in order to understand the *genius loci* of a given plot or area.

To apply the methods of ethnographic research, the following elements need to be considered (Schensul, Schensul and LeCompte 2012):

Observation – it is important to actively engage with the subject of study by physically entering and observing the field for a given amount of time.

Language – using the native language can be an important instrument where possible.

Note-taking – it is essential to keep an ethnographic diary to systematically record various aspects of behavior, a chronology of events, recurring stories and narratives, rituals, and habits.

Pictorial notes – taking photographs, collecting or drawing maps, and writing tables and diagrams to systematically record certain aspects of cultural life.

Concrete instances – when interviewing research participants, it is helpful to ask about the specificities of concrete phenomena rather than asking about their take on an abstract analysis.

Focus on a specific aspect – while the breadth of "culture" has to be taken into account and borne in mind, it can be helpful to ground the general in the specific by focusing on specific phenomena, rituals, or habits.

Endnotes

1 Kozol, J. **Amazing Grace. The Lives of Children and the Conscience of a Nation.** New York: Broadway Books. 1995. See also Wacquant's excellent ethnographic investigation on male prize-fighting as a chance to gain social capital, e.g. Wacquant 2011, see above.

2 Benedict, R. **Patterns of Culture**. New York: Houghton Mifflin, 1934.

	gestures mimics	statements	actions
1	friendly	„conservative"	distance
2	shocked grossed out		distance
3	friendly	„chose to be gay?"	curiosity
4	amicable		touch
5	⋮	„you are changing me!"	HUG! ♡
6	✓	„I really like you"	

Anthony Grujic (2015) **Behavior table**. Observation notes taken during research about the importance of cultural exchange with regard to homophobia in Poland.

Both the strengths and limitations of ethnographic research lie in the very nature of the method: It is, in the end, an abstraction of a deeply personal experience, as the researcher enters a field that he or she engages and corresponds with physically, mentally, and emotionally. The results of the research are therefore inextricably linked with the individual capabilities and suitability of the researcher within the given field of study.

On a political level, this means that power plays an important part in the research experience; for example, how will a disadvantaged community respond to a privileged researcher? Can ethnographic research go beyond the dynamic of the encounter?

On a more personal level, the accuracy and relevance of ethnographic research strongly depends on the perceptiveness, focus, and reflective capability of the researcher, as well as his or her ability to understand their findings within the greater context of the field.

This text is based on the writing of Anthony Grujic and was edited by Martina Löw.

#B.13

ANALYZING AND VISUALIZING ACTORS

Brugha, R. and Varvasovszky, Z. "Stakeholder analysis. A review." **Health Policy and Planning** 15, no. 3 (2000): 239–246.
Bryson, J. M. "What to do when stakeholders matter. Stakeholder Identification and Analysis Techniques." **Public Management Review** 6, no. 1 (2004): 21–53.
Enserink, B., Hermans, L., Kwakkel, J., Thissen, W., Koppenjan, J., and Bots, P. **Policy Analysis of Multi-Actor Systems**. The Hague: Lemma, 2010.
Healy, Patsy "Collaborative Planning in Perspective." **Planning Theory** 2, no. 2 (2003): 101–123.
Latour, Bruno **Eine neue Soziologie für eine neue Gesellschaft. Einführung in die Akteur-Netzwerk-Theorie**. Frankfurt am Main: Suhrkamp, 2007.
Harrison, J.S., Freeman, R.E., and Cavalcanti Sá de Abreu, M. "Stakeholder Theory As an Ethical Approach to Effective Management. Applying the theory to multiple contexts." **Review of Business Management** 17, no. 55 (2015): 858–869.
Mitroff, I.I. **Stakeholders of the organizational mind**. San Francisco: Jossey-Bass, 1983.

Actor analysis is a combination of methods used to create an overview of systems of actors related to a design problem. It is used to clarify different perceptions, positions, and relationships among actors and can therefore lay the groundwork for strategic actions.

The method as described here originates from stakeholder analysis in strategic management. The term *stakeholder* was already being used in the 1930s to describe major interest groups such as customers, employees, the general public, and shareholders. In the 1980s, stakeholder analysis was developed into a more systematic approach with clearly defined steps. The adaptation of actor analysis for spatial planning was linked to paradigm shifts from top-down comprehensive planning to more collaborative, inclusive strategic approaches (Brugha and Varvasovszky 2000, 240; Healy 2003, 102 onwards).

In the reviewed literature, the terms *stakeholder* and *actor* are often interchanged. Enserink et al. (2010) define an actor as "a social entity, person, or organization, able to act on or exert influence on a decision … actors are those parties that have a certain interest in the system and/or that have some ability to influence that system, either directly or indirectly." (2010, 80). In this quote, the authors emphasize the actors' ability to act rather than focusing solely on their interest, as the term stakeholder would imply (2010, 80).

Actor analysis is based on stakeholder analysis methods, which focus on the perceptions, values, resources, and networks

Makoko/Iwaya Waterfront Regeneration Plan[1]

The city of Lagos is the largest city in Africa and has been one of the fastest-growing cities in the world over the past few years. The impact of urbanization in the metropolitan area presents big challenges, including resource management, housing policy, mobility infrastructure, and developing ecologically sustainable environments. In addition to this host of issues, some of the coastal areas of the city are directly threatened by climate change and a continuously rising sea level. Makoko, an informal settlement located on the coast, faces shrinking land resources for urban development of any kind. As a reaction to this situation, various projects have been initiated that deal with this vulnerability by using innovative approaches. These include, for example, the projects Floating School by NLÉ, and Decentralized Neighborhood Hotspots by Urban Fabulous, both of which have contributed to the Makoko/Iwaya Waterfront Regeneration Plan (2013). The existing local knowledge of Makoko's inhabitants, who have lived and worked under these conditions for some years, and a new resource-based local economy for and by locals, should help the area face the urbanization and climate-change challenges of the future. To achieve this, however, all actors – from government institutions to investors and inhabitants – must work together effectively. The office of Urban Fabulous conducted an actor analysis on the macro, meso, and micro of actors. For a detailed exploration of different aspects, a variety of methods with different theoretical backgrounds are available. These include, for example, social network analysis, game theoretic models, and discourse analysis. Actor analysis has also been influenced by actor-network theory, but follows a different approach. In contrast to the rather classic approach discussed here, actor-network theory assumes that not only humans have agency in processes, but that the nature and technology they are connected with do as well (Latour 2007, 9–38).

Instructions for the Application of Actor Analysis: Steps

The different steps in actor analysis include problem formulation, identifying the inventory of actors, mapping formal relationships, clarifying interests, objectives, and perceptions, mapping actor interdependencies according to power and interest, and finally comparing the results with the initial problem formulation (Enserink et al. 2010, 83).

Actor analysis starts out with an initial definition of the problem, which is necessary in order to specify the focus and scope of analysis. The problem formulation can start from the point of view of a problem owner or that of the researcher or designer conducting the analysis (Enserink et al. 2010, 83).

As a second step, the actors involved are identified. Mitroff (1983) describes different actor identification techniques, which are best used side-by-side to obtain a representative picture of relevant actors. These techniques include a variety of approaches:

levels of Nigeria, Lagos, and Makoko and visualized the interrelationships – for example, projects connecting the different actors, and the actors' roles in the development processes (world-architects n.d.).

Lekki Free Trade Zone[2]
In 2003, the Nigerian government formed an alliance with a Chinese corporation to build a Free Trade Zone around the city of Lekki, located in Lagos State east of the city Lagos. The aim was to improve national economic structures and development as well as to enhance business relationships between China and Nigeria. The development of the Free Trade Zone was to be carried out according to existing Chinese practices, where Free Trade Zones have proven to be regional and economic development boosters. Originally, the Chinese company, the Lagos State government, and local investors joined together to develop the Lekki Free Trade Zone. However, since most financial investments came from Chinese investors, they strongly influenced the planning process. The master plan, for example, was adapted to Chinese construction norms, and finally revised by the urban planning and design institute of Shenzen in China.
In 2016, local researchers in cooperation with the Heinrich Böll Foundation did an actor analysis and visualized power shifts during the development process of the Free Trade Zone using a power interest matrix. It shows relationships between actors according to their

- the imperative approach (based on the actors' felt interests in the problem)
- the positional approach (based on formal decision-making structures)
- the reputational approach (based on key informants' identification of important actors)
- the opinion leadership method (Who shapes actors' opinions?)
- the demographic approach (identifying actors by age, gender, occupation, religion, and so on)
- and using problem diagrams and causal maps for the defined problem (identifying who influences the system factors) (Mitroff 1983, 33; Enserink et al. 2010, 85 onwards).

As a third step, the formal aspects of the actors should be mapped, as they shape the interaction and resource dependencies between actors and form the basis for informal relationships. These include formal positions, formal relationships and laws, tasks and responsibilities, legislation, procedures, and authorities. Next, the interests, objectives, and problem formulations of the different actors are identified. Finding out their specific interests shows the main relationship actors have to the problem and points out possible solutions. Where interests can be understood as a general feature of a group of actors (such as the interest of a company to make a profit), the objectives, in turn, are the specific goals for a certain situation. Both shape the actors' perception of the

interests in and their ability to exert an influence on the project (Heinrich Böll Stiftung Nigeria and Fabulous Urban 2016).

LGBT Community Space in Sheffield
In 2013 and 2014, architecture students from the University of Sheffield carried out research and a design project concerning urban spaces for Sheffield's LGBT community. Since minority sexual and gender identities often face exclusion, the goal of the project was to create an LGBT community center in Sheffield that offered people a focal point for information and support. Therefore, the needs and desires of various LGBT groups in Sheffield, as well as those of similar groups in other British and international cities, were investigated. Afterwards, multiple workshops were organized to determine the best location within the city of Sheffield for the new community center. The students also looked at other relevant actors related to the LGBT community. These were organized according to their involvement and motivation, as well as categorized into groups of different power levels. The results were visualized in a stakeholder circle diagram created by students of the University of Sheffield. This diagram places the design problem at the center and lists all the different actors and roles surrounding it. The closer actors are to the center of the circle, the greater their importance to the problem-solving process.

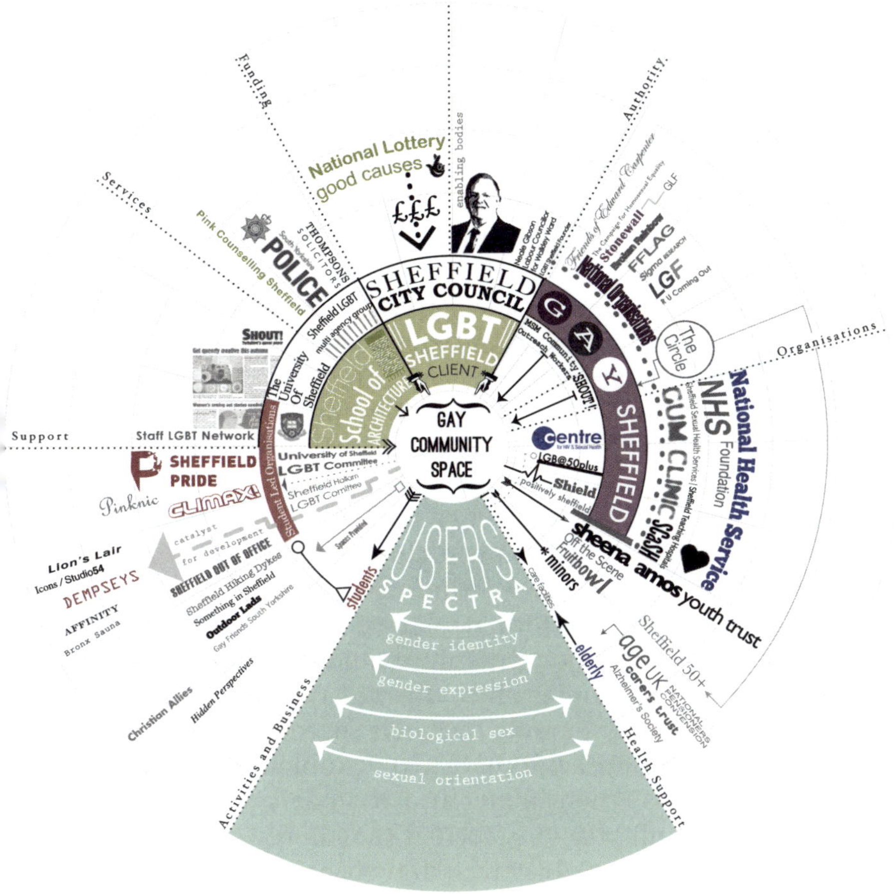

LGBT Sheffield Live Team (2013) **Live LGBT. Sheffield LGBT stakeholder map.**

Mapping Climate Communication[3]

The Mapping Climate Communication Project started in 2014 as a collaboration between EcoLabs, a non-profit graphic design research lab and studio, and the Center for Science and Technology Policy Research at the University of Colorado. The goal of the project was to research and visualize how different discourses on climate change are influenced and manipulated by different actors according to their resources.

The researchers used a matrix to visualize networks of actors based in the United Kingdom, Canada, and the United States of America. The resulting graphics illustrate the discursive positions taken as well as the relationships between the institutions, organizations, and individuals. All actors are characterized through their color-coding and arrangement, which signify their position within and between different discourses. The sizes of the actors' circles represent their relative influence on general communication. Actors are differentiated by the use of various circle circumferences, which on the one hand categorize the actors into different types and on the other hand visualize their level of internet presence.

problem, which can be defined as the gap between a desired and the actual situation. Problem perceptions also differ insofar as actors have different understandings of the causal relationships between the factors within a given system. These problem perceptions shape the behavior of actors and can be compared by using an overview table, which includes differences or conflicts as well as common ground in problem perceptions, interests, and objectives (Enserink et al. 2010, 92 onwards).

The fifth step in actor analysis consists of identifying interdependencies between the actors and the power structures. The problem owner depends on other actors and their willingness to cooperate in solving the problem. Therefore, it is important to investigate the problem owner's dependency on the other actors' resources, their replaceability (the criticality of the actors), and the importance of the problem to them (the dedication of the actors). These factors will determine whether actors are able or willing to exert influence on the situation, whereas the similarity or difference of their interests from those of the problem owner will determine whether their agency is constructive or not. These dependencies can be put together in a table or visualized in stakeholder maps or power-interest matrices (see p. 135). This step of analysis can be used (for example) to include further interests in the problem formulation and to identify necessary coalitions and possible compromises (Enserink et al. 2010, 96–100).

As a last step, the analysis is compared to the initial problem formulation. The insights from the different steps are put together

São Paulo Social Housing
One-third of São Paolo's population lives in *favelas* (slums) and on informal land subdivisions, facing issues of social inequality, poverty, and environmental problems. In order to address these problems, the project Strategies for the Planning, Financing, and Sustainable Implementation of Housing and Urban Development Policy was developed by the São Paulo Municipal Housing Secretariat, which is responsible for housing policy, in cooperation with the Cities Alliance and the World Bank. The goal of the project was to establish management tools as well as a strategic planning process.
For a better understanding of complex planning processes, multiple public actors involved with municipal housing policy, as well as actors involved with planning regulations, were analyzed and categorized according to their ability to operate on a municipal, state, or federal level.

Project Documentation[4]
The 2016 research studio Simulizi Mijini focused on the creation, curation, and perception of urban heritage. It questioned the power relationships within urban heritage determination processes. Instead of focusing exclusively on top-down decision-making processes, the project posed the question "What is urban heritage?" directly to the public. Perceptions of urban heritage depend on different circumstances, experiences, and perceptions, and can be unique to and adjustable for every human being.
An analysis of all the public

to conclude threats and opportunities. This can be used to reformulate the problem, inform the interaction with the actors, and necessitate further research activities when knowledge gaps are identified (Enserink et al. 2010, 96–100).

Actor analysis provides a comprehensive overview of multiple actors, interests, and perspectives. It is useful for identifying common ground or potential conflicts as well as the actual interdependencies of actors in strategic design problems. Thus, the range of potential fields of application is very broad. Actor analysis can be used wherever strategic decision-making relies on systems of multiple actors. When all actors are taken into consideration and when data collection is conducted as an inclusive process, the full potential for mediating and democratizing planning and design processes can be achieved (Enserink et al. 2010, 80; Harrison et al. 2015, 859 onwards; Bryson 2004, 27).

Some of the information necessary for actor analysis, such as actor perceptions and informal relationships, is not easy to gather and correctly interpret. Even where it is possible, broad research of these aspects may require substantial time and resources. In any case, results may be distorted by incorrect information or wrong assumptions, which is why it should be clearly indicated where information has come from and what data may be ambiguous (Enserink et al. 2010, 104). The analysis produces static images of situations and relationships and should therefore be understood as an iterative process during and after each cycle of analysis (Enserink et al. 2010, 105).

institutions involved in defining urban heritage exceeded the scope of the project. From the beginning, the organizers strived to discover alternative ways of curating and perceiving urban heritage from a different point of view while gathering stories from a variety of people. The process of archiving these multiple stories transformed all the interviewees into actors, granting them the power to decide what urban heritage is and what it is not.
The first part of the studio examined urban heritage in Dar es Salaam, Tanzania, while the second part focused on the Berlin district of Moabit. In both cases, stories concerning perceived urban heritage were collected, documented, and curated for the public. The results were then juxtaposed and compared in order to detect similarities and differences.
After wandering through the district in Berlin, we identified the topic of food and migration as our starting point. By doing so, we limited the group of relevant actors to migrants who ran food shops, who we then approached for interviews. We asked people about their relationships within the district of Moabit, which provided us with valuable information about the interviewees' personal networks. This information was documented in a digital archive illustrating the networks between people, places, and cultural practices. The interests, objectives, and the actor's views of the problems they faced were also queried in the interviews and represented in the archive.

This text is based on the writing of Andrea Protschky and Hannes Mundt and was edited by Xenia Kokoula.

In order to address the question of how the archive would be curated, we identified and categorized possible actors who might be able to take on this task. Throughout our work we were able to apply some aspects of actor analysis and critically reflect on the questions of different interests, abilities to act, and powers to influence the main question of determining what constitutes urban heritage (Habitat Unit TU Berlin, n.d.).

Endnotes

1 World-architects. **Makoko/Iwaya Waterfront Regeneration Plan**. [Online]. n.d. Available at https://www.world-architects.com/es/fabulous-urban-zurich/project/makoko-iwaya-waterfront-regeneration-plan/ Accessed: 18.12.2018.

2 See the chapter on the Lekki Free Zone (IFZ) in: Heinrich Böll Stiftung Nigeria and Fabulous Urban, **Urban planning processes in Lagos**. Nigeria: Heinrich Böll Stiftung Nigeria and Fabulous Urban, 2016, 191–204.

3 EcoLabs. **Mapping Climate Communication. No. 1 Climate Timeline and No. 2 Network of Actors**. [Online]. Updated October 16, 2014. Available at: https://ecolabsblog.com/2014/10/16/the-mapping-climate-communication-project-publishes-the-climate-timeline-and-the-network-of-actors/ Accessed December 18, 2018.

4 Habitat Unit TU Berlin. **Simulizi Mijini / Urban Narratives.** [Online]. n.d. Available at: https://urbannarratives.org/de/forschung/ Accessed December 18, 2018.

B.14

GETTING LOST: UNFOLDING CREATIVE THINKING

Groves, M.L. "Baudelaire, a Portrait of a Flâneur." [Online]. n.d. Available at: http://mlgroves.com/baudelaire-a-portrait-of-a-flaneur/ Accessed July 7th, 2015.

Benjamin, W. **Städtebilder**. Frankfurt am Main: Suhrkamp Verlag, 1936.

Benjamin, W. (1987), **Berliner Kindheit um Neunzehnhundert**. Frankfurt am Main: Suhrkamp Verlag, 1987.

Flaneur Society. "Guide to Getting Lost." [Online]. n.d. Available at: http://www.flaneursociety.org Accessed: July 7th, 2015.

Riedl, E. **Die Spur des Flaneurs, Zur Konzeption des Flaneurs bei Walter Benjamin und W.G. Sebald**. Saarbrücken: CVM Verlag Dr. Müller Aktiengesellschaft & Co. KG, 2008.

Siebel, W. "Talent, Toleranz, Technologie: Kritische Anmerkungen zu drei neuen Zauberworten der Stadtpolitik." In **Georg Simmel und die aktuelle Stadtforschung**, edited by Mieg, H.A., Sundsboe, A.O., and Bieniok, M. Wiesbaden: Springer Fachmedien VS Verlag für Sozialwissenschaften, 2011.

Sonntag, S. Introduction to **One Way Street and Other Writings**, Benjamin, W. London, NLB, 1979.

This paper explores parts of Walter Benjamin's work and their relevance to urban design and planning – that is, both his ways of thinking and the inherent (not scientific but rather artistic and creative) methods of developing different perspectives and innovative thoughts about the city and the task at hand. The methods Benjamin used in his work have obvious similarities with qualitative tools of the social sciences like comparative studies and participant observation, and can serve as inspiration for those involved in designing and researching our built habitat. Very importantly, architecture, urban design, and planning as disciplines work not only with science and theory, but also with praxis. Working at both ends of this spectrum, as well as linking these two poles together, is dependent on finding ways to free one's thoughts, find new perspectives, and develop ideas about space.

Walter Benjamin was born in Berlin in 1892. He wrote many scientific and artistic books, papers, articles, and essays on a wide range of different topics, ranging from literature, theater, philosophy, and art to cities and history. The passages and perspectives most relevant to urban design are contained in his books *Städtebilder*, *Berlin Childhood around 1900*, and *Passages*.

The role and perspective of the flaneur, and his or her efforts to get lost within a city in order to explore and to find new insights through unplanned and unexpected detours, is a recurrent motif in Benjamin's work. In *Berlin Childhood around 1900*, for instance, he explores his childhood memories by reminiscing, wandering through the streets and parks of Berlin's past, and thinking of the

Stadtwandern Donaustadt – Die Totale Landschaft
This film by Andreas Bernögger, Christoph Kirchberger, and Patrick Klein (which can be accessed at https://vimeo.com/43599393) aims to confront theory with the spatial actualities experienced and shown through the perspective of the Wanderer. In working on the project, the method of estranging oneself from the investigated area was as important as the aimless "hunt" for the phenomena described in the theory, which was guided by subjective impressions. As described above, a book on theory (Rolf Peter Sieferle's *Rückblick auf die Natur*) became "another space in which to stroll" and as such the lens for critical reflection through comparison – binoculars with which to sharpen one's perception of complex spatial phenomena in Vienna's "total landscape."

Stadtgeflüster: Kagran zwischen Stadt und Utopie
This project by Niklaas Baudet von Gersdorff, Andreas Bernögger, Franziska Lind, Julia Pyszkowski, and Klara Seltenhammer deals with the urban development of the Kagran district in Vienna. The authors chose an audio play in which the fictional protagonist Sophie accompanies the listener through the past and possible futures of the district (available at http://www.kulturflatrate.net/projects/stadtgefluester/). The audiobook plays through headphones and all the listener needs to make the walk autonomous is a map.

treasures and thoughts discovered during previous strolls. Benjamin seldom reflects on his methods in his texts – preferring to do so in a huge body of secondary literature – but he very prominently does just this in the chapter he wrote about the Tiergarten:

> Not to find one's way in a city means little. But to lose oneself in a city as one loses oneself in a forest requires practice. Then the street names must call out to the lost wanderer like the snapping of dry twigs, and the small streets of the city-centre must reflect the time of day as clearly as the mountain hollow. (Walter Benjamin quoted in the Flaneur Society n.d.).

In this passage, Benjamin refers to the difficult task of getting lost within a familiar environment (which "requires practice"), and of letting oneself be led and taught by the city itself (Riedl 2008, 74). However, this quote also provided the inspiration for the *Guide for Getting Lost* published by the Flaneur Society. It contains a simple description of the benefits of an unplanned walk as well as some blunt hints for those unable to point their feet in an unknown direction and onto an arbitrary trail (Flaneur Society n.d.).

The act of getting lost, which sounds (and is) so easy in unknown surroundings, and is an obvious approach for curious explorers of the urban – and which might also apply to a Sunday walk, or to a keen-witted traveler encountering a new city without a tourist map or travel guide – is certainly also a tool for urban designers. It should therefore be consciously performed in professional practice when dealing with design or research tasks.

During the walk, Sophie informs the listener about the history of Kagran and about recent urban development in the area. She also asks questions about the landscape, thereby opening a one-sided dialogue. She not only confronts the "consumer" of the audiobook with the reality of the city, but also tries to estrange the listener from the scenery, drifting more and more into an imaginary Kagran, her own utopia, where things work in a completely different way. The goal of this approach is not only to introduce an audience to a place and to certain abstract and specific ideas about it, but also to set utopian thinking about urbanity and the development of that place into motion through estrangement and the generation of critical distance, forming the contribution of some initial ideas, and starting a political debate.

An Urban Design Project in Warsaw

A further example is an urban design project by Professor Pahl-Weber of the Department of Urban Regeneration at TU Berlin in which I and some colleagues massively benefited from engaging in Benjamin's process of *flânerie* – to some degree consciously, but also partly accidentally. After being left with the feeling that we had grasped nothing about the place and the task ahead early on, we left the other hard-working groups in the seminar room and went for a walk, magnanimously interrupted by lunch and ice cream (which gave us time to think and talk).

Siquans, Bernhard (2018) **Stadtgeflüster 1**.

This is because creative processes are not linear, and are therefore unpredictable – especially when they are complex. Taking a step off the beaten path, making a detour (metaphorically and physically), and pondering while encountering new impressions (all elements inherent in the behavior of the flaneur) can help to find… well, who knows what? But whatever it is, it may lead to satisfying results in the end.

So far we have discussed the flaneur as a tool for exploring and as a (literary) narrative perspective. In his work *Passages*,

Distracted frequently by a large number of points and items of interest, we followed an uncertain path – inhaling different atmospheres, liking and disliking different places, and getting more and more of a feeling for the idiosyncratic city of Warsaw. The two people who had grown up in Warsaw and the two to whom it was completely unknown talked constantly about their impressions. One small park drew us in, and we watched the children play in the water while our Polish colleagues talked to an old woman (until she outed herself as anti-Semitic). I had a nap until the sun went behind a nearby skyscraper (a second one is planned to be built right next to it). After some more strolling, we ended up at the location our project centered on, a completely run-down old industrial site with no more than a few lonely and damaged (but heritage-protected) buildings. Getting a good impression of the atmosphere and ideas surrounding it, we took a close look at our site, not letting ourselves be deterred by the fences. Of course, this long detour took a lot of time from the two workshop weeks allocated to designing an urban design project. In the end, however, I think that the strength of our approach (including in comparison to the approach of other designers) was that it most closely "inhaled" the genius loci and identified a very specific – and very different – way of dealing with a protected ensemble of buildings in surroundings deformed by WWII and

Siquans, Bernhard (2018) **Stadtgeflüster 2**.

Benjamin aims to recount the history of Paris as the capital of the nineteenth century. Here, the figure of the flaneur is supplemented with yet another facet: that of a paradigmatic symbol and the personification of an (urban) era. Importantly, Benjamin again meets the flaneur in the texts of Charles Baudelaire (1821–1867), whose work he partly translated.

> For the perfect flâneur, for the passionate spectator, it is an immense joy to set up house in the heart of the multitude, amid the ebb and flow of movement,

a speculative real estate industry. In the end, we found a well-adapted approach that implemented many little details and characteristics from the site itself as well as the treasures we discovered during our walk through Warsaw. The project could not have included these many useful facets if we hadn't first allowed ourselves to get lost as flaneurs.

Bermögger, Andreas (2018) **A small park in Warsaw that inspired the professional flaneurs.**

Bermögger, Andreas (2018) **A close look of the protected building from outside as well as inside revealed ideas on how to deal with them and find the specific genius loci.**

> in the midst of the fugitive and the infinite. To be away from home and yet to feel oneself everywhere at home; to see the world ... and yet to remain hidden from the world. (Baudelaire quoted in Groves n.d.).

The flaneur is not merely a person exploring a city (for the purposes of amusement and lifestyle or out of intellectual interest), but also a product of the city: *flânerie* is only conceivable in large cities, not in towns or villages. It is only possible in the big industrial conurbations that arose from the eighteenth and nineteenth century onwards, where a single inhabitant (due to the size and plurality of the city) simply cannot know the whole city or cope with all the impressions and events it generates. It is also in such cities that the flaneur is able to experience freedom from "daily

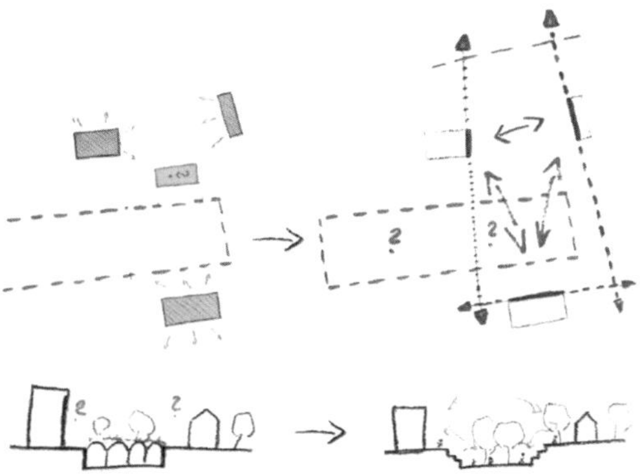

Bermögger, Andreas (2018)
Sketch showing basic ideas on how to form an ensemble out of the doomed-looking and run-down remnants of an old brewery.

work" (see, for instance, Georg Simmel, *Die Großstädte und das Geistesleben* – a work which Benjamin also referred to as highly relevant). Paris, therefore, as one of the first and greatest examples of this new type of human settlement, became the birthplace of *flânerie* – which is both an activity and a way of dealing with manifold perceptions and memories (see Riedl 2008, 54–76).

Considering Benjamin's flaneur in more details, we can see similarities with another philosophical figure: *the wanderer*. Friedrich Nietzsche describes the wanderer as someone "stepping outside the city to see how high the towers are" – that is, as an intellectual reflecting on existing structures. Georg Simmel, on the other hand, sees the wanderer as someone "coming to a city" – a stranger new to a setting, thereby uniting remoteness and proximity, for whom reflection is thereby "enforced." Critical distance – which enables reflection – is the common denominator of both. For Nietzsche it is an individual achievement, but for Simmel it is a social role systematically generated by urbanity and migration (Siebel 2011, 79 onwards).

Leaving one's home city and coming to a new city as a stranger, and thereby being estranged from home and enabled to reflect on both, is the theme of Benjamin's urban descriptions in *Städtebilder*: "You learn to see Berlin from Moscow faster than Moscow itself," (Benjamin 1963, 7; translation by Andreas Bernögger). It is not only the method of comparison that is important in doing this, but also the process of estranging oneself from the familiar to create the critical distance that forms the basis of productive thinking. You "need the gap, need the distance of time or space," (Szondi in Benjamin 1963, 91; translation by

Andreas Bernögger). This method of distancing (combined with the viewpoint of the flaneur) was also used to reflect on the past by Benjamin in *Berlin Childhood around 1900* and *Passages*.

> [A] book is not only a fragment of the world but itself a little world … which the reader inhabits. …. The book for him was another space in which to stroll (Sontag 1979, 21).

This is another highly interesting thought, because it extends the methods of *flânerie*, comparison, and estrangement described above to the creation of a critical distance to books and imaginary worlds. It immediately brings to mind both utopian (Aldous Huxley's *Island*) and dystopian (George Orwell's *1984*) novels, as well as the utopian visions of planners like Le Corbusier (in his plans for Paris or Algiers), Ludwig Hilbersheimer (Hochhausstadt), Frank Lloyd Wright (Broadacre City), and groups like the Metabolists (Kenzo Tange's Tokyo City Bay Project) or Archigram (Walking City, Plug-in-City). Such ideas inspire creative thoughts as well as dissent, and nourish reflections on and criticisms of the built and planning reality. But urban designers, who are necessarily employed in thinking about and participating in the designing of the future, find inspiration and the chance to compare and estrange themselves not only in this virtual "other world":

> … this corner of the Zoological Garden bore traces of what was to come. It was a prophetic corner. For just as there are plants that are said to confer the power to see into the future, so there are places that possess such a virtue. …. In such places, it seems as if all that lies in store for us has become the past. (Benjamin 1987, 43; translation based on Fraser 2013).

Just as Foucault's heterotopias depict utopias within real spaces, Benjamin evokes a similar concept of past, present, and future processes being intrinsic in certain places – places where tomorrow can be found today. In reflecting on his childhood, Benjamin also searches for the "present contained in the past" and the traces left by it.

This text is based on the writing of Andreas Bernögger and was edited by Angela Million.

B.15

NARRATING THROUGH GRAPHICS

Abrams, J. and Hall, P., eds. **Else/where. Mapping New Cartographies of Networks and Territories**. Minneapolis: University of Minnesota Design Institute, 2006.

Angelil, M. and Siress, C. "Mapping Flows. Switzerland as Operational Landscape." In **Flowscapes, Designing infrastructure as landscape. Research in Urbanism Series** Vol. 3, edited by Nijhuis, S., Jauslin, D., and van der Hoeven, F. Delft: TU Delft, 2015.

Bertin, J. Semiology of **Graphics: Diagrams, Networks, Maps**. Madison: University of Wisconsin Press, 1983. First published 1967.

Corner, J. "The Agency of Mapping: Speculation, Critique and Invention." In **Mappings**, edited by Cosgrove, D., 213–252. London: Reaktion Books, 1999.

Howard, E. **Garden Cities of Tomorrow**. London: Swan Sonnenschein & Co. Ltd, 1902.

Imhof, E. **Cartographic Relief Presentation**. Bern: Wabern, 1965.

Kramer, J. "Is abstraction the key to computing?" **Communication of the ACM** 50, no. 4 (2007): 36–42.

Lutter, W.G. and Ackerman, M.S. **An introduction to the Chicago School of Sociology**. Interval Research Proprietary, 1996.

Lynch, K. **The Image of the City**. Cambridge: MIT Press, 1960.

Topalov, C. "The city as terra incognita. Charles Booth's poverty survey and the people of London, 1886–1891." **Planning Perspectives** 8, no. 4 (1993): 395–425.

Tufte, E. **Envisioning Information**. Cheshire, Connecticut: Graphic Press, 1990.

Narrative graphics are tools for visually communicating complex information, ideas, systems, and networks to an audience in a simplified, accessible, and attractive manner. The goal is not to present the raw data itself, but to gather, organize, and reduce the data in order to provide concise insights and information about the topic. As Edward Tufte put it, "to envision information – and what bright and splendid visions can result – is to work at the intersection of image, word, number, art" (Tufte 1990, 9). This section focuses on visual representations of space and time as maps and diagrams in the field of urban design. It is also informed by the evolution of narrative graphics in their application across a broad array of related fields throughout the twentieth century.

Following the revision of key literature and the review of reference projects (among others, Bertin 1983; Tufte 1990; Abrams and Hall 2006) alongside the definition of narrative graphics above, five possible but by no means exhaustive categories of application emerge: research analysis and (re)presentation; manifestos; design processes and visualizations; networks and systems; and awareness and debate. These categories even represent an evolution in the way narrative graphics have been used; more broadly, they also represent changes in the understanding of space and consequently in design thinking and design processes. Narrative graphics are a snapshot in time, reflective of society and its priorities and ideals, that help us understand the spaces that we inhabit.

London Poverty Maps, Charles Booth, 1902[1]
A social investigation initiated by Charles Booth in 1886 resulted in a series of maps visualizing the extent and spatial distribution of poverty amongst the approximately six million inhabitants of the ever-expanding metropolis. The London Poverty Maps were published in several editions – the last in 1903 – and used survey data along with ethnographic observation to create a potent and precise image of social inequality. A palette of colors ranging from black to yellow was used to distinguish the different social classes, which were in turn associated with other attributes such as income, criminality (for example, the lowest class in black is further described as "vicious, semi-criminal"), health, and so on, creating a compelling narrative.

Boston Cognitive Mapping, Kevin Lynch, 1960[2]
American planner Kevin Lynch's famous graphics were developed as part of his wide-ranging study of the perception of urban form. They are best known for visualizing the theory of the five basic elements (paths, edges, districts, nodes, landmarks) which, according to Lynch, help urban dwellers form mental maps of their environment. It is important to understand, however, that these maps were not simply derived from a theoretical argument but were based on extensive field research, including site visits and interviews as well as oral descriptions and sketches from the residents themselves. The evocative

Imhof, E. (1962–1976) **Mount Everest Map**.
Printed map of Mount Everest 1:100 000.
From a Swiss secondary-school atlas.

power of the cognitive maps, therefore, lies in the combination of a theoretical, academic perspective with the insights of the public.

Mount Everest, Eduard Imhof, 1962[3]
Eduard Imhof's hand-drawn maps of mountainous regions explore the potential of cartography to illustrate the third dimension through the use of color and shading. Also noteworthy are his theoretical contributions to the aesthetics of cartography and his use of scientific as well as artistic arguments to explain the working process of drawing a map.

Autobahnplanung Oranienplatz, Fotomontage, Kohlmaier and von Sartory, 1969[4]
The iconic collage by architect Georg Kohmeier and artist Barna von Sartory is a critical commentary on postwar urban planning in Berlin, and specifically the planning principles of the car-friendly city. The existing, dense, and compact urban fabric was being razed to make place for new developments with little, if any, consultation of the residents. This collage juxtaposes a Los Angeles highway with an aerial image of Oranienplatz in Kreuzberg in order to demonstrate the scale and extent of demolition that a new planned highway would necessitate.

Facemap Toronto, Julie Bogdanovicz, 2013[5]
This map of Toronto focuses on social inequality between the three clearly distinguished classes of poor, middle class, and

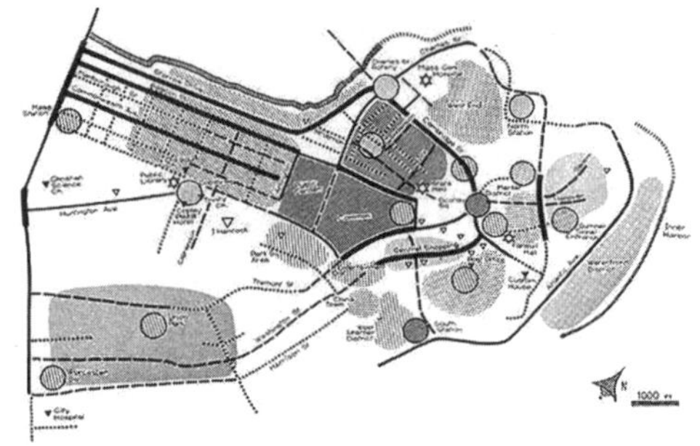

FIG. 35. *The Boston image as derived from verbal interviews*

Lynch, K. (1960) **Boston Cognitive Mapping**. An image of Boston as derived from verbal interviews. featured in **The Image of the City**.

Although the fields of application have largely remained the same over time, the production, medium, perception, and understanding of narrative maps and diagrams have developed and changed, particularly due to socio-technical developments.

Originally, the key challenge in producing successful narrative graphics was reducing three-dimensional or even four-dimensional information (that is, including time) onto two-dimensional, static planes. Tufte described this challenge as "how to reduce the magnificent four-dimensional reality of time and three-dimensional space into little marks on paper flatlands" (Tufte 1990, 119). With the development of computer-aided design, as well as of digital representation methods, we are no longer bound to a static piece of two-dimensional paper. Narrative graphics can now utilize the dynamic, interactive, and inexpensive medium of computers to communicate increasingly complex networks and ideas. Interestingly, the level of abstraction can be

wealthy. The "three cities of Toronto" – one for each of the three classes –demonstrate the extent of segregation. While this phenomenon is already well-documented, the Facemap uses a collage of real faces instead of a more abstract color scheme. The intention is to narrate the complex correlation of class, income, and race and confront the viewers with the lived, human reality of segregation.

IABR—Project Atelier Rotterdam: The Urban Metabolism, .FABRIC and JCFO, 2014[6]

The IABR—Project Atelier Rotterdam was commissioned for the Rotterdam Biennale in 2014 to examine the different flows in the city and the opportunities they present for sustainable urban development. The Atelier developed a design methodology to identify and map the flows using different graphics, including mapping that links specific flows (cargo, waste, energy, and so on) to locations within the greater Rotterdam area. Beyond making these flows visible, the mapping of different flows is used as a tool in generating design strategies and demonstrating how these strategies work within the urban context.

viewed in relation to the evolution in technology: "Before the advent of aerial photography ... a map was expected to represent its territory with comprehensive accuracy. Freed of that responsibility, cartographers can manipulate their data into any number of visual representations" (Abrams and Hall 2006, 12). Rather ironically, now that computer-aided design allows us to draw to the highest level of accuracy, narrative graphics no longer require this type of precision. Instead, the objective of narrative graphics is increasingly to communicate relationships, ideas, and systems.

Regardless of the choice of medium or approach, the challenge remains the same: to produce understandable, insightful, and information-rich graphics from a broad range of complex raw data. As Tufte asserts, "confusion and clutter are failures of design, not attributes of information." He states that we must "find design strategies that reveal and detail complexity, rather than fault the data for an excess of complication," or "fault viewers for a lack of understanding" (Tufte 1990, 53). Although there are no absolute and universal standards or conventions, guidelines for narrative graphics do exist. Some authors – such as Imhof in *Cartographic Relief Presentation* (1965), and Bertin in *Semiology of Graphics* (1983) – have even written specific and detailed rules, although

Project Atelier Rotterdam (2014) **Goods-City**.

these can and have been challenged. Additionally, a host of tools and guidelines are now readily available online.

Based on this literature, the most important points to consider when producing a narrative graphic include layering and separation, composition, simplification and abstraction, color, scale, aesthetics, and interest. Each of these elements can be implemented in a variety of ways; for example, color can be used to label, to measure, to represent reality, to enhance legibility, and to increase the aesthetic appeal of the graphic. An appropriate method or combination of methods should be selected in order to best communicate the subject or information.

Narrative graphics run the risk of being abstracted to the point where information is manipulated, unfairly represented, or lost due to over-simplification. Maps and diagrams thus become powerful political tools, as acknowledged by James Corner (1999) and more recently Marc Angelil and Cary Siress (2015). This has become a greater concern with the development of technology, as anyone can now produce and distribute graphics online.

On the other hand, the key strength of narrative graphics is their ability to communicate complex information not only understandably but beautifully. Successful narrative graphics allow for the discovery and transfer of knowledge; they raise awareness and help facilitate decision-making. Computer-aided design and the Internet have facilitated greater complexity, accessibility, interaction, and a greater range of representation methods. While new media such as blogs and newsgroups are often

Endnotes

1 Booth, C. **Life and Labour of the People in London. Volume 1**. London: Macmillan, 1902.

2 See also: Fig. 35 on p. 146 of Lynch, K. **The Image of the City**. Cambridge: MIT Press, 1960.

3 Imhof, E. **Cartographic Relief Presentation**. Bern: Wabern, 1965.

4 Kohlmaier, G. and von Sartory, B. **Autobahnplanung Oranienplatz**. 1969. Photo montage. Available at http://derarchitektbda.de/von-der-auto-imme-zum-rollenden-gehsteig/museum-berlin_radikal-modern_kohlmaier-sartory_oranienplatz_4mb_kl/ Accessed April 22, 2020, and Schulz, B. "Die Vergänglichkeit großer Ideen." **Bauwelt** 34 (2015). Available at http://www.bauwelt.de/dl/936771/artikel.pdf Accessed April 22, 2020.

5 Bogdanovicz, J. "Facemap von Toronto—Soziale Segregation im Spiegel der Gesichter." **ARCH+** 213, no. 12 (2013): 156–157.

6 IABR–2014–PROJECT ATELIER ROTTERDAM: THE URBAN METABOLISM. [Online]. Available at https://iabr.nl/en/projectatelier/2014parotterdam

Kohlmaier and von Sartory (1969) **Fotomontage Autobahnplanung Oranienplatz**.

fragmented and messy, and do not necessarily provide people with clear and complete answers, they can make us "capable of asking better questions" (Abrams 2006, 14). Consequently, discussion of the key issues raised and represented in these forums is encouraged.

This text is based on the writing of Madeleine Appelros and Benedikt Wieser and was edited by Xenia Kokoula.

B.16

ADDING, DIVIDING, SUPER-IMPOSING

Avermaete, T. "Climat de France." **Oase Journal for Architecture** 74, (2007): 116–134.
Ching, F. **Architecture: Form, Space and Order**. New York: Van Nostrand Reinhold, 1979.
Curdes, G. **Stadtstrukturelles Entwerfen**. Stuttgart: Kohlhammer Verlag, 1995.
Deplazes, A. **Constructing Architecture: Materials, Processes, Structures. A Handbook**. Basel: Birkhäuser, 2013.
Frankl, P. **Die Entwicklungsphasen der neueren Baukunst**. Leipzig: Verlag von B.G. Teubner, 1914.
Frankl, P. **Das System der Kunstwissenschaft**. Berlin: Gebr. Mann Verlag, 1998.
Mühlenthaler, E. **Großformen im Wohnungsbau**. Berlin: Universitätsverlag der TU Berlin, 2007.
Norberg-Schulz, C. **Intentions in Architecture**. Oslo: Universitetsforlaget, 1963.
O'Gorman, J. **ABC of Architecture**. Philadelphia: University of Pennsylvania Press, 1997.
Schweizer, O. **Die architektonische Großform**. Berlin: Brauch Verlag, 1957.
Wienand, R. **Grundlagen der Gestaltung zu Bau und Stadtbau**. Basel: Birkhäuser, 1985.

A designer is always confronted with the question of how his environment was made and how new elements have been and can be added to it (Wienand 1985, 135). "The first valuable contribution to the understanding of architectural compositions was made by Paul Frankl in 1914," (Norberg-Schulz 1968, 97). Frankl established the basic concept of *additive*, *divisional*, and *superimposing* (*interpenetrating*) spatial organizations. Each of these approaches is characterized by a different relationship of the single piece to the whole. Recognizing the most dominant method means detecting the predominant characteristics of the whole (design).

Additive approach: The additive approach begins with a single piece, and once assembled leads to a complex whole. As a result, the perimeter or boundary seems jagged and chaotic. On the other hand, additive expansion of the amorphous whole is always possible (Ching 1979, 73). Additive organizations occur in environments of tough competition where resilience and flexibility are needed. Informal settlements represent this kind of "state of emergency," in which the compatibility of single components is of more importance than the design quality of the whole. Another characteristic, besides the undefined boundary of the whole, is the connection between each piece and the whole. It is this feature that ensures the flexibility of the whole. The replacement of each component is only possible as a result of the existence of this seam. In a continually advancing and differentiating society, this grade of adaptability leads to a continuing imbalance of the whole (Wienand 1985, 136).

Climate de France, Algiers Fernand Pouillon, 1954–1957
In the early 1950s, the French government decided to solve the problem of an increasing housing crisis in the French colony with large-scale social housing. Located on the outskirts of Algiers, the site was completely encircled by highways and was projected to become an urban island. However, its main characteristic was the uneven topography. Pouillon chose to introduce an orthogonal grid (see figure on page 158 of superimposition approach), which generated varying typologies depending on the slope (Avermaete 2007, 120).
The urban organization of the whole, including the smaller parts, "appear at first sight as a collection of autonomous entities. They present themselves as a juxtaposition of isolated building blocks" (Avermaete 2007, 124) with the main building at the center (see figure on page 158 of additive approach).
The block goes by the name *200 Columns*, referring to the three-story-high colonnade surrounding the central courtyard. Pouillon used this element to outline the whole and rhythmize the building as well as the courtyard see figure on page 158 of divisional approach). Its monumental portico entrances are located on the two transversal sides, while smaller gates traverse the long sides. Pouillon isolated himself from the modernist movement, which propagated the open plan. Instead, he described this approach as *paysage intérieur*, which "suggests

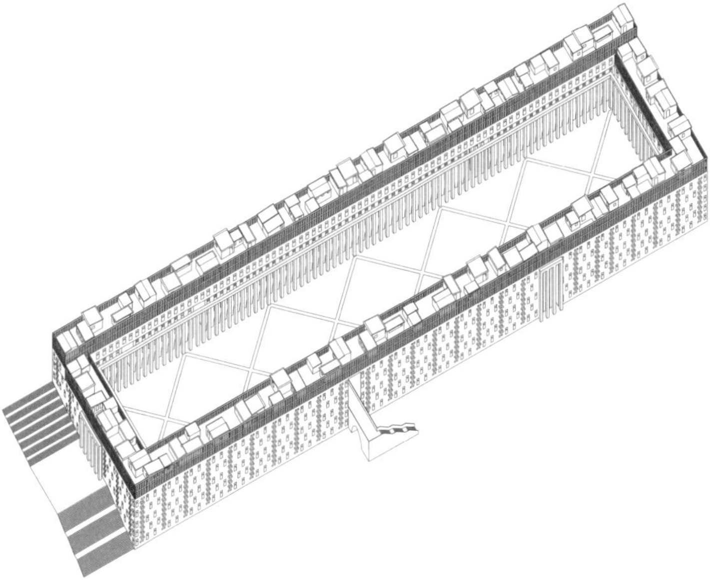

Rico Samuel Diedering (2016) **Axonometric drawing of housing complex Climat de France**. Designed by Fernand Poullion in 1954.

Divisional approach: The opposite of spatial addition is spatial division. "The components … are no longer complete isolated pieces but fractions of a pre-existent whole. The structure does not consist of many units; it is one unit divided into parts or fractions," (Frankl 1914, 71). One can find such organizations in situations that favor a clear demarcation between inside and outside, such an urban approach in which the landscape is interiorised and defined by surrounding elements," (Avermaete 2007, 124).

Urban Design Studio: TRANSTOPIA - Hybridized Building Practices[1]

The assignment of the Transtopia studio was to conceive a micro-neighborhood addressing various cultural identities. We based the design on urban types and narratives we derived from interviews about migration. The proposal should be conceived as a *transtopia*: as a heterotopia and a realization of a Third Space in which various cultural trajectories are hybridized to form a new urban reality. We detected a high degree of fragmentation within the life paths of our interviewees. This applied particularly to the time before they actually started to migrate. However, the experiences on their journey were what influenced their new life in Germany. Older people in particular found themselves in situations where they did not "belong" anywhere; they were trapped between idealizing and disparaging the past, as well as their reality in Berlin. In accordance with the typological research on several types of courtyards, we transferred both – interviews and typology research – into our programmatic framework. It was important to us to confront the future dwellers with different development options, so they were asked to position themselves within these two poles. Our assumption was that we would be able to create stable spaces for this positioning, regardless of location.

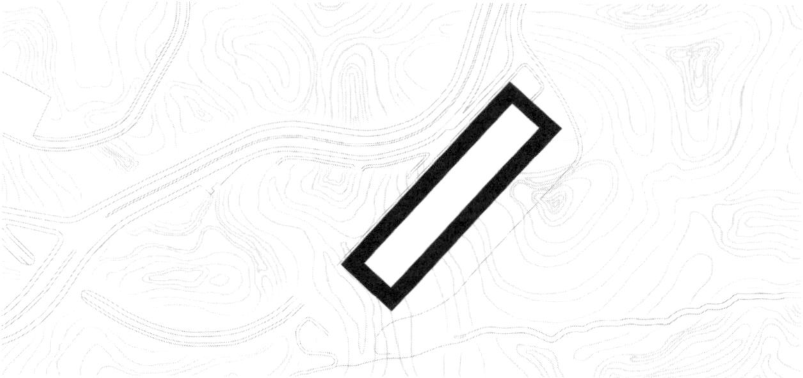

Rico Samuel Diedering (2016) **Site plan**. Superimposition of the orthogonal grid system onto the hilly site.

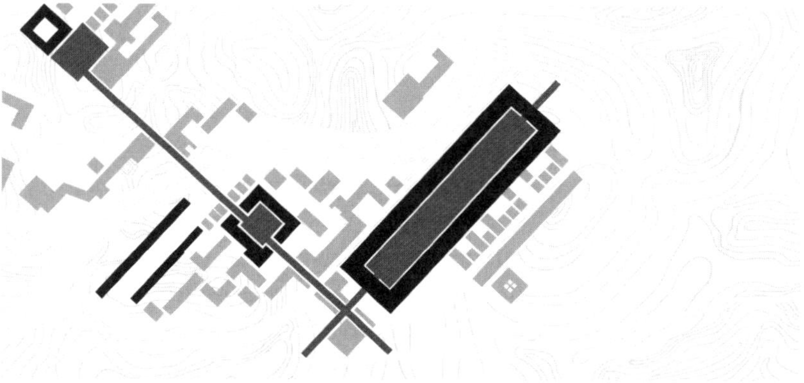

Rico Samuel Diedering (2016) **Site plan**. Adding a specific quality to the complex sequence of public spaces, which are declined in an extensive number of typologies with different morphologies.

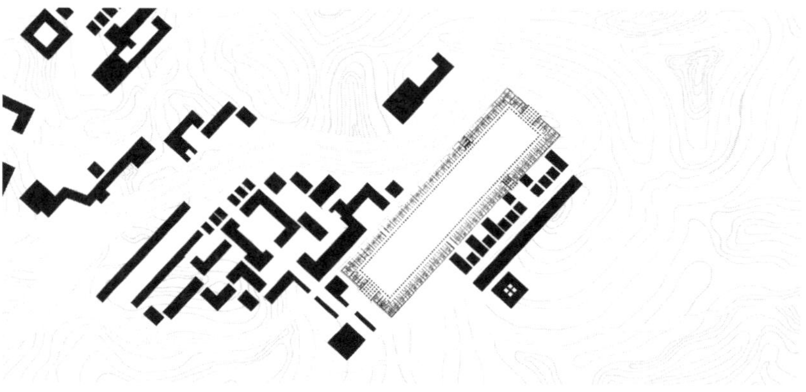

Rico Samuel Diedering (2016) **Site plan**. Dividing the spatial arrangement of the plan of the ground floor into smaller components.

as fortifications. The whole dominates and controls its smaller parts, but they still depend on each other. There is an intrinsically dialogic relationship between the components concerning how much autonomy each element can have before the whole irreparably collapses (Johnson 1994, 379). Divisional decisions are made in every planning process. The whole becomes subdivided and organized into smaller, assessable units; for example, land use plans or construction schedules on building sites use a divisional approach.

Superimposing approach: In contrast to the spatial subdivision of the whole into simpler units, superimposing is about the spatial complexification of the whole (Frankl 1914, 72). The existence of two or more reference systems at the same time leads to a certain degree of ambiguity. Whether the whole is still legible or becomes too undefined to comprehend depends on the number of overlapping systems. As such, overlapping historical patterns, supply systems, legal zones, or social distribution can easily be discovered in complex systems such as cities. However, superimposition as a method can also be used in designs at a smaller scale. A conscious use of ambiguity by the designer that constitutes connections to specific identities (provided by e.g. the history of the place) enables residents to choose between different reference systems. These situations become built symbols of freedom within the urban landscape; the limitations of the city are confronted with the freedom of choice (Wienand 1985, 166).

We designed on one of the rare sites that still belong to the Senate. The project is located in the east-Berlin district of Marzahn, next to an S-Bahn track and the highway cloverleaf of Landsberger Allee and the B158. Since 1990, the area along this infrastructure has undergone an unprecedented commodification. In *Die architektonische Großform*, O.E. Schweizer said that future development will happen along the linear lines of infrastructures.
And indeed, almost 60 years later new typologies such as cinemas, drive-in restaurants, drive-in furniture stores, and malls gather along this link (an example of additive development). All have one thing in common: they isolate themselves from the outside world in order to establish their own (commercial) reality. Thus, one can enjoy a coffee in a dense and lively shopping street even in suburban Marzahn. The Mall exemplifies that idea: the City within the building, in the best possible way.
We were also interested in creating our own reality within a set boundary. According to O.M. Unger, we created a "framework for an undefined, unplanned, for a spontaneous process" (Mühlthaler 2007, 7). To strengthen the spatial quality of the large form, we hijacked the most common building type of Marzahn and set it at the top of the abovementioned framework.
In an environment with almost no spatial coherence, we decided to emphasize the direction of the infrastructural link, as this is what most strongly defines the whole area. At

The classification of spatial organizations into additive, divisional, and superimposition is rooted in gestalt psychology. As such, it follows the assumption that human beings in a complex world create a holistic view of the whole. Architects like Wienand, Norberg-Schulz, and Frankl applied this assumption in order to establish a formal concept of architectural theory that counters the absence of "a common basis [and of] the architects depressing [reality] to work without any objective criticism and self-criticism," (Norberg-Schulz 1968, 13). This concept for the description and evaluation of spatial organization evolved in an academic context. It therefore applies the same method for analyzing the architectural object that scientists do when carrying out research projects: they obtain a deeper knowledge about a certain issue "through dissecting it into smaller components to draw conclusions about the whole" (Wienand 1985, 7).

Owing to its scientific links, there are a huge number of references for this theory in architectural history. These make it apparent that each method has intrinsic features that will influence any further evolution of the project under consideration. The connection between design quality and the divisional approach or superimposition is a highly relevant factor for every designer. By contrast, the additive approach meets many programmatic demands for resilience and flexibility – but at the expense of design quality. A critical question is to what degree this knowledge is helpful if the methods are executed according to the preconditions on site (Wienand 1985, 136 and 150). There

the same time, the two adjacent housing slabs defined the realm for the third-space implementation. But instead of ceding the space to commerce, we wanted to establish a place that would enable people with a migration background to position their identity within this imaginary environment. It is for this reason that we activated the last remaining remnants (buildings) of the socialist era, which were also connected to the infrastructural link. As these remaining social institutions – such as schools, post offices, and even a swimming bath, as well as several gymnasiums – are of an additive nature, we decided to add three more within our set framework: a language school, library, and a theater.

Endnotes

1 TUB Students. "TRANSTOPIA – Hybridized Building Practices." Design studio for the Master in Urban Design at the Technische Universität Berlin, supervised by Misselwitz, P., 2016. See also: https://www.architektur.tu-berlin.de/fileadmin/i41/KVV/kvv-arch-ss16.pdf

also needs to be a discussion on whether additive, divisional, or superimposing design (or a combination of approaches) is the best way of dealing with challenging – and sometime already built-up – environments. In urban and architectural design, each of these options (or their combinations) demonstrates the motivation of and position taken by the designer towards the given social and spatial context. These are either focused on expanding high-quality elements that already exist by blending in new building developments, or alternatively on "putting a new building in the foreground and thus disregarding existing design criteria. The focus here is on the independence of the new architecture, which can only be judged as uncritical if the existing situation does not give rise to any of its qualities and the new building and design can therefore be understood as a positive approach" (Curdes 1995, 80; translated from German by the author).

This text is based on the writing of Rico Samuel Diedering and was edited by Angela Million.

B.17

CREATING CONCEPTUAL MODELS

Alberti, L.B. **On the Art of Building in Ten Books**. Cambridge, MA: The MIT Press, 1988.

Arpak, A. "Physical and Virtual: Transformation of the Architectural Model." Thesis, Middle East Technical University Graduate School of Natural and Applied Sciences, 2008.

Elser, O. and Schmal, P.C., eds. **Das Architekturmodell: Werkzeug, Fetisch, kleine Utopie**, Zurich: Scheidegger & Spiess, 2012.

Evans, R. **Translations from Drawing to Building and other Essays**, London: Architectural Association, 1976.

Frampton, K. and Kolbowski, S. **Idea as Model**, New York: Rizzoli, 1981.

Knoll, W. and Hechinger, M. **Architectural Models: Construction Techniques**, 2nd edition. Munich: Deutsche Verlags-Anstalt, 2006.

Moon, K. **Modeling Messages: The Architect and the Model**, New York: Monacelli Press, 2005.

Morris, M. **Models: Architecture and the Miniature**, Chichester, West Sussex: Wiley Academy, 2006.

Porter, T. and Neale J. **Architectural Supermodels: Physical Design Simulation**, Oxford: Architectural Press, 2000.

Reynolds, C. "The Fourth Register of Architecture: "Model as..."" MArch thesis, UCL Bartlett School of Architecture, 2015.

Rowe, P. **Design Thinking**, Cambridge, MA: The MIT Press, 1986.

Smith, A. **Architecture Model as Machine: A New View of Models from Antiquity to the Present Day**, Oxford: Architectural Press, Elsevier Ltd, 2004.

In order to define conceptual models, we must first describe "models" as a broader term and give a short overview of the different types that may be used. Models can be concisely described as three-dimensional representations of a design idea. They have always been a part of the architectural and urban design process, but the first definition of architectural models is found in Leon Battista Alberti's Renaissance work *On the Art of Building in Ten Books* (1988), originally published between 1443 and 1452. He considered models to be the most important tools of the design process. He also pointed out that their importance – apart from being a tool for communicating with clients – lies in their ability to be altered and adapted during the design process (Arpak 2008; Reynolds 2015). Before the Renaissance, two-dimensional representation played a more important role as the quickest and easiest means of demonstrating a design. Models gained in importance during the Renaissance as they were considered suitable for communicating design ideas with clients (Reynolds 2015).

Arpak (2008) distinguishes between four different types of models in his master's thesis: conceptual models, working models, structural models, and presentational models. The boundary between these categories can be blurred, however, and other types of models may be added to the list according to the stages of the design process. Distinctions can also be made based on the scale and size of the models, which can range from a 1:1 tactile model to a much smaller-scaled topographic or site model. The latter has a great significance for urban design professionals, as

Europan 11: Nynäshamn competition entry, Franz Reschke Landschafts-architekten[1]
This entry for the Europan 11 competition in Sweden (2010) was developed using an "accident of form" methodology. Photographs of the site were analyzed and traced. The tracings were overlaid on Styrofoam, which was then carved and cut along the lines. Following this, the Styrofoam boards were used as molds to create abstract cast models. Details of the models were then selected, carved, and cut in an iterative process.

OMA – Styrofoam models
Rem Koolhaas's office is famous for the unique methodology used in its working process. The office places great emphasis on the modelling phase and produces several Styrofoam mass studies or conceptual models for each design process. This enables the testing of different variations and typologies. These models are archived and stored, giving the office the opportunity to revisit past creative processes, learning from them again and again.

The MAXXI Museum, Zaha Hadid (2009)
The design of the MAXXI museum of contemporary art in Rome responds to the existing urban structures of the surrounding area. The dominant urban grid directions were formalistically transferred to the design as parallel curves. Based on a study model, these forms were then realized as walls. The curved, parallel walls are the core elements of the

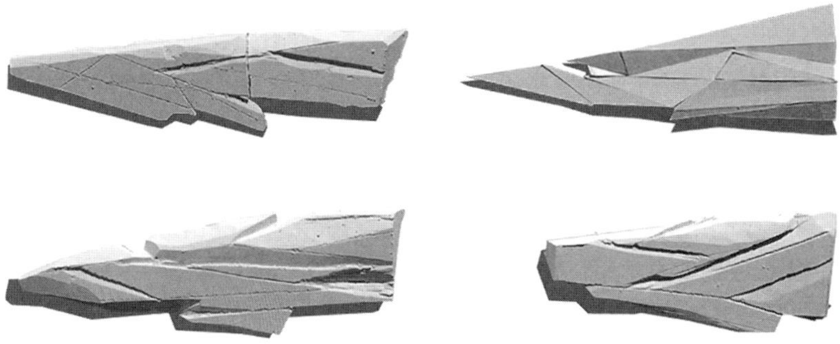

Franz Reschke Landschaftarchitektur (2010) **Concept Cast Models**.

site models are part of the design process from the very beginning and provide a representation of the existing structure as well as of masses and correlations in the urban space.

This initial categorization demonstrates that conceptual models are the ones created during the very first phase of the design process. They are manifestations of ideas that function as three-dimensional sketches. They are the most important tool for capturing thoughts and ideas and developing them further. Conceptual models can empower the design process and clarify design principles. They are usually built quickly and simply and can be easily adjusted over the course of the process. They are tests of existing ideas while at the same time acting as catalysts for creativity. Conceptual models often exist without scale; they communicate a core concept in an abstract way while generating new ideas.

project, functioning as exhibition surfaces and creating both interior and exterior spaces at the same time. The spatial effect generated by this structure intertwining with the surrounding urban grid was tested using various study models.

Urbanes Spüren[2]
Several different types and scales of concept models were produced for the *Urbanes Spüren* project as part of the Master in Landscape Architecture program at TU Berlin. The project site was Mettmann-platz, a piece of land at the border of Berlin's Wedding and Moabit districts. The site is crossed by three bridges, with a fourth one under construction. As these structures strongly defined the characteristics of the site, the first task for students was to build a site surrounding model at a scale of 1:500. This model was intended for use throughout the whole semester for working models and tests. Six people worked on this site in the course of their master's degree, and the site surrounding model made it possible for each student to test their own design principles.
The main goal of the studio was to produce a design based on a subjective atmospheric approach. After three different levels of analysis (subjective, inter-subjective, and objective) students were required to define a particular atmospheric effect to be achieved in the course of the eventual design process. Abstract models based on a reference project were created during this step. The steps of this phase

Conceptual models – based on a variety of materials, scales and purposes – are a fundamental part of architect, landscape architect, urban professional, and artist toolkits. As they are suited to delivering an abstract message as well as representing a particular design principle, they have a wide variety of applications.

When facing an actual design problem, the very first step is to produce principal sketches. After collecting a range of possible design solutions, the different suggestions are tested using new sketches and conceptual models. It is an iterative process in which one goes back and forth, gradually narrowing the spectrum of appropriate solutions.

After starting with several design ideas, the ones that demonstrate the most potential are selected for further development. These are then tested in conceptual models, usually in the way that best fits the problem. This means that – for example – the solution to an urban-scale problem may be tested using quickly built styrofoam models. Paper or cardboard are also appropriate for this phase, as they are easy to work with and allow for a large number of adjustments. The next step is studying and comparing the models, defining the potential as well as any problematic aspects of the different ideas. Compared to two-dimensional sketches, conceptual models offer an increased potential for achieving spatial understanding. The issues and opportunities identified are then once again tested using sketches, leading to new solutions which are in turn tested on an adjusted version of the existing model. Decisions are made at the end of

were as follows: firstly, to find a reference space or picture with a strong atmosphere; secondly, to create an abstract model with the same spatial effect; and thirdly, to transfer the result onto the actual design site.
After identifying the atmospheric goal, designing commenced by defining spatial elements that might generate a similar effect. Conceptual models were essential to testing the generated effects during this phase. Different formalistic tests were developed and carried out, and the result always differed as a result of the material used. This once again underlined the importance of material choice: clay, cast, and cardboard models built along the same principles prompted completely different conclusions and led to different directions for the design.
As the project was intended to reflect a realistic design perspective and process, more detailed models were also worked out at a larger scale, ultimately becoming an important part of the final concept.

each step of this iterative process. The combination of decisions slowly leads to a more and more detailed design idea, one that is changed and adapted over and over again. The following list is a summarization of the steps of the first phase of a design process in which conceptual models are created:

1. First design concept sketches
2. Selecting ideas for further development
3. Testing the selected ideas with conceptual models
4. Comparing the design ideas based on the models
5. Further development using new sketches
6. Adjusting the conceptual models based on the new sketches
7. Repeating the process

Certain choices must be made before the actual model-building begins: those of choosing the scale and the material.

As mentioned above, conceptual models can be a big help for architects and urban professionals because they allow for more detailed spatial analysis. The availability of a wide range of materials enables the analysis of a problem from a variety of different angles. Finding the right material for a design problem is crucial – not only to save time, but also because it is necessary for arriving at the conclusions that will ultimately lead to the best answer to a problem.

Consequently, this tool's most significant limitation lies in the necessity of finding the right material. All materials have their own structure, and an incorrect choice may mislead designers

Endnotes

1 Franz Reschke Landschaftsarchitekten. "EUROPAN 11 competition entry." [Online]. 2010. Available at https://www.franzreschke.de/arbeiten/stadtpark-nynaeshamn-2/

2 TUB students. "Urbanes Spüren." Seminar project for Master in Landscape Architecture students at Technische Universität Berlin, supervised by Holz, S., 2016. Further details: http://www.planen-bauen-umwelt.tu-berlin.de/fileadmin/i43_praktika/160215_Projektbeschreibung_Master.pdf

when they are considering design options. Working with any given material tends to define the paths of thinking: if the wrong tool is selected, following the material's path could lead to the wrong answers, and important solutions and hidden problems may remain undiscovered.

This text is based on the writing of Piroska Szabó and was edited by Andreas Brück.

B.18

INTERVENING THROUGH SYSTEM THINKING

Austin Center for Design. **An Introduction to Wicked Problems**. [Online]. n.d, Available at https://www.wickedproblems.com/table_of_contents.php Accessed July 29, 2016.

Brenner, N., ed. **Implosions/Explosions. Towards a Study of Planetary Urbanization**. Berlin: Jovis, 2013.

Brown, V. Harris, J.A., and Russel, J., eds. **Tackling Wicked Problems. Through the Transdisciplinary Imagination**. London: Earthscan, 2010.

Buchanan, R. "Wicked Problems in Design Thinking." **Design Issues** 8, no. 2 (Spring 1992): 5–21. Available at http://web.mit.edu/jrankin/www/engin_as_lib_art/Design_thinking.pdf Accessed July 29, 2016.

Gibbons, M. and Nowotny, H. "The Potential of Transdisciplinarity." In **Transdisciplinarity. Joint Problem Solving among Science, Technology, and Society. An Effective Way for Managing Complexity**, edited by Thompson Klein, J., Grossenbacher-Mansuy, W., Haberli, R., Bill, A., Scholz, R.W., and Welti, M., 67–80. Berlin: Springer, 2001.

Orr, D. "Systems Thinking and the future of cities." In: **Solutions** 5, 1 (2014), 54-61. Available at http://www.thesolutionsjournal.com/node/237149 Accessed July 29, 2016.

Renn, J. and Scherer, B., eds. **Das Anthropozän. Zum Stand der Dinge**. Berlin: Matthes und Seitz, 2015.

Rittel, H. and Webber, M. "Dilemmas in a General Theory of Planning." **Policy Sciences**, 4 (1973): 155–169. Available at http://www.uctc.net/mwebber/Rittel+Webber+Dilemmas+General_Theory_of_Planning.pdf Accessed July 29, 2016.

Urban Metabolism Group. **Urban Metabolism**. [Online]. n.d. Available at http://www.urbanmetabolism.org/ Accessed July 29, 2016.

Walloth, C. **Understanding complex urban systems. Multidisciplinary approaches to modeling**. Cham: Springer, 2014.

A reductionist perspective on planning problems seemed to work well for a long period of progress and prosperity; today, however, we are increasingly confronted with the limits of this way of thinking (Orr 2014). Faced with the proclamation of the *Anthropocene* – the age when humankind started to have a significant global impact on the earth's biological, geological, and atmospheric systems (Renn and Scherer 2015) – and the theoretical claim that the whole world has been urbanized (Brenner 2013), as well as with the complex interdependencies of urban and natural systems, we increasingly realize that reducing complexity today often means ignoring reality, if not violating it altogether. It is therefore an insufficient strategy for solving the wicked problems of modern societies in the twenty-first century.

The term *wicked problems* was coined by the planning and design theorists Horst Rittel and Melvin Webber in 1973 in their article "Dilemmas in a General Theory of Planning." In contrast to tame problems, wicked or evil problems lack a clear definition, goal, and path of action. They are difficult or even impossible to solve because of contradictory, incomplete, and changing requirements (Austin Center for Design n.d.). Wicked problems are complex issues that resist conventional approaches to problem-solving. There are no good or bad and no right or wrong solutions to them; only better or worse solutions. The effort to solve one aspect of a wicked problem always reveals or creates new problems. Most of the concrete problems that urban planners and designers are facing touch upon much larger issues, such as

Dune, Magnus Larsson[1]
In his master's thesis *Dune* (2008), the Swedish architect Magnus Larsson attempts to tackle the wicked problem of the desertification of the Sahel Zone in Africa. The term *desertification* describes the expansion of the desert, which goes along with a series of problems like drought, water scarcity, famine, death, forced migration, political instability, and armed conflict. Larsson's systemic solution is as follows: he suggests building a 6,000-kilometer-long inhabitable anti-desertification wall ("the dune") that functions as a physical support structure for vegetation. Larsson's anti-desertification wall would be a sand-stopping device made of sand: a type of bacteria would be flushed through the dune to cause a biological reaction that turns the loose sand into solid sandstone. Working with the existing and abundant material of sand and using only bacteria could effectively stop desertification, and – in theory – help to prevent most of its potential negative consequences from occurring. By collecting condensation water, habitable green spaces could be created that transcend state and ethnic borders. However, as Larsson himself admits, there are many unresolved political, practical, ethical, and financial questions concerning this speculative project.

Petrochemical America, Richard Misrach and Kate Orff[2]
Petrochemical America is a multi-layered assemblage

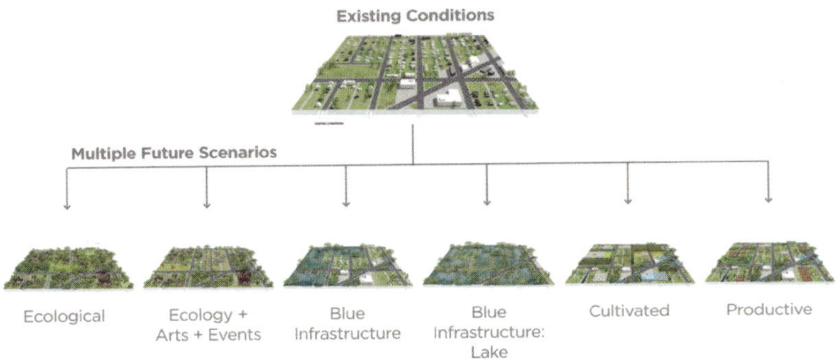

Stoss Landscape Urbanism (2013) **Illustrative Scenarios**.

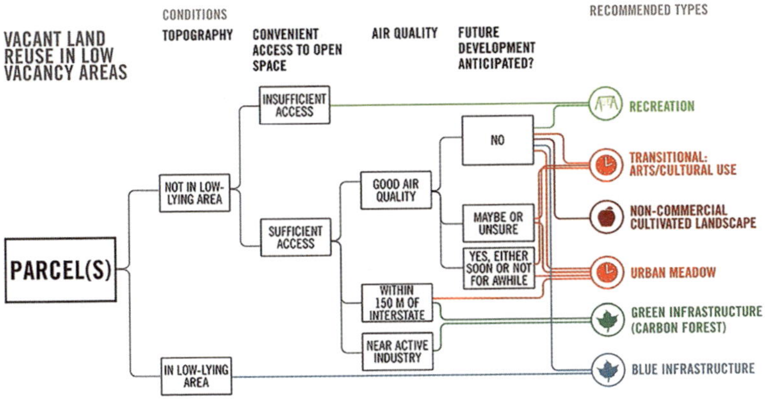

Stoss Landscape Urbanism (2013) **Decision-Making Matrix**.

of narrative visual information, developed through research and data mapping along the Mississippi River by the photographer Richard Misrach and landscape architect Kate Orff. It analyzes the environmental impact of the petrochemical industry and the complex interdependencies of the cultural, physical, and economic systems in the region known as Cancer Alley, an area of intense chemical production known for its high rates of the disease. The publication draws attention to the environmental destruction caused by petrochemical landscapes and the global impact of industrial landscapes as a whole to prompt a more in-depth discussion about the relationships between energy production, climate change, and the landscapes produced by humans. By integrating photography, emotion and analysis, and research and speculation, *Petrochemical America* illustrates how design can address the public interest in order to remake a place and problematize the complex systemic relations of cultural and natural systems, as well as the wicked challenges that go along with humankind's intervention in them.

Detroit Future City, Stoss[3]
The city of Detroit is facing overwhelming challenges. The decline of the local industrial economy has led to rapid shrinking of the population, causing a subsequent erosion of the urban fabric as well as other socio-economic problems. A poor transportation system and a lack of public services are just

The Open Workshop (2014) **Bird's-Eye View of the City's Waterfront**. The Open Workshop's project is proposing a systemic intervention in the dredge-cycle of the city of Toledo, USA.

some of the most urgent issues. In order to tackle these complex problems, a multi-pronged, multi-scalar approach was needed both in the short- and long-term. Between 2010 and 2013, and in collaboration with an interdisciplinary team of planners, designers, and community leaders, the landscape architecture office Stoss developed the *Detroit Strategic Framework*, a decision-making roadmap for improving the quality of life and business in Detroit. The project identifies and establishes links between social, economic, and ecological systems. These integrated solutions include new forms of urban living, new modes of production in the city, and new productive green infrastructures. The project recognizes that a single solution to one specific problem would not be able to address the complexity and interrelatedness of the issues Detroit faces, and acknowledges that the strategies must work across different scales and time frames. Landscape is rethought as a greater system – one with the potential to be reproductive, generative, and structural.

Dredgescaping Toledo, The Open Workshop, 2014[4]
The growth of the global shipping industry and the increased sizes of ships have created new logistical routes that approach the shallower depths found closer to urban areas. Maintenance of these routes requires continuous dredging to counter the natural tendencies of erosion. Dredging, the process of excavation, and the gathering, transport,

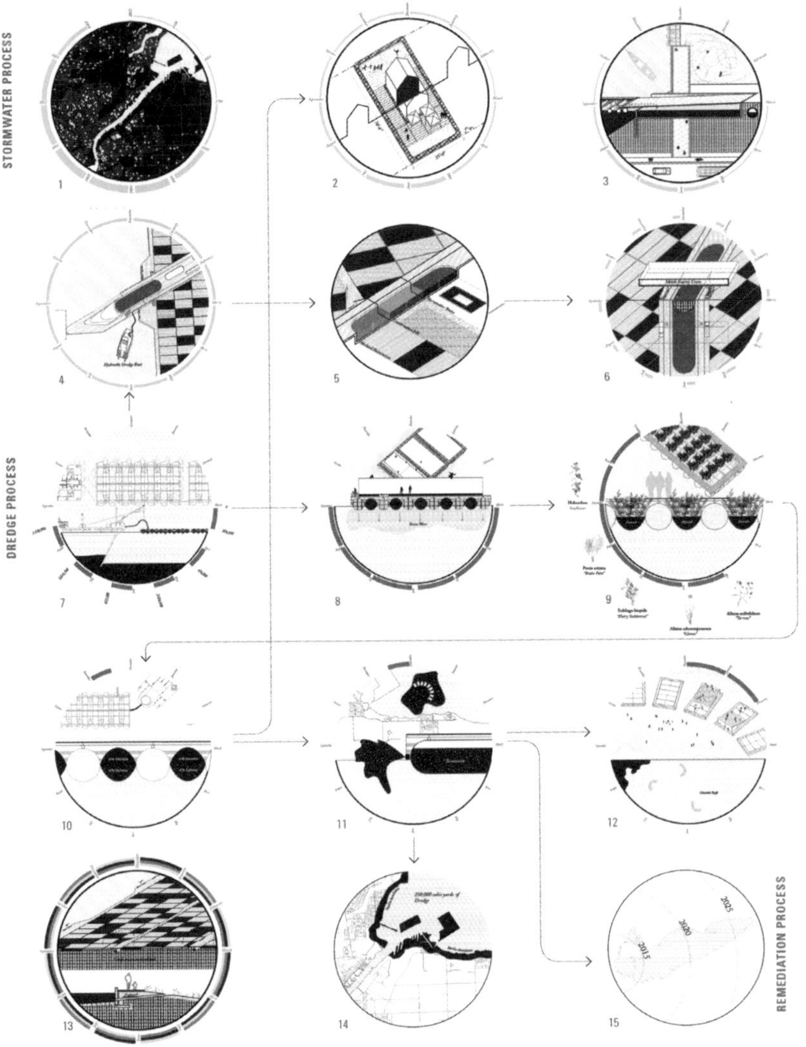

The Open Workshop (2014) **Dredge Land Processing**. Confluence of the dredge, civic and watershed subsystems.

and disposal of sediment from coastal areas therefore continue to be one of the largest anthropogenic spatial interventions on our planet. Ironically, the *dredge cycle* – the cyclical process of dredging – is itself catalyzing the erosion that it was established to counter, thus reinforcing a never-ending process. This becomes a significant wicked problem for urban, terrestrial, and aquatic (eco)systems. The Open Workshop's design proposal *Dredgescaping Toledo* (2014) incites a systemic confluence of the subsystems of the dredge-shed, watershed, and civic-shed of the city of Toledo, USA, into a comprehensive meta-system called the *soft shed* – a resilient, multi-scalar, malleable, and productive system that creates new climate change, inequality, sustainability, and health; issues for which there is no easy fix. A further reason that wicked problems are so hard to tackle is that they exist at the interface of different systems, thus requiring transdisciplinary approaches and a systemic thinking perspective (Brown, Harris, and Russel 2010).

The term *systemic thinking* describes a broad and diverse analytical tradition with various fields of application. According to this way of thinking, a social or planning problem cannot be approached in isolation but must be understood as a part of systems and sub-systems. Systemic thinking seeks to deal with complexity by understanding the complex logic, rules, and relations of diverse urban and natural systems. Instead of separating out single elements, systemic thinking focuses on relations, connections, interdependencies, and causalities. Instead of ignoring complexity, it is a holistic approach that tries to live up to it (Orr 2014).

The concepts of wicked problems and systemic thinking have been used as analytical tools in various disciplines. Today, there are a host of different interpretations, methodologies, and concepts in fields as diverse as ecology and political studies (political ecology), sociology (actor-network theory), and mathematics and computer science (cybernetics). Recently, these two concepts have been increasingly adopted in space-related disciplines such as geography, urban planning and design, and landscape architecture. One emerging and very influential field of research here is urban metabolism, which analyzes material flows within urban settlements, as well as the interconnections

relationships to make each individual shed more robust as a way of countering the dredge cycle's negative consequences. This is done using a series of spatial strategies that include lakes, islands, and tributaries.

IABR—Project Atelier Rotterdam: The Urban Metabolism, .FABRIC and JCFO, 2014[5]

Like all cities in the world located on deltas, the harbor city of Rotterdam is extremely vulnerable to the impacts of climate change. Rotterdam today faces a major challenge: (How) can further economic growth be ensured in a sustainable way? The 2014 project *Atelier Rotterdam: The Urban Metabolism* for the IABR by design offices .FABRIC and JCFO uses the systemic perspective of an urban metabolism approach to analyze the urban systems of Rotterdam and to develop strategies and specific design proposals in answer to this question. In order to visualize the urban metabolism, nine primary flows within the city-system are identified: goods, people, waste, biota, energy, food, fresh water, air, and sand and clay. In a next step, four strategies are identified that would contribute to an urban metabolism with fewer negative and more positive effects on Rotterdam's sustainability: collecting resources (the extraction of raw materials from waste and food); creating biotopes (improving urban nature through the local use of fresh water, sand, and clay); channeling waste and energy waste (through the use of the byproducts of of anthropogenic and natural systems and sub-systems (Urban Metabolism Group 2016).

In urban design, two different approaches to dealing with wicked problems can be distinguished: the *problematizing approach* and the *problem-solving approach*. In the former, design methods are used as analytical tools to define and illustrate the complexity and uncertainty – or in other words, the wickedness – of a problem by visualizing its position within interrelated systems (see Misrach and Orff 2012; Tillie et al. 2014). In the latter, design methods are implemented on the basis of a systemic perspective in order to tackle a wicked problem. The methods and tools being used may be traditional, but in many cases they are applied in unorthodox ways in order to deal with a wicked problem that requires unorthodox solutions, leading to the invention of new methods and tools or even new emerging fields of research (see Larsson 2008; Stoss n.d.; The Open Workshop 2014).

Although systemic thinking is characterized by the non-determination of a fixed set of steps to be applied (Rittel and Webber 1973), there are some general guidelines designers should consider if they want to tackle wicked problems on the basis of a systemic thinking perspective. These include:

Problem definition: Designers should recognize the complexity of the context in which they act and define the specifics of the problems they are confronted with.

Analyzing the urban-natural complex as a system: In order to develop an understanding of the problem's wickedness,

energy extraction); catalyzing re-industrialization (boosting the quality of the flows of goods, people, and air).

Endnotes

1 Larsson, M. (2008): **Dune**. [Online]. 2008. Available at http://www.magnuslarsson.com/architecture/dune.asp Accessed July 29, 2016.

2 Misrach, R. and Orff, K. **Petrochemical America**. New York: Aperture, 2012.

3 Stoss. **Detroit Future City**. [Online]. n.d. Available at https://www.stoss.net/projects/planning-urbanism/detroit-future-city Accessed April 22, 2020.

4 The Open Workshop **Dredgescaping Toledo**. [Online]. 2014. Available at http://www.theopenworkshop.ca/Pages/A_Projects_Toledo.html Accessed July 29, 2016.

5 Tillie, N., Klijn, O., Frijters, E., Borsboom, J. and Looije, M., eds. **Urban Metabolism: Sustainable Development of Rotterdam**. [Online]. 2014. Available at http://iabr.nl/media/document/original/urban_metabolism_rotterdam.pdf Accessed July 29, 2016.

designers need to analyze its relation to systems (Buchanan 1992).

Circular instead of linear design-thinking: Wicked problems cannot be solved with a single design proposal. Designers have to predict and take into consideration long-term (and rebound) effects on related systems and the possibility of generating new wicked problems (Buchanan 1992).

Transdisciplinary/cooperative approaches: To tackle wicked problems, designers need to think beyond the scope of their discipline and incorporate the perspectives of a variety of actors (scientific, civil, political, etc.) (Gibbons and Nowotny 2001).

The strengths of both concepts lie in their potential to critically address the reduction of complexity that is still embedded in many methodological research and design approaches. Nevertheless, we must acknowledge that even though the two concepts were developed with the ambitious aspiration of dealing with the complex problems of modern societies, they are ultimately theoretical frameworks that unavoidably introduce a certain reduction of complexity themselves. When tackling wicked problems on the basis of a systemic thinking perspective, the task for designers is to find an adequate balance between being overly reductionist and being capable of acting – so as to avoid violating reality on the one hand and getting lost in chaos on the other.

This text is based on the writing of Hisar Ersöz and was edited by Xenia Kokoula.

B.19

DESIGNING GRID PRINCIPLES

Benevolo, L. **The History of the City**. Cambridge: MIT Press, 1980.

Bott, H. "Stadtraum und Gebäudetypologien im Entwurf." In **Lehrbausteine Städtebau. Basiswissen für Entwurf und Planung**, 6th edition, edited by Bott, H. et al. Stuttgart: Städtebau-Institut, Universität Stuttgart, 2010.

Curdes, G. **Stadtstruktur und Stadtgestalt**, 2nd edition. Stuttgart, Berlin and Cologne: Verlag W. Kohlhammer GmbH, 1997.

Fehl, G. "Stadt im Nationalen Grid: Zu einigen historischen Grundlagen der US-amerikanischen Stadtproduktion." In **Going West? Stadtplanung in den USA – gestern und heute**, edited by Petz, U. Dortmund: Kolander & Poggel GbR, 2004.

Frick, D. **Theorie des Städtebaus**. Tübingen: Ernst Wasmuth Verlag, 2008.

Korda, M. **Städtebau – Technische Grundlagen**, 5th edition, Stuttgart: Teubner Verlag, 2005.

Kostof, S. **The City Shaped: Urban Patterns and Meanings through History**. London: Thames and Hudson, 1991.

Lindemann, H**. Stadt im Quadrat: Geschichte und Gegenwert einer einprägsamen Stadtgestalt**. Basel: Birkhäuser, 1999.

Marcuse, P. "The Grid as City Plan: New York City and Laissez-faire Planning in the Nineteenth Century." **Planning Perspectives** 2, issue 3 (1987): 287–310.

Morris, A.E.J. **History of Urban Form: Before the Industrial Revolutions**. New York: Longman Scientific & Technical, 1994.

Schenk, L. **Designing Cities: Basics, Principles, Projects**. Basel: Birkhäuser, 2013.

Shpuza, E. "Urban Shapes and Urban Grids: A Comparative Study of Adriatic and Ionian Coastal Cities." Paper presented at the 6th International Space Syntax Symposium, Istanbul, June 2007.

Weston, R. **100 Ideas that Changed Architecture**, London: Laurence King Publishing Ltd, 2011.

A *grid plan* is an urban pattern in which every street crosses another at a right angle (*Dictionary of Urban Regional Planning* 2015). To this day, it is the most commonly applied organizing principle in urban design (Schenk 2013). As it has been in use for such a long time, it has also been discussed a great deal. Curdes (1997) described grids as continuous two-dimensional connection and division elements. Shpuza (2007) later discussed urban grids as independent systems with an internalized global logic tied to patterns of connectivity between the streets. Similarly, Weston (2011) wrote that a modular grid was meant to be both rational and universally applicable.

Throughout the long history of the city, grid patterns have proven successful as a universally valid organizing principle that is both adaptable and resilient (Schenk 2013). Nevertheless, they are discussed critically, particularly where the regular grid is concerned.

Generally speaking, grids offer easy navigation through parallel and orthogonal structures. A clear and simple development pattern within a city enables residents and visitors to understand the organization of an area and make their way around (Curdes 1997). All the functions within a grid are automatically connected. Grids enhance the efficiency of transport networks for pedestrians as well as for public transportation and cars (Kostof 1991).

In our constantly changing cities, grids provide a good mechanism for reacting to new social, technological, and economic requirements by altering connections or shifting uses

The ancient Greek city of Miletus
Kostof (1992) argues that the grid is geographically and historically universal. No other urban structure can be applied as a standard at any site. As a result of this universality, a wide range of diverse references in terms of scale, project size, geometry, historical background, adaptability, contemporary design, and so on can be named. Throughout the long history of this structure, many cities have been founded based on a grid design. We will therefore begin our references here with a short review of historic examples.
A grid was often used in the foundation of Greek and Roman cities, thereby serving as examples for the later development of major cities in Europe. In circa 500–400 BC, Miletus was designed as a grid-planned town. Its design is most probably attributable to Hippodamus, who is considered to be the father of urban planning, and the city used his basic design of regular, orthogonal squares. The Roman grid was organized with the Cardo Maximus (the main north-south-oriented street and the Decumanus Maximus (the main east-west-oriented street) acting as the main axes for the city plan. The forum was found at the intersection of these two principal streets and the city was surrounded by rectangular defensive walls. This arrangement is still recognizable in many European cities founded as parts of Roman colonies.
Like many other American cities – such as Washington D.C., Portland, Chicago, and

Hippodamos of Miletus (circa 500–400 BC) **Plan of the city of Miletus**. Miletus was designed as a grid-planned town. It is attributed to Hippodamus of Miletus, who is considered to be the father of urban planning, and features the basic design of his rhythmic and orthogonal squares.

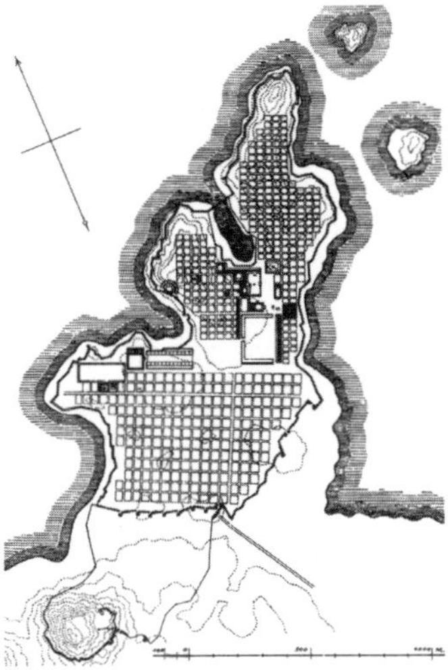

within the network. Instead of being limited by blocks of the same size, a grid may eventually be adjusted by connecting or splitting blocks, or by removing and relinking the connections (Schenk 2013). A heterogeneous mix of compatible housing and building types, as well as land uses, are possible even with similar block sizes. As such, it is possible to develop a diversity of neighborhoods within the city by accommodating different building typologies. The use of irregular grids, in contrast to very straight grids, allows specific urban spaces to be created (Schenk 2013). Grids are usually easily expandable, and the regular grid is particularly so (Curdes 1997). A grid pattern is both robust and flexible, and is suited to being adapted to meet changing needs without abandoning the basic urban design and its qualities (Schenk 2013).

Individual areas within the grid design possess a high spatial quality of their own. It is therefore not necessary to change

Philadelphia – New York City is a representative example of a city that uses a grid pattern on an urban scale. The New York City Commissioner's Plan was first presented by a commission appointed by the New York State Legislature in 1811. Despite criticism, it is currently viewed favorably by urban planners, and discussion of its size and associated functions have been fruitfully discussed. One of these discussions concerns the benefits of shorter blocks: as there are many ways to get to a specific destination, it is possible to choose the fastest and shortest way. Short blocks prioritize pedestrians, making walking an easier and faster option. With its unique block size of 200 by 200 feet (approximately 61 m × 61 m), Portland serves as a good example of this, whereas most other American cities have much larger block patterns. Most blocks in New York were built at the 200-foot scale in order to create a pedestrian-friendly downtown. Barcelona should also be named as a well-known example: the Barcelona Grid, also called Cerdà's Plan after its original designer Ildefons Cerdà, dates from 1859 and is renowned for its unique octagonal geometry and the size of its squares. Cerdà's focus on greenery created green spaces as walkable spaces, which have proven to be advantageous to the city. Milton Keynes in Great Britain and Chandigarh in India, both built in the 1960s, were designed based on more recent requirements, such as an increased volume of traffic.

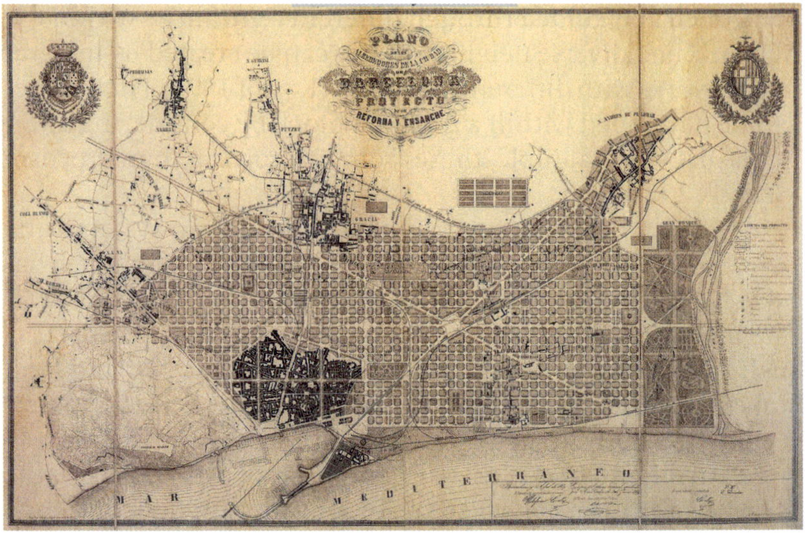

Ildefons Cerdà i Sunyer (1859) **Barcelona – Cerda's Plan**. The Barcelona grid, first designed by an urban planner, Ildefons Cerdà, in 1859, was known for its unique octagonal geometry and square-size. His focus on greenery resulted in walkable green spaces that have been advantageous to the city.

or develop the entire grid to ensure completeness. Changes and adaptions can be caused by drawn-out realization processes resulting from e.g. political or economic situations (Schenk 2013). Continuous grids with small blocks have the highest percentage of land used as streets. The number of streets may be reduced for ecological reasons, also leading to a decrease in infrastructure costs. Creating different street hierarchies allows traffic to be

Both grids were designed as cities with superblocks and roundabouts at the intersections of the most important streets. While Chandigarh is set in a valley without topographical obstacles, Milton Keynes aimed to integrate the existing topography and to use cul-de-sac streets within the blocks to connect the entire plan to the surrounding area using bike and footpaths (Kostof, 1991).

At the scale of site projects, grid patterns are most frequently implemented on conversion sites or city extensions, depending on the specific conditions of each site. A good example are Berlin's urban extensions in Friedrichstadt (1688) and those later carried out by James Hobrecht: various parts of these extensions are based on a grid pattern between the main roads.

The conversion of Munich's airport in Riem in 1992 shows the adaptability of the grid design. The overall concept of the 560-hectare area revolved around the spatial concept "compact, urban, green," and was implemented using a superimposed grid. The new block structure, featuring a mix of uses including commercial, residential, public open space, and trade fair facilities, was designed using a basic grid and then deformed to allow the landscape and existing structural facilities of the airport to be integrated.

The Beijing Technology Park Masterplan by Gabrysch + Partner (2004) calls for the regular grid to be transformed step-by-step into an organic structure: the highly geometric section is for controlled and guided through different centralities within the network, and diverse neighborhoods can be created by integrating networks with different functions (Kostof 1991). Hierarchies can be developed within a grid or a block by considering different layers – for example, those from macrocosm to microcosm (Schenk 2013).

Grids provide an easy and efficient way to systemically parcel – and thereby equally distribute – land, a quality which has been particularly important in the past (Kostof 1991, Fehl 2004). The limitation of grids is their dependence on external factors such as topography, existing connections, and urban and landscape structures such as existing buildings and trees. Geographical features can be dealt with through deformations, tilted shifts, and curves in the grid plan (Schenk 2013). Another disadvantage is the potential for a regular grid to result in a monotonous cityscape. For easy orientation within the grid system, it is necessary to ensure that not every street looks the same and that orientation points (landmarks) are implemented (Schenk 2013). Compared with cities that have grown more organically, grid-based cities are prone to losing their own character as a result of standardization. It is therefore important to look for the special features within each city or site (Fehl 2004).

The grid as a method is used in many different disciplines and, as such, in many different approaches concerning structure and scale. In urban planning it is applicable at the regional and urban scale, as well as the scale of individual sites. Grids can also

industry and business, while the more organic area provides space for housing. Culture and sport, as well as research facilities, are located between these sections and integrated with public green areas. Hierarchies and clusters are clearly recognizable, as is the integration of water structures.
Grid patterns have also been implemented at the architectural scale, for example at the Free University in Berlin. The design of the Free University (1963) is based on an open-grid design – which was typical for universities in the 1960s. It was therefore later able to accommodate changes, such as Foster and Partners' extension building, which was completed in 2005 (Weston, 2011). Many of the aspirations of the architects Candilis, Josic, and Woods were realized in the paradigmatic Free University of Berlin (Chousein, 2013).

be applied in landscape architecture, and are common even at smaller scales, such as that of individual buildings. In addition to the clearly recognizable regular grid, different grid structures can be used. The main characteristic of the regular grid is an even and orthogonal net structure that forms the basis for square or rectangularly formed blocks. However, tilted, deformed, transformed, and superimposed grids are frequently more suited to the considerations of planning requirements, topography and existing urban structures, visual connections, and orientation points. It is often necessary to use such modified grids because an orthogonal structure is unsuitable for the specific shape of the planning site (Schenk 2013). As mentioned above, grids can be applied at different scales. It would be possible to combine grid systems with a network-based approach on a regional, urban, project-related, or building-expansion scale (Frick 2008). Walkability, public space, traffic connections, and so on need to be considered with regard to grid size.

This text is based on the writing of MinJi Kim and Selina Schöller-Mann and was edited by Angela Million.

B.20

PRODUCING AND REDUCING COMPLEXITY

Colander, D. and Kupers, R. **Complexity and the Art of Public Policy – Changing Society from the Bottom Up**, Princeton: Princeton University Press, 2014.

Crawford, R. **What Can Complexity Theory Tell Us About Urban Planning?** New Zealand Productivity Commission, 2016.

de Brujin, J. and ten Heuvelhof, E. **Networks and Decision Making**. Meppel: Boom Koninklijke Uitgevers, 2000.

Edelenbos, J. "Design and Management of Participatory Public Policy Making." **Public Management Review** 1, no. 4 (1999): 569–576.

ElMaraghy, W. et al. "Complexity in Engineering Design and Manufacturing." **CIRP Annals – Manufacturing Technology** 61, no. 2 (2012): 793–814.

Guinée, J.B., ed. **Handbook on Life Cycle Assessment: Operational Guide to the ISO Standards**, Dordrecht: Kluwer Academic Publishers, 2002.

Hendriks, C. **Sustainable Construction**, Boxtel: Aeneas, 2001.

Holland, J. **Complexity: A Very Short Introduction**, Oxford: Oxford University Press, 2014.

Mayer, I., van Bueren, E., Bots, P., and van der Voort, H. "Collaborative Decision-making for Sustainable Urban Renewal Projects: A Simulation - Gaming Approach." **Environment and Planning B: Planning and Design** 32, no. 3 (2004): 403–423.

McLoughlin, J.B. **Urban and Regional Planning: A Systems Approach**. London: Faber, 1969.

Moroni, S. "Complexity and the Inherent Limits of Explanation and Prediction: Urban Codes for Self-organising Cities." **Planning Theory** 14, no. 3 (2014): 248–267.

Portugali, J., Meyer, H., Stolk, E., and Tan, E. **Complexity Theories of Cities Have Come of Age: An Overview with Implications to Urban Planning and Design**. Heidelberg: Springer, 2012.

There is no general consensus on the meaning of complexity. Etymologically, *complexity* comes from the Latin word *complexus*, which means *interwoven*. A complex system is one in which elements interact and affect each other in such a way that it is difficult to isolate the behavior of individual elements. Complexity in systems is invariably multidimensional. A complex system usually consists of many members, elements, or agents that interact with one another and with the environment (ElMaraghy 2012).

Generally speaking, two types of complexity can be distinguished in complex decision-making: system complexity and political complexity. System complexity, particularly the sustainability of technological and design options, can be addressed by using substantive modelling (Hendriks, 2001). Political complexity can be addressed through a participatory planning approach or through process management (De Bruijn and Ten Heuvelhof 2000; De Bruijn et al. 2002; Edelenbos 1999).

Urbanists have viewed cities as complex systems at least since the 1960s. An eclectic range of approaches have looked at how implicit economics and cultural rules have shaped cities, as well as how networks can enhance effective relationships among a city's agents. Complexity and unpredictability challenge the feasibility of urban planning beyond a certain point (Crawford 2016).

Complexity theory is a young science that draws on many disciplines and has yet to establish a unified framework (Crawford 2016). One of the main features and problems of complexity is that it can be found almost everywhere. Thanks to this feature,

Songzhuang Arts and Agriculture City[1]
In most parts of the world – and especially in China – populations and cities are rapidly growing, leading to a steady increase in the demand for food and resources. This also results in an increasing division between urban and agricultural land as farmland is moved to the outskirts of the cities. As a result, the food industry and supply chain have developed into a complex, globally operating system that on the one hand pollutes the environment (among other things through long transport distances) and on the other weakens the connection between urban dwellers and nature.
The Chinese city Songzhuang is located next to Beijing. For its Songzhuang Arts and Agriculture City master plan, the interdisciplinary planning office Sasaki envisions the creation of a series of self-sustaining communities by closely interlinking urban and agricultural uses. Most of the area's existing settlements will be retained and supplemented with a highly diverse range of building typologies and uses. Urban agriculture is also deeply embedded in the plan. By creating a highly complex urban and agricultural fabric with several urban cores, the plan not only targets the ecological dimension but also a number of economic and social aspects. At the same time, this complexity is reduced by the championing of agriculture and food provision in urban developments, which also demonstrates the plan's conceptual shortcomings. While the planners provide

complexity concepts can, in principle, be applied to many different fields. The approach of increasing and reducing complexity was first applied in physics, as physical systems are relatively less complex. Disciplines such as biology, sociology, and mathematics soon followed (Crawford 2016).

Complexity-based approaches are now also applied in the fields of urban planning and urban design – for example in investigating the pattern of land use in cities, the spatial segregation of ethnic, cultural, and socio-economic social groups within a city, the size distribution of cities in a region, the economic and geographical spatio-hierarchical patterns of central places in cities, metropolitan regions, and countries, the structure of city road networks, the structure of communications between cities, and other urban phenomena (Portugali 2009).

There are two broad approaches to planning in complex urban systems. One bases city development on a few simple, universal spatial rules, while the other takes a participative, collaborative approach to city development (Crawford 2016). The former could be considered an approach that reduces complexity, while the latter produces (or increases) complexity.

The first of these responses to the problem of planning in complex systems builds on the observation that a complex order can arise spontaneously from the consistent and persistent application of (often implicit) spatial laws over time. In this approach, a government enacts a few simple and universal rules to guide the behavior of urban agents, who are then free

a comprehensive examination of the distribution of the different urban and agricultural uses, it is not clear to what extent the needs shown reflect actual needs. Furthermore, the plan barely addresses the issues of transport infrastructure and means of transportation, and how the city will be connected to its surroundings and Beijing. The master plan would also have benefited from a stronger perspective on local food distribution and local food service cultures as ways of fostering locally driven economies and benefits for both the residents and ecology.

Ananas New Community.[2] The Ananas New Community plan for the Indonesian city Silang, located around 50 kilometres from Manila and largely responsible for the capital's food supply, seeks to interlink existing urban uses with (until now adjacent) agricultural ones in order to encourage a sustainable food network and a new way of living. Although it appears to have the same focus as the Songzhuang Arts and Agriculture City development concept at first glance, the plan shows more consideration of a complex variety of environmental aspects – for example, dealing with different seasons and their impacts (for example, monsoons) and sun and wind planning for a comfortable microclimate. Eco-corridors, which are used for farming and farmhouses as well as for (agri)cultural programs aim to create a close-knit network of side-by-side food production and food processing, as well as

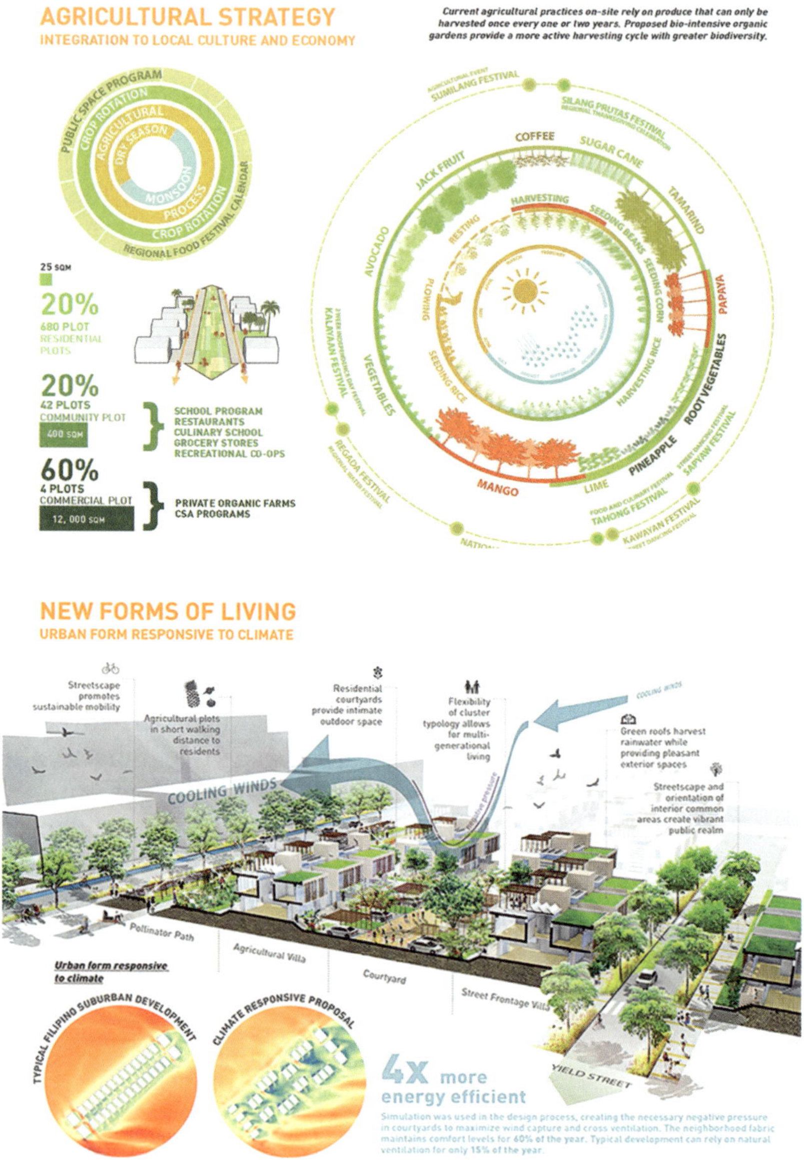

Sasaki (2015) **Ananas New Community urban development strategy**. The plan combines a functional landscape network of agricultural plots, eco-corridors, and parks in Silang, Philippines.

to realize their own plans as they see fit in line with those rules (Crawford 2016).

The second of these responses is to use a participative, collaborative, and iterative approach to engage urban agents in the evolutionary development of a city. Planning is essentially provisional and is adapted to the emerging form and behaviors of the city through collective action (Crawford 2016). As Crawford

introducing newer residents to and fostering learning about local farming practices. Thus, the plan for urban agriculture is supposed to help create better-quality food, economic efficiency, and community. At the same time, the plan does not consider whether residents will actually want to contribute to the community gardens planned throughout the city. This demonstrates that complexity can also produce or hide blind spots.

Potsdam à la Card – Modelling Density for the inner city of Potsdam[3]
A strategic way of dealing with complex systems of urban development is to set options and rules by urban design and let actors cooperatively negotiate or play about them. This project uses a macro-scale concept of urban density to create a planning strategy for the future inner city of Potsdam. The proposed spatial model originates from the historic housing structure of the baroque city extension: blocks and the five-axis-residential building. The existing urban fabric, as well as new themed development blocks, are communicated through the images of a card game. Used as a planning strategy, it offers a variety of local open- and green-space identities and building-block typologies with the aim of defining the inner city blocks in their density and function. This approach results in a flexible city collage of structure and vegetation flows operating with local built environment traditions.

(2016, 10) points out, a collective action process in spatial planning might involve:

1. Understanding the structures of the urban sub-system, organizing collective actions within them, nesting the sub-system and its connections or integrating the sub-system within and across different levels of the larger system;
2. Identifying relevant resources and key actors (with decision-making rights and the knowledge needed to move things forward) within the sub-systems;
3. Building collective action institutions at a workable scale and scope;
4. Identifying what system-wide support functions (e.g. data collection, analysis and feedback on system development) are required.

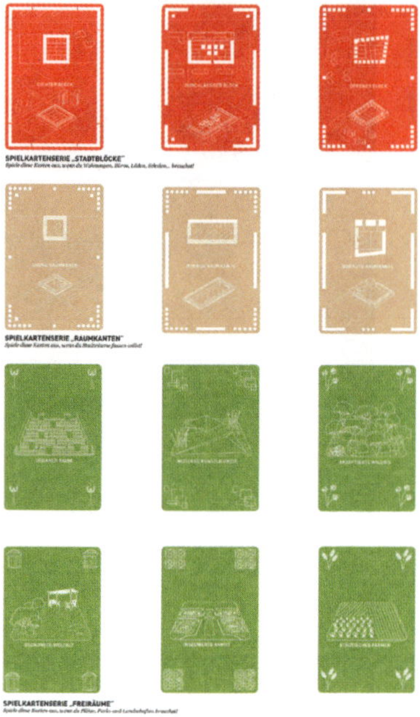

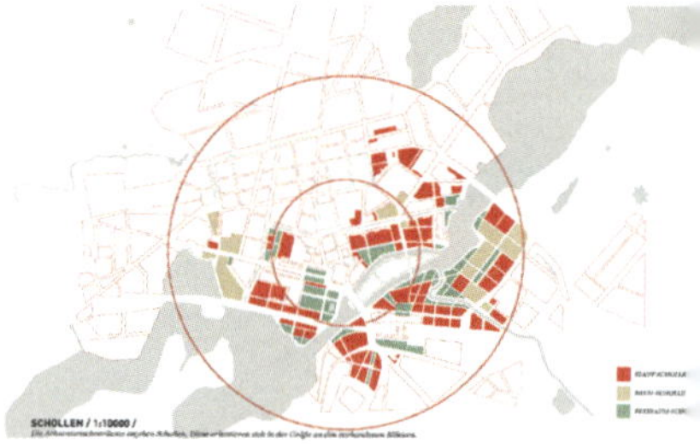

Producing and reducing complexity in cities has provided a sound theoretical basis supported by mathematical formalism for use in urban planning and urban design. The aim here is generally not to identify new urban phenomena, but rather to create a single, sound theoretical basis for a variety of urban phenomena and properties that were hitherto perceived as independent of each other, and thus interpreted with reference to different theoretical bases. All of these phenomena have already been interpreted as emerging from local interactions between agents and ultimately giving rise to global structures (Portugali 2009). Contemporary developments and situations such as globalization and urbanization are reflected in the increasing popularity and dominance of theories and perceptions of reality that emphasize change

Felix Bentlin, Arlett Gehrke, Johannes Hipp, Peter Mackensen (2012) **Potsdam à la Card**. Planning strategy inspired by gamification aimed at sparking discussion about different green-space identities and building-block typologies in order to define the future use and density of inner-city blocks of Potsdam, Germany.

and instability; in the shifts from modernism to postmodernism, from structuralism to post-structuralism, from constructivism to deconstructivism, from systems in equilibrium to systems out of equilibrium, from closed to open systems, and from entropy to self-organization and complexity that recognizes notions such as chaos, the edge of chaos, fractal structures, and nonlinearity (Portugali 2005).

There are four main limitations when dealing with complexity. Firstly, simulation models originally designed for the study of complexity and self-organization have become the message itself. Secondly, the complexity of cities tends to overlook the fact that complexity theory is a new science that is critical of the "first culture" existing within cities themselves, which sees cities as simple systems (Portagali 2005, 17–38). Thirdly, and as a consequence of the above, most studies on the complexity of cities do not engage with the qualitative assessment of cities raised by the pertinent complexity theories. Fourthly, students investigating the complexity of cities have indiscriminately applied theories and models that were originally developed to deal with natural phenomena to cities, ignoring the implications resulting from the fact that cities are not natural phenomena but rather artefacts of their creators and surroundings (Portugali 2009).

This text is based on the writing of Yijie Bu and was edited by Angela Million.

Endnotes

1 Sasaki Associates. **Songzhuang Arts and Agriculture City.** [Online]. 2012. Available at http://www.sasaki.com/project/265/songzhuang-arts-and-agriculture-city/ Accessed April 24, 2020.

2 Sasaki Associates. **Ananas New Community**. [Online]. 2015 Available at http://www.sasaki.com/project/389/ananas-new-community/ Accessed April 24, 2020.

3 TUB students. "Postdam à la Card." Design studio for the Master in Urban Design and Urban and Regional Planning TUB, supervised by Million, A., winter term 2011/2012.

B.21

ENGAGING HUMANS AND NONHUMANS IN DESIGN

Fink. R.D. and Wayer. J. "Interaction of Human Actors and Non-Human Agents. A Sociological Simulation Model of Hybrid System." **STI Studies** 10, no. 11 (2014).
Grusin, R. Introduction to The Nonhuman Turn, edited by Grusin, R., 7–29. Minneapolis: University of Minnesota Press, 2015.
Harrison, A.L. "Introduction: Charting Posthuman Territory." In **Architectural Theories of the Environment. Posthuman Territory**, edited by **Harrison, A.L**. New York: Routledge, 2013.
Latour, B. "On Actor-network Theory. A few Clarifications." **Soziale Welt** 47, no. 4 (1996): 369–382.
Latour, B. "On recalling ANT." In **Actor-network theory and after Blackwell**, edited by Law, J. and Hassard, J. Oxford: Blackwell, 1999, 15–25.
Loenhart, K.K. "Superfast Jellyfish. Matter, Agency and Emergent Properties of Landscape." In **GAM 07. Zero Landscape. Unfolding Active Agencies of Landscape**, edited by Technische Universität Graz, Fakultät für Architektur. Graz: Technische Universität Graz, 2011, 142–159.
Morton, T**. Ecology without Nature**. Cambridge. Massachusetts: Harvard University Press, 2007.
Morton, T. "Here Comes Everything. The Promise of Object-Oriented Ontology." **qui parle** 19, no. 2 (Spring/ Summer 2011): 162–190.
Reed, C. "The Agency of Ecology." In **Ecological Urbanism**, edited by Mostafavi, M. and Doherty, G. Baden: Lars Müller Publishers, 2010, 324–329.
Roncken, P., Stremke S., and Paulissen, M. "Landscape machines. Productive nature and the future sublime." **Jola Journal of Landscape Architecture** 6, no. 1 (2011): 68 – 81.

Under the term *the nonhuman turn*, Richard Grusin has tried to bring together a variety of postmodern theoretical developments from the late twentieth century interested in "decentering the human" (2015, 7) as the sole focus of the humanities and social sciences. He lists these approaches as follows: actor-network theory, affect theory, animal studies, assemblage theory, brain sciences, new materialism, media theory, speculative realism, systems theory, and science and technology studies. The nonhuman can be literally interpreted as everything that is not human, which Grusin illustrated with "animals, affectivity, bodies, organic and geophysical systems, materiality or technologies" (2015, 7). This applies at different scales and includes the immaterial.

The aim of the nonhuman turn is to dismantle human exceptionalism, ending the dualism that problematically privileges humans while also eroding subject-object relations along the way. One of the approaches that seeks to study the existence and understand the agency of the nonhuman is radical or object-oriented ontology (Morton 2011). Under this school of thought, the human and the nonhuman merge and the presumed fundamental differences between natural and (cultural) built environments become blurred. This opens up ecological thinking to new fields. Timothy Morton (2007, 4) develops this very idea, arguing that as long as the field of ecology sees nature as a "surrounding medium that sustains our being," it can never develop its full potential for change (see also: Loenhart 2011).

Oyster-Tecture, Moma Rising Currents[1]
In this vision for Brooklyn, a comprehensive ecosystem is designed using oysters as the main agent. The oysters would initially be grown in the Gowanus Canal, following which the oyster culture would be transferred to a human-made reef (constructed of simple, sustainable materials such as rope) in the shallow waters of the Bay Ridge Flats. The oysters would help clean the harbor's water through their metabolic processes and at the same time provide the bay with protection against storm surges and rising tides. In the short term, the project would enable community-based development of the waterfront. In the long term, it would even be possible to grow edible oysters, increasing the productivity of the ecosystem.
This design concept engages nonhumans with multiple capabilities (oysters) that are connected to hyper-local conditions in the canal and bay and are actively supported by various technologies. The potential of this concept and the possible benefits for the whole urban and natural system are being showcased in an ongoing small-scale pilot project (SCAPE 2010).

Butterfly Bridge[2]
The *Butterfly Bridge* is an intervention that provides butterflies with the opportunity to navigate obstacles they encounter in urban settings. Crossing above a street with a high volume of traffic, the bridge is planted with

José Hasse Velez (2015) **Areal view with proposal**. The storage lake is shown at its maximum water level. It is possible to see submerged walking paths that appear when the level becomes lower. The water also crosses under the street to irrigate small biospheres near the church and town hall.

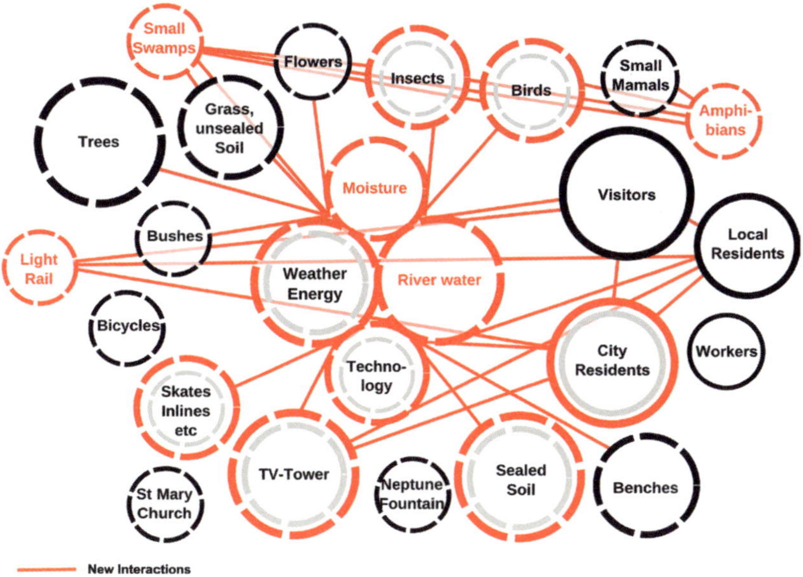

José Hasse Velez (2015) **Spatial practice assemblage proposal**. Proposed spatial practice assemblage with new actors and connections in red. The new "composite" actor is shown in the middle. Only new connections are shown.

Scape Studio (2014) **Living Breakwaters**: South Shore of Staten Island.

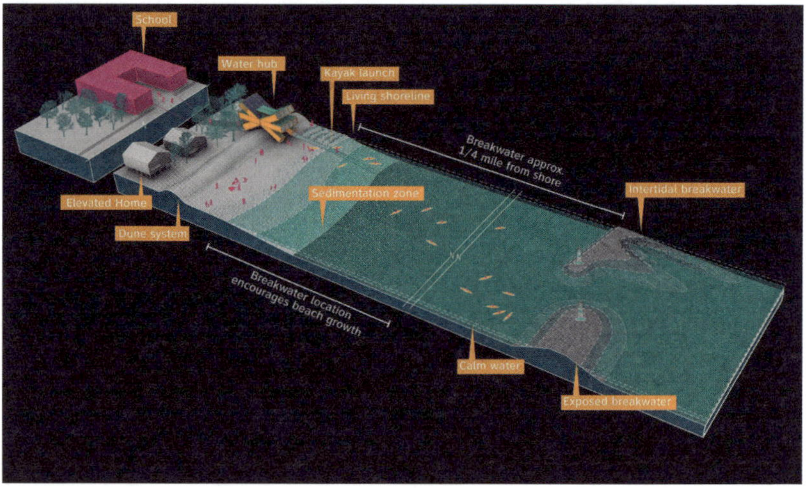

Scape Studio (2014) **Living Breakwaters**: schematic section showing the integration of community spaces, waterfront and breakwaters.

enticing flowers and plants that lure butterflies away from speeding vehicles. This project reimagines urban infrastructure for the diverse species with which we share space and resources (Natalie Jeremijenko n.d.).

The Landscape Machine at the Rathausforum, 2015[3]
Some of the ideas reviewed here were tested during an academic exercise. Since 2015, the area around the Rathausforum in Berlin has been the subject of an organized public debate concerning a possible comprehensive redesign. In this alternative approach to the redesign by José Hasse Velez, the challenge was to bring nonhumans into center stage and draw attention to the fact that the natural and cultural systems are interwoven. The main aim was to develop a prototype for the site in which the role of nonhumans would be equal to that of humans.
After considering abundance and scarcity at the site, a number of the nonhuman actors representing possible

Posthuman theory and the Anthropocene are two recent approaches that critically examine the dichotomy between humans and nonhumans and are thus related to the nonhuman turn. If humans are now just another force of nature at a planetary scale, as the term *Anthropocene* implies, then they are ontologically comparable with other forces, such as geology or the climate. Posthuman discourses explore similar theoretical possibilities, proclaiming the fusion of nature, humans, and technologies to be an evolutionary process that radically transforms the human subject. The nonhuman debate, however, rejects this notion of evolution, arguing against the distinction between humans and nonhumans in the first place (Grusin 2015).

Engaging the nonhuman is not yet an established method in design. Although some of its principles have been used before, its theoretical agenda has not been consciously or explicitly addressed. Considering the nonhuman can take very different forms depending on how it is understood, the levels of agency involved, and the working scale. It is up to the designer to determine where and how the application of this method can be most productive. Some of the theories listed above as ideas traced by Grusin at the origin of the nonhuman turn could offer different approaches; actor-network theory and systems theory are examples that have already been explored in a design context. Landscape architecture and environmental planning are generally considered to be the design fields that have traditionally engaged with natural rather than human-made systems, and have as such taken into account

capabilities and synergies – such as infrastructure components and specific animal species – were identified. The final concept focuses on the collection and storage of energy, with the double objective of trying to increase energy autonomy on site and simultaneously making this process highly visible. The height of the nearby television tower presents an ideal opportunity to harvest wind energy. This can then be stored in the form of an artificial lake at the former Marx-Engels-Forum using water from the river Spree. The landscape machine is located in a key public urban space, and technology acts as an agent in supporting a new ecosystem. The design of the new waterscape aims to engage humans and nonhumans alike, taking into account their respective spatial practices. To achieve this, the topography of the site is designed to accommodate existing infrastructure as well as the activities of humans and selected animal species, and offers a variety of spatial configurations (water reservoirs, islands, and paths). The configuration of the urban space and the activities of the humans (such as skating and bathing) and animals depend on the stored energy levels, which are determined by weather conditions such as precipitation and wind. The consequences of changing microclimatic conditions would not only be visible in the landscape, but would also be directly experienced by the humans and animals that inhabit it.

the actions and influences of nonhuman elements such as animals, natural processes, infrastructure, materials, space, and so on.

When determining the impact of this approach, there are two major dimensions to consider: engineering (complex problem solving) and culture (values transmission and aesthetics). Roncken (Roncken et al. 2011) explores these two aspects in his proposition for *landscape machines*: not only do these dynamic ecological systems operate autonomously to address problems through what he calls their "productive nature" (the engineering dimension), but they also reward the observer with an understanding of how they work – something Roncken calls the "sublime," an experience that goes beyond that of purely visual perception (the cultural dimension). When designing or intervening in an ecosystem, there are different levels of interaction between humans and nonhumans that can be strategically employed. Chris Reed (2010) addressed four ecological strategies for interaction: structured (humans create only the scaffolds and the ecosystem develops by itself), analog (humans design non-living agents that work like living agents), hybrid (the system works using environmental, engineering, and social dynamics simultaneously), and curated (humans set the dynamics and interact sporadically over time). Another variable in this method is supplied by the different categories of the nonhuman – for example, living creatures (animals and plants), other natural phenomena (hydrology, geology, meteorology, etc.) and less tangible agents such as technologies, affects, and so on (Reed 2010).

Endnotes

1 Adaptation strategy by SCAPE / Landscape Architecture PLLC commissioned by the Museum of Modern Art in 2009 for the exhibition "Rising Currents: Projects for New York's Waterfront", which dealt with New York City's challenges in relation to climate change and sea level rise.
SCAPE. **Oyster-Tecture / MoMA Rising Currents**. [Online]. 2010. Available at http://www.scapestudio.com/ Accessed December 12, 2018.

2 Martin, C. "Wondrous engagement: Natalie Jeremijenko." [Online]. Updated August 27, 2015. Available at https://architectureau.com/articles/natalie-jeremijenko/ Accessed April 23, 2020, and Beatley, T. **Handbook of Biophilic City Planning & Design**. Washington, D.C.: Island Press, 2016, 242–243.

3 Hasse Velez, J. "The landscape machine at the Rathausforum – an academic exercise." Coursework for the Urban Design Method and Tools Seminar, supervised by Giseke, U. and Kokoula, X. Technische Universität Berlin, Summer Term 2015.

In our attempt to systematize the method within the limited scope of this paper, we suggest the following workflow:

A possible starting point is a descriptive analysis of the power and agency of both the human and nonhuman actors within the design field. If (nonhuman) resources are recognized as actors as well, an integrated actor network (inspired by Latour's actor-network theory; see 1996, 1999) can be described, detailing the relationships and acting competences of the involved actors – whether they are human or nonhuman. The non-linear and non-hierarchical approach of Latour's actor-network theory can help indicate which actors are involved in a design task and what power they have to interact. Their impact can be specified in different categories of agencies. An integrated network would include the main components of the ecological and the urban system and consider how they interact. This includes narratives and descriptions developed from the perspectives of the engaged nonhuman actors. Depending on the engineering problem, the designer could look for patterns of abundance and scarcity or do an analysis of capabilities for the most relevant actors. A further step would be to rethink the existing relationships between the actors and imagine new ones, looking at the implications for each actor's level of agency. This could lead to minor and/or major adjustments within the actor network (or, depending on the design problem, within the ecosystem). During this step of rethinking the agency of and interaction between the actors, additional design methods, such as media research or dynamic role-playing games, may be applied. The key is to bring the capacity of the nonhumans to (inter)act into play and regard the method of doing so as a reality filter that provides a deeper understanding of the strategies involved.

In a world where the distinctions between natural and cultural processes and environments and between subject and object become blurred, it is essential to engage both human and nonhuman actors in design. Arguably, the most fruitful examples of this approach come from hybrid and complex situations featuring many intersections and interactions that challenge symmetrical approaches. They are to be found in suburban spaces, green infrastructures in dense cities, industrial complexes in less dense areas, and similar spaces. However, less complex cases, involving the nonhumans that are closest to us and easiest to recognize – such as the animals in our urban habitat – also present ample opportunity to experiment with and showcase the potential of this method (see, for example, the work of Natalie Jeremijenko).

The consequences of applying this method reach beyond broadening designers' palettes with more diverse interpretation tools. Engaging nonhumans in design allows for less biased analysis and helps promote environmental justice. It can also be used to draw attention to nonhumans by giving them a voice within a narrative with a radical agenda. Here, Grusin (2015, 7) sees the possibility of a "way forward ... in light of the difficult challenges of the twenty-first century" (such as climate change).

This text is based on the writing of José Hasse Velez and was edited by Xenia Kokoula and Undine Giseke.

#B.22

BUILDING KNOWLEDGE THROUGH CHARRETTES

Kegler, H. "Charrette – neue Möglichkeiten effektiver Beteiligung am Stadtumbau." **Die Alte Stadt** 4 (2002): 299–307.

Nanz, P. and Fritsche M. **Handbuch Bürgerbeteiligung. Verfahren und Akteure, Chancen und Grenzen**. bpb Bundeszentrale für politische Bildung, Bonn, 2012.

Lennertz, B. "The Charrette as an Agent for Change." [Online]. 2003. Available at http://www.kolleg.loel.hs-anhalt.de/studiengaenge/mla/mla_fl/conf/pdf/conf2005/12lennertz_c.pdf Accessed April 23, 2020.

ITA Institut für Technikfolgenabschätzung **Leitfaden partizipativer Verfahren. Ein Handbuch für die Praxis**. Brussels and Vienna: König-Baudouin-Stiftung, viWTA and ITA, 2006. Available at http://www.planet-austria.at/0xc1aa500d_0x0010b22c.pdf Accessed 21 July, 2016.

A charrette is a participatory open design process that brings together a variety of actors, such as citizens, planners, and decision makers, in order to develop new solutions and find consensus in a short amount of time. Along with the New Urbanism architecture movement, which argued for walkable cities and an avoidance of urban sprawl, the charrette was developed as a planning method in the USA in the 1980s. During this time, the National Charrette Institute (NCI) was founded in Portland, Oregon. The NCI continues to promote the charrette as an "Agent for Change" (Lennertz 2003) with the potential to bring about "true collaboration in community planning" (Lennertz 2003). Today, charrettes are a widely used method in the US, as well as being very well-known in Great Britain and Germany (Nanz and Fritsche 2012, 53). The German urban and regional planner Dr. Harald Kegler defines the method as a public, and consequently open, procedure for the optimization of urban planning processes featuring direct planning democracy, vital interdisciplinarity, and concrete decision-making (Kegler 2002). In architectural education, "charretting" is used in a broader sense to mean making the final efforts in completing a design proposal.

The term *charrette* is derived from the French word for cart. In the nineteenth century, art students in France used carts to transport their work to the academies for their final presentation. As they did so, the population offered the students hints and tips so that they could make final changes to their artwork. Correspondingly, the planning process of charrettes today is led

Wohnumfeld Schorfheideviertel, 2020 and Güterbahnhof Grunewald, 2014
The charrette *Wohnumfeld Schorfheide*[1] in the Marzahn-Schorfheideviertel was organized on behalf of the local *Quartier-Agentur* (neighborhood management agency) and dealt with the future possibility of shrinking communities at the edge of Berlin. The design of the open spaces was an essential part of the participation. These were to become a park accessible to the public and used by local residents. Among the design features developed through the charrette were multifunctional boxes that could be used for storage, workshops, or as recreational spaces. The built project, planned by the landscape architects gruppeF, was awarded the Deutscher Landschaftsarchitekturpreis in 2011.
Another approach was taken at a former railyard in Grunewald,[2] Berlin, where a charrette was organized to collect ideas for the planned development of the site. During the workshop, a design vision for the huge, empty site was developed by residents living around it. The charrette was supported by the local council of Berlin-Charlottenburg, and organized by Heinrich-Böll-Stiftung and a group of young architects and planners. Even though the plans were not put into action, the charrette is considered exemplary in the way it was executed.

by professional planners. Involving the population is intended to foster a creative atmosphere and bring forward new solutions for complex planning tasks in a short amount of time (Nanz and Fritsche 2012, 53 onwards). But instead of just giving hints and tips, citizens can actively take part and come up with their own planning proposals. In this sense, the role of the planner is changing. As Kegler states, the planner is leaving the role of "the 'lonesome mastermind' or 'neutral moderator' behind. The planner is mediator, activator, listener, constantly open dialogue partner, and responsible expert regarding the requirements of integrated urban development." (Kegler 2002, 302, translated by the author) The charrette can be characterized by three main principles that distinguish the method from other participatory design processes: it is completely open, so that everyone can participate; there are no hierarchies amongst the participants, whether they are experts or not; and the process takes place in a short amount of time.

As Nanz and Fritsche state, charrettes are suited to developing solutions for concrete questions about spatial development, as well as to the formulation of general goals for different municipal scales (Nanz and Fritsche 2012, 54). Various different starting points and intentions may result in the decision to organize a charrette process. On the one hand, municipal administrations primarily choose charrettes for neighborhood development, as well as for the reorganization of public and semi-public spaces like parks and squares, the large-scale development of wasteland,

Endnotes

1 Gruppe F. "Wohnumfeld Schorfheideviertel." [Online]. n.d. Available at https://gruppef.com/wohnumfeld-schorfheideviertel/ Accessed April 23, 2020.

2 Bezirksamt Charlottenburg-Wilmersdorf. **CHARRETTE(VERFAHREN): BürgerInnen planen ihre Stadt am Beispiel der Konversionsfläche Güterbahnhof Grunewald**. [Online]. March 2014. Available at http://siedlung-eichkamp.de/Web_BI/2014/140324_Doku_Charette.pdf Accessed April 23, 2020.

and the elaboration of a city's overall integrated visions and concepts. This approach aims to foster citizen participation in the existing and official development process of a project. It focuses on the collection and review of problems in a largely conceptual manner, as well as on the discussion of sometimes very detailed design ideas.

On the other hand, charrettes can also be used in a bottom-up approach – for example to satisfy the desire of a citizens' initiative for active participation, or to deal with an existing problem. The aim of this kind of charrette is to gain publicity and raise awareness of perceived problems.

The charrette process is time-limited. The main charrette lasts at least four consecutive days. A couple of weeks before the main event, a mini-charrette introduces the planning task and intended project. A public evaluation takes place after the main charrette, which informs the actors involved about further proceedings based on the results and outcome of the process (Nanz and Fritsche 2012, 53 onwards). A charrette is flexible concerning the use of different methods. A formulation for the process, using different methods and formats to generate a productive discussion and a planning proposal in a short amount of time, should be developed in relation to the specific context of the issue at hand. There is no one particular scheme for a charrette (Kegler 2002). Formats and methods used in the process should guarantee that the ideas of all participants are collected and discussed, and then fed back into to the possibilities and constraints of the initial situation and compared with the interests of the different actors and with the visions of the municipal administration. Professional planners contribute by being able to condense the results into frameworks and development concepts (Nanz and Fritsche 2012, 53). Charrettes should take place close to the project site or area and be easy to access (Kegler 2002).

The charrette process puts the focus on concrete decision-making for complex planning problems. At its best, it deals with context-related issues and produces a clear image, vision, and design for a specific project. Everyone who could potentially be concerned should be involved, meaning that citizens as well as experts and stakeholders work together to develop a planning approach. The process is shaped by direct feedback from everyone involved. (Kegler 2002) Furthermore, due to the integration of a variety of perspectives and interests, charrettes help to produce development concepts that are likely to be approved by a majority of the involved parties (Nanz and Fritsche 2012, 54). The flat hierarchy of the process enables more effective participation by non-experts and can increase their identification with the design approach chosen. The main limitation of this tool is similar to the challenge faced by other participation formats: how can a broad and diverse group of citizens be reached? Charrettes can only lead to public acknowledgment of the result if they are able to successfully mobilize a wide variety of participants. If the process lacks transparency and fails to develop and entertain a broad discourse, it may not meet the local and/or wider public expectations and lose their political support (see Nanz and Fritsche 2012). Moreover, there is a risk that the results of the process may not become a crucial element of the continuing project, and that the participation turns out to be nothing more than a manipulative front.

This text is based on the writing of Phil von Lueder and Johanna Ulmer and was edited by Katharina Hagg.

#B.23

PARTICI-PATION AND ENACTMENT GAMES

Abt, C. **Serious Games**. New York: Viking, 1970.

Duke, R. **Gaming: the Future's Language**. New York: Sage, 1974.

Duke, R. "Origin and Evolution of Policy Simulation: A Personal Journey." **Simulation & Gaming** 42, no. 3 (2011): 342–358.

Hagg, M. and Schetter, O. "Procedural Fairy Tales about Teaching Productive Urban Design in Germany." **City Observer** 2, no. 1 (2016): 134–153.

Hofmann, S. **Partizipation Macht Architektur: die Baupiloten – Methode und Projekte**. Berlin: Jovis, 2014.

Ministerium für Wirtschaft, Energie, Industrie, Mittelstand und Handwerk NRW / MWEIHM, ed. **Werkzeugkasten Dialog und Beteiligung. Ein Leitfaden zur Öffentlichkeitsbeteiligung**. Düsseldorf: Eigenverlag, 2012.

Play The City. **Play Brussels**. [Online]. 2013. Available at https://www.playthecity.nl/page/8986/play-brussels Accessed July 28, 2016.

Ratner, N. and Bruner, J. "Games, Social Exchange and the Acquisition of Language." **Journal of Child Language** 5, no. 3 (1977): 391–401.

Sanoff, H. **Design Games**. Los Altos, CA: William Kaufmann, 1979.

Sanoff, H. **Community Participation Methods in Design and Planning**. New York: John Wiley & Sons, 2000.

Tan, E. **Negotiation and Design for the Self-Organizing City. Gaming as a method for Urban Design. A+BE Architecture and the Built Environment Volume 11**. Delft: TU Delft, 2014.

Tan, E. "The Evolution of City Gaming." In **Complexity, Cognition, Urban Planning and Design: Post-Proceedings of the 2nd Delft International Conference (Springer Proceedings in Complexity)**, edited by Portugali, J. and Stolk, E. Zurich: Springer, 2016.

As a structured form of play, games are a kind of activity that always has two purposes: amusement and education. Ratner and Bruner developed theories on the educational function of games in their study of how children acquire language skills (1977). Clark Abt defined games that have an explicit educational purpose and are not intended to be played primarily for amusement as *serious games*. Richard Duke traces the history of serious games from their earliest forms – as war games such as checkers and chess – to their being "copied first by the business schools and then by the social sciences" (Duke 1974).

Games have been a participatory tool since the 1960s. In 1964, Duke was the first to apply games to the field of urban planning (Duke 2011). He developed a game to help city council members in Lansing, Michigan to solve the complex budgeting issues they faced. This exercise later became known as *METROPOLIS*. According to Duke, gaming professionalism increased rapidly during the 1970s in the US, and organizations such as the International Simulation and Gaming Association and the National Gaming Council were formed (1974, xii). Sanoff defines these kinds of games as "participation games," which are useful for organizing group decision-making in design and planning processes (2000, 77).

Today, participation games are increasingly integrated in educational programs for design and communication. Early on, Duke and Sanoff identified the use of educational games for "skill development by business people, police officers, and diplomats

Urban Enactment Game, 1st year studio for the Master in Urban Design at TU Berlin, 2016
The Urban Enactment Game is an educational roleplaying game and an integral part of the urban design studio taught by the Habitat Unit and the Chair for Urban Design and Urbanization at TU Berlin. In the 2015/16 winter semester, a group of about forty-five students adopted the roles of different stakeholders involved in the urban development dispute concerning the BEHALA site, an inner-city freight port area in Berlin-Friedrichshain. In the scenario, it had not yet been decided whether the location should become a site for media companies and office buildings and/or housing developed by private or public bodies. With this scenario setting, the game aimed to give the students a wider perspective on urban design and on decision-making processes involving private developers, the media, citizen groups, and the city and local administration. Although the roleplaying game was only a three-day workshop within the semester, it had a significant influence on the development of the students' design projects. Students researched the agendas and agencies of their assigned stakeholder roles. Real-life formats such as council meetings and demonstrations were reproduced and performed. In this way, participants gained an understanding of how decision-making processes unfold and how strategies and tactics to influence these processes are employed. The game had a very clear procedural structure. However, as the

to develop skills in persuasion, bargaining and strategic planning" (Duke 1974; see also Sanoff 2000, 77), and Sanoff published a manual on design games to be employed in design practice and education (1979). In this tradition, participation games are used in design and planning processes as communication and decision-making tools to involve participants and let them "develop a better understanding of themselves and others" (Sanoff 2000, 77).

The method can be used in different phases of the design process. Firstly, participation games can work as a research tool to "analyze the interests of users" (Hofmann 2014, 15). As part of an analysis, they can also generate a better understanding of the complex actor networks and agencies in urban development processes (Hagg and Schetter 2016). Secondly, thanks to their playful nature, games can help to engage people in the design and planning phase (Sanoff 2000, 219). They can be used as a tool to facilitate the communication between professionals and non-professionals. Participation games are also a way to "stimulate collective intelligence and knowledge production" through negotiation among players (Tan 2016, 273–274).

With regard to the players, participation games can be divided into two categories: ones that are played with the direct actors, and ones that are played with indirect representatives through the "interview and represent method" (Tan 2014, 182). Many participation games are played out through models, drawings, and cards, like board games. Even though Duke argued as early as 1974 that, with the development of computer science,

stakeholder groups had their own offices, meeting places, and newsrooms, the game developed a dynamic that mimicked real-life disputes with e.g. demonstrations, secret agreements, and media disclosures. "By way of ex-post evaluation, it became clear that most students understood the possibilities and limitations of their role models and that they became aware of what sort of spaces and programmes different stakeholders demand in the city and why they are associated with specific locations and urban products. They gained a better understanding about the importance of alliances and compromise; in fact, the dynamics of the game made the students more willing to compromise and also opened their minds for a more experimental contextualization of design tasks." (Hagg and Schetter, 2016, 7). The Urban Enactment Game model was based on the War Game model developed by Prof. Jürgen Schulz at Universität der Künste Berlin.

Nachbarschaft 3000, baupiloten, 2014[1]
Nachbarschaft 3000 is a project that gathered together local people in the Kottbusser Tor neighborhood in Berlin who – because of fear, shame, or culture or language barriers – do not usually take part in the neighborhood planning process (Hofmann, 2014). The game allows people to interact with each other and propose new and creative ideas for improving their neighborhood in a playful way. Nachbarschaft 3000 was developed by baupiloten,

the method could be applied using software, most of the practice is still analogue. A specific form of indirect planning games are "role enactment games" or "role-playing games," a gaming method in which decision-making processes, conflict situations, or real events are (re-)enacted. During the game, participants adopt their assigned roles to represent the perspectives, interests, and arguments of specific stakeholders. These games are most effective when players have to adopt a role that is antagonistic to the one they would choose outside the game. Through embodiment and acting out, they can get to know completely different points of view (MWEIHM 2012). The modern role-play was introduced through the "psychodrama" method developed by the Austrian-American doctor, psychiatrist, and sociologist Jacob Levy Moreno (1889-1974).

Games are designed to challenge players to solve the given issues, and the aim of most games in urban planning is to portray a pseudo-realistic situation in which people can interact with each other and find solutions for contested urban issues. The first step in designing a city game is simulation. Most of the games are defined by a scenario inspired by a real and complex urban dispute or planning problem. In order to make it possible to play in a limited amount of time and with limited equipment, the scenario should be a simplified version of reality. The next step is the definition of stakeholder roles. As it is not possible to reach out to all the involved stakeholders, the most important and determining ones should be identified and

an architecture practice founded by Susanne Hofmann in 2001 that engages in participatory and social design.

Play Brussels, Play the City, 2013[2]
Play Brussels is a negotiation and design game that was played by designers and local stakeholders in the city's Porte de Ninove or Ninoofse Poort neighborhood in 2013 (Play the City, 2013). In response to the creation of an urban park (intended to be part of a planned urban development) being repeatedly postponed, over forty locals from different interest groups in the area engaged in a week-long game session to generate proposals for the temporary public use of the local wasteland and adjacent vacant buildings. The resulting low-maintenance proposal was to make the land publicly accessible and to connect it to the wider Brussels Green Network. The strategic result was an open letter to the mayor of the city written by the players. In the letter they asked him to support the concepts drawn from the game and to allow their bottom-up implementation. The design practice that developed the game was Play the City, founded by Ekim Tan in 2008.

Katharina Hagg (2016) **Urban resistance movement interrupting a local council board meeting**. From a three-day Urban Enactment game within the Master in Urban Design Studio in the 2016/17 winter semester (Habitat Unit & CUD TU Berlin).

included in the game. The roles could be played either by the stakeholders themselves or by other players who take on their roles. Games are based on a set of simple, compulsory rules. If the rules are followed strictly, players will face many unpredictable complexities throughout the game (Tan 2014, 49). Sanoff identifies rule systems and methods of procedure as one of the key factors of games. He argues that the rules of games should refer to reality (2000).

Endnotes

1 Hofmann, S. **Partizipation Macht Architektur: die Baupiloten – Methode und Projekte**, Berlin: Jovis, 2014.

2 Play The City. **Play Brussels**. [Online]. 2013. Available at https://www.playthecity.nl/page/8986/play-brussels Accessed July 28, 2016.

Depending on the type of the game, different preparatory steps are necessary. These can include researching the topic of the game and its aims, building a model of urban elements or an abstracted layout of the scenario as a physical "board" on which the game is to be played, researching the players' roles, attitudes, and agencies, establishing where the game is going to be played, and so on. Before the game starts, the instructions and rules should be explained to all players.

Tan argues that the aim of games in participatory planning and design, whether for educational or practical purposes, is to arrive at outcomes that have an effect on reality or could be implemented in reality (2014, 368). The actual circumstances and incidents outside the game may also have an impact on the game, and may improve or hinder its execution. As much as games and reality are intertwined, they also differ substantially. The process of negotiating and decision-making in games, as much as it tries to apply rules similar to reality, often idealizes the relations of power. Urban design and development gaming tends to integrate a wider variety of stakeholders from top-down and bottom-up flows into the game. In reality, many decisions continue to be discussed and made by experts, planners, politicians, and/or developers behind closed doors. In the game, these processes are usually portrayed as being much more open, and information is shared with all the interest groups. In order to implement the outcome, this discrepancy should be considered (Tan 2014, 369).

Jörg Stollmann (2016) **The local mayor's office.** From the three-day Urban Enactment game within the Master in Urban Design Studio in the 2016/17 winter semester (Habitat Unit & CUD TU Berlin).

Despite all this, absolute democracy is not possible even in the game, because not all stakeholders can be reached and represented and because non-human actors are largely excluded from the process (Tan 2016). Another difficulty faced by gaming in participatory planning is a certain resistance among architects and urban designers to integrating the results into the design process, as they believe it compromises the level of design quality. One possible way of overcoming this limitation is for designers to customize a set of design-related rules for the game in question (Tan 2014, 369). Finally, a challenge shared by both games and all other participatory tools is the question of power: how much agency are the players granted not only within the game, but within the planning process it informs – and who is ultimately responsible for the outcome and its implementation?

This text is based on the writing of Saba Khanghahi and Yue Zhang and was edited by Katharina Hagg.

#B.24

VISUALIZING POSSIBLE FUTURES

Duden. "Szenario." [Online]. 2017a. Available at http://www.duden.de/node/707326/revisions/1388556/view Accessed April 23, 2020.

Duden. "Szenarium." [Online]. 2017b. Available at http://www.duden.de/node/707325/revisions/1620786/view Accessed April 23, 2020.

Hallding, K. "Scenarios to Envision Urban Futures in a Changing World." In **Access to Resources - an Urban Agenda**, edited by Palmer, H. Braunach: Spurbuchverlag, 2014.

Reed, C. and Lister, N. (2014): **Ecology and Design: Parallel Genealogies**. [Online]. April 2014. Available at https://placesjournal.org/article/ecology-and-design-parallel-genealogies/ Accessed July 2, 2015.

Salewski, C. "Totale Gestaltung - Vom Nutzen und Missbrauch von Szenarien und Utopien in Architektur und Städtebau." **Arch+** 222 (Projekt Bauhaus 1: Kann Gestaltung Gesellschaft verändern?) (2016): 174–176.

Scenario Journal. "Scenario 03: Rethinking infrastructure. Wild Innovation: Stoss in Detroit." [Online]. Spring 2013. Available at http://scenariojournal.com/article/wild-innovation/ Accessed April 23, 2020.

Schoemaker, P. "Scenario Planning: A tool for Strategic Thinking." **Sloan Management Review** 36, no. 2 (1995): 25–40.

T?F. **The Why Factory**. [Online]. n.d. Projects by the Delft University of Technology, Faculty of Architecture and the Built Environment. Available at http://thewhyfactory.com/project/ Accessed July 28, 2016.

MoMA. **Uneven Growth - Tactical Urbanisms for Expanding Megacities**. [Online]. n.d. Website for the Exhibition at MoMA NYC, November 22, 2014–May 25, 2015. Available at http://uneven-growth.moma.org/ Accessed January 20, 2016.

Weller, R. "Planning by Design. Landscape Architectural Scenarios for a Rapidly Growing City." **Journal of Landscape Architecture** 3, no. 2 (2008): 18–29.

The term *scenario* is widely used. It is derived from the Latin word *scaenarium*, meaning the location where a stage is built or an act is set (Duden 2017b). In planning, a scenario is a hypothetical sequence of events designed for the consideration of causal relationships (Duden 2017a).

In other words, a scenario is a medium or a platform. It is used in many different fields, including literature, theater, and the film industry, as well as in economics, politics, and ecology. A scenario is a construct that makes it possible to think about developments (usually, but not necessarily, in the future) in order to make risks and chances of success visible. Even within the planning profession, scenarios can look very different from each other. In fact, every design in planning can be seen as scenario. We as planners design a vision for a building, an urban space, a city, or a region. Karl Hallding's definition is helpful when considering the visualization of scenarios: "Scenarios are, in essence, stories about the future told to inform current decision-making. They are used to expand the understanding of possible future developments beyond what can be achieved by conventional future projections" (Hallding 2014, 49). The urban future depends on many uncertainties, each of which may determine its development. Scenario thinking can be used as "a structured tool for expanding the range of possible outcomes" (Hallding 2014, 48). A good scenario in planning should offer new perspectives beside normative guidelines, and it should be extreme yet plausible. (Hallding 2014). The most prominent users of scenarios in planning are urban plan-

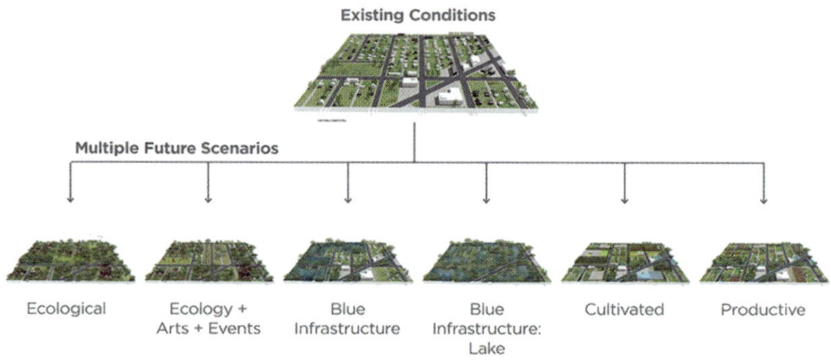

Desimini, Jill (2013) **Wild Innovation: Stoss in Detroit**. Illustrative future scenarios for Detroit.

ners and urban designers, because scenarios are a simple tool for illustrating city development. Other planning professions, such as architects, landscape architects, and spatial planners, also use scenarios to test interventions that would lead to specific futures. The visualization of a designed scenario is crucial to communicating an idea. Regardless of the profession, visualization is responsible for conveying the full extent and complexity of relevant information from the planner's mind to that of the reader.

The visualization of scenarios helps us to imagine alternative futures and to translate our imagination into a format all people, regardless of their language and technical knowledge, can understand. Clear communication of the story is necessary to enable the next step: discussing the scenario with other people. "Good scenarios are [always] the result of people working together to ensure that future challenges are illuminated from different perspectives" (Hallding 2014, 57).

Ideas must be visualized not only for ourselves but for others – both professionals and non-professionals. To get the

Lisa Kirchner, Gabrielle Mainguy, Luisa Multer (2016) **Studio Project on Urban-Rural Linkages. Living with the river – Architecture adapted to flood areas**.

best results when explaining a concept to others, any number of methods, skills, techniques, and planning tools may be used – but visualization helps to convey the information and tell a story more than any other mechanism. It is difficult to categorize visualized scenarios because of their diversity, even though they are united by the aim of being as plausible and convincing as possible. In order to achieve this aim, atmospheric and narrative tools are especially common. Extremely frequently, a combination of two or more visualization methods are used for each illustration of a design. To develop a scenario, a framework must first be constructed using the following steps:

1. Develop the key question(s) for the work (What is the topic or issue?)
2. Set boundaries (concerning factors such as time, focus, and scale)
3. Identify important drivers (such as climate change and demographic change)
4. Categorize those drivers (Is their impact high or low?)
5. Construct a matrix in which you can play with the uncertain developments of the drivers
6. Visualize the different scenarios generated with the matrix
7. Analyze the scenarios (from a quantitative and/or qualitative perspective)
8. Evaluate and discuss the scenarios (see also: Hallding 2014, 58–59).

Boomtown 2050: Scenarios for a Rapidly Growing City, Richard Weller, 2009[1]
In his 2009 study, Richard Weller developed different scenarios for the future of Perth, Australia. As a starting point, he presented Perth's historical development until the present day, as well as the city's anticipated growth if it continues developing in line with current trends. He then developed three scenarios relating to different structural city models. In his *Garden City* future scenario for Perth, the focus is on multiple towns with compact structures linked by new light-rail public transport. By contrast, the *Seachange City* future scenario highlights a type of low-density urban development along the coast. Weller not only contributes to the debate about how the city could develop through his work, but also criticizes development as it stands today. To do this, he uses several tools for the visualization of his scenarios. Crucially, a timeline is used to show the temporal integration of certain developmental stages. Their physical extents are shown using maps, perspectives, axonometric views, and collages.

Bremen Bewegen, Nexthamburg, 2014[2]
In collaboration with Nexthamburg, an office for public participation, the city of Bremen developed scenarios as part of a large-scale participation process around the creation of the city's Strategic Transport Development Plan 2025.

When the sixth point is arrived at, it is necessary to visualize the outcomes set by the framework. Remember what it is you wanted to demonstrate. Your idea should be visible in the visualizations. It is easier to choose the right combination of tools if you keep your main drivers in mind, as well as what uncertainties generate the scenario you want to visualize.

Scenarios are a good method for examining future developments because they do not show the real world but different variations of it. They present the world as it *could* look. It is easier to be daring in scenarios; to show more extreme and unconventional versions of the future world. Another significant characteristic of the visualization of scenarios is a highly expressive, narrative, and intense way of presenting information that always has the goal of convincing the reader.

At the same time, a scenario always has weaknesses in situations where decisions are made about uncertain developments and forecasts. Visualizations can compensate for missing facts, but they can also be responsible for blurring the facts that do exist through the use of atmospheric pictures.

This text is based on the writing of Luisa Multer and was edited by Andreas Brück.

Citizens were asked to contribute their suggestions and ideas for improving the city's transport system, as well as to create their own future scenarios. Scenarios could be developed and submitted via an interactive online platform and at a mobile, interactive engagement station (*Bremen Bewegen on Tour*), which stopped at different locations in the city. Out of 419 submissions, the top thirty scenarios were then showcased. The results and recommendations of the citizens were integrated into the further development of the strategic transport development plan.

New Tribal Territories, Elizabeth Yarina[3]
This project by Elizabeth Yarina points out the disadvantages faced by tribal communities in the Indian state of Orissa due to the intrusion of outside value structures. Although the forests of Orissa once served as commons, landscape industrialization has turned the region into a production and extraction site led by a state-sponsored private sector. The project creates a framework for a local agency involved with promoting local participation and control over the transformation processes. By empowering local groups and bringing their knowledge into a concrete framework, this project also provides a framework for tribal modernity. The project uses several tools to visualize its ideas. It combines maps, diagrams, and collages into one graphic with different layers of information. A timeline is used to show

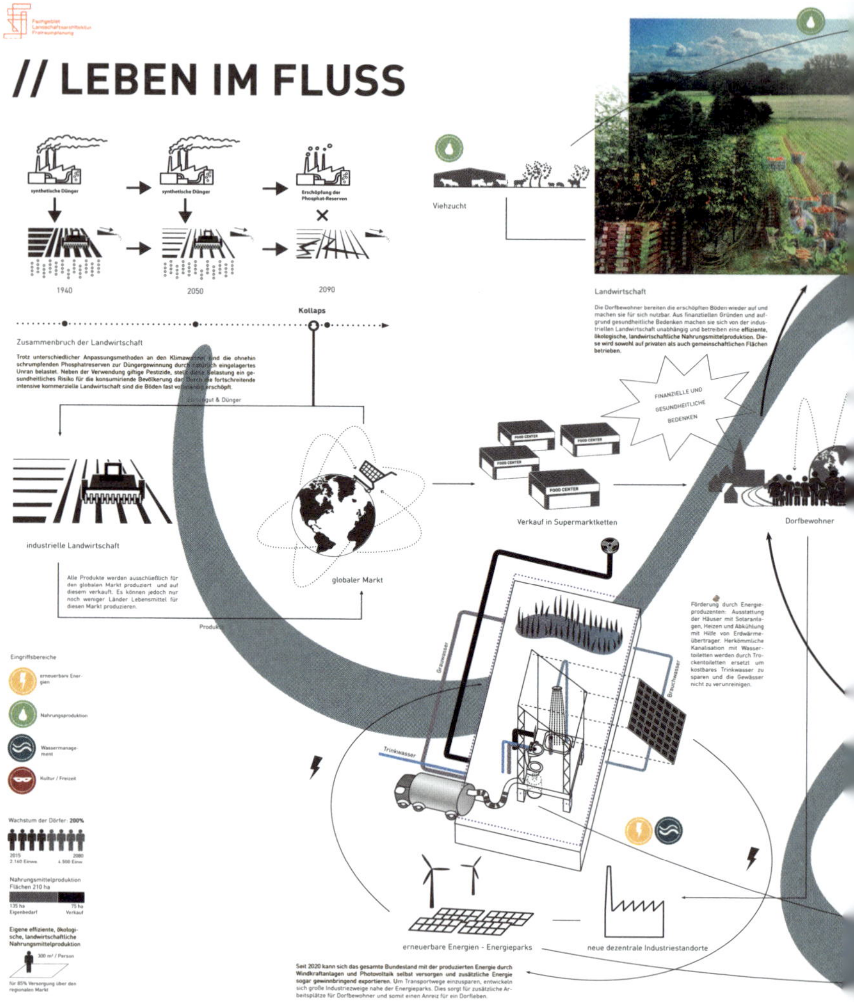

the historic relations and present the genesis of transformation.

The Why Factory[4]
T?F dealt with the topic of biodiversity, developing different scenarios with varied locations, focus and visualization styles. These explore how urban design and architecture could facilitate interactions between human and non-human actors. One project focuses more on the visualization of strategic diagrams and typologies, while the other project works with atmospheric axonometric views and perspective drawings. Many scenario projects operate on a large scale, but these projects focus down to a very small, architectural level and demonstrate in detail the consequences of different degrees of increased biodiversity.

Downsview Park, Stan Allen, James Corner, and Nina-Marie Lister, 1999
For Toronto's 1999 Downsview Park Competition, Stan Allen, James Corner and Nina-Marie Lister contributed a project proposing "scaffolds that would sponsor the propagation of emergent ecologies, natural systems that would be seeded initially and evolve over time with increasing levels of complexity and

Lisa Kirchner, Gabrielle Mainguy, Luisa Multer (2016) **Studio Project on Urban-Rural Linkages**. Complex systemic diagram showing the "Climate Migration" scenario applied to a local detail of the villages Wickerstedt, Flurstedt, Niedertebra, and Obertrebra, and Eberstedt near the river Ilm.

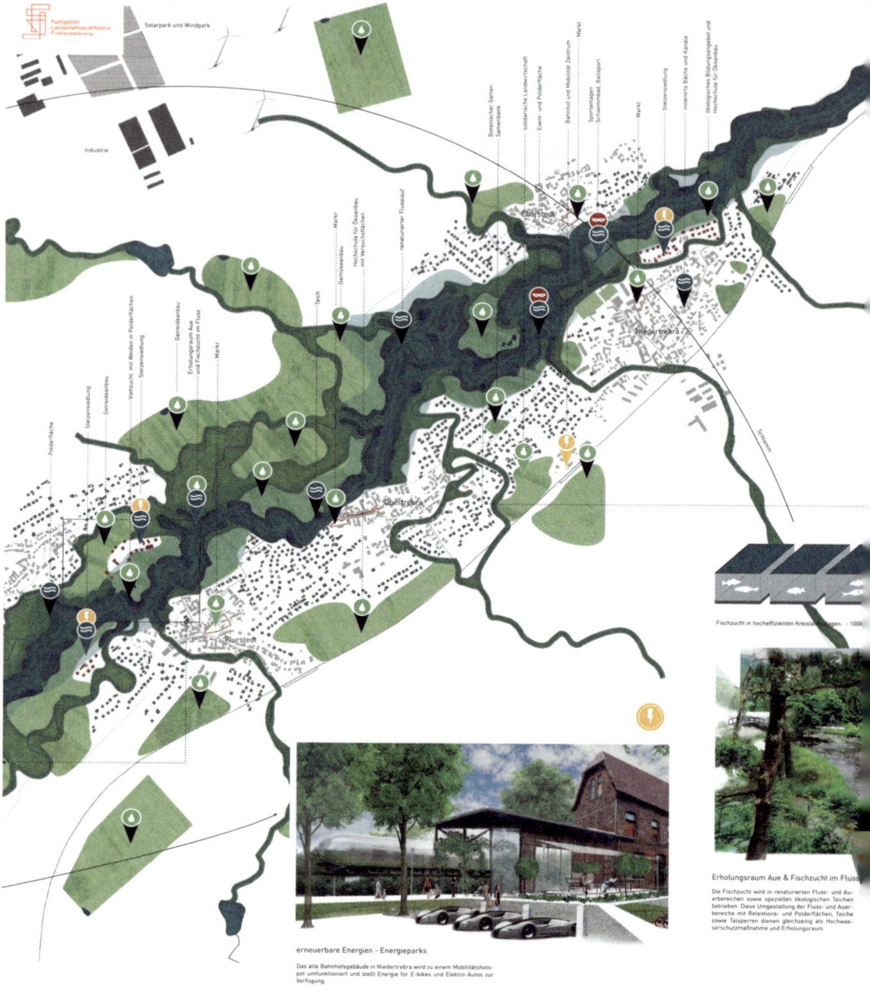

adaptability" (Reed and Lister 2014). The competition task involved long-term process planning. Allen, Corner, and Lister's project included clear predictions about the future, involving the steps needed for implementation, the constellation of actors, and procedures, potentials, and predictions concerning the natural environment (Reed and Lister 2014). They used various tools – such as diagrams, graphics, plans, and combinations of all three – to illustrate the possible future, making the development of explanations and proposals concerning the scenario easy to identify and understand. In this case, with the help of the scenario method, a variety of ideas were gathered together under the same concept for the long-term future. Following this, a collection of critical and multi-layered scenarios was generated.

Lisa Kirchner, Gabrielle Mainguy, Luisa Multer (2016) **Studio Project on Urban-Rural Linkages**. Complex systemic diagram showing the "Climate Migration" scenario applied to a local detail of the villages Wickerstedt, Flurstedt, Niedertebra, and Obertrebra, and Eberstedt near the river Ilm.

Endnotes
1 Weller, R. **Boomtown 2050: Scenarios for a Rapidly Growing City**. Perth: UWAP. Available at https://uwap.uwa.edu.au/products/boom-town-2050-scenarios-for-a-rapidly-growing-city Accessed April 23, 2020.
2 Freie Hansestadt Bremen. **Bremen Bewegen.** [Online]. n.d. Available at http://bremen-bewegen.de Accessed April 23, 2020.
3 Yarina, E. "New Tribal Territories." **ARCH+** 223 (Planetary Urbanism: The Transformative Power of Cities) (2015): 48–51.
4 T?F. **The Why Factory**. [Online]. n.d. Projects by the Delft University of Technology, Faculty of Architecture and the Built Environment. Available at http://thewhyfactory.com/project/ Accessed July 28, 2016.

B.25

URBAN CODING

Ahlert, M., Becker, M., Kreisel, A., Misselwitz, P., Pawlicki, N., and Schrammek, T. **Moravia Manifesto – Coding Strategies for Informal Neighborhoods**. Berlin: Jovis, 2018.

Alexander, C. **A Pattern Language**. Oxford: Oxford University Press, 1977.

Czenki, M., Schäfer, C., and Zander, L.M. **PlanBude - Ohne Vertrauen geht es nicht.** [Online]. 2017. Available at https://www.designondisplay.de/planbude Accessed May 14, 2019.

Greenspan, E. "Top-down bottom-up urban design." **The New Yorker**. October 2016. [Online]. Available at http://www.newyorker.com/business/currency/top-down-bottom-up-urban-design Accessed April 10, 2019.

UN-Habitat. **Habitat III Issue Papers 11 – Public Space**. New York: UN-Habitat, 2015.

Lynch, Kevin **Good City Form**. Cambridge, Massachusetts and London: The MIT Press, 1981.

Mikoleit, A. and Pürckhauer, M. **Urban Code. 100 Lessons for Understanding the City**. Cambridge: MIT and Zurich: gta Verlag and ETH Zürich, 2011.

PlanBude. **PlanBude.** [Online]. n.d. Available at http://planbude.de/results-of-planbude-process-the-st-pauli-code-groundwork-for-the-architectural-competition/ Accessed May 14, 2019.

Sennett, R., Burdett, R., Sassen, S., and Glos, J. **The Quito Papers and the New Urban Agenda**. London and New York: Routledge, 2018.

Siebel, W. **Die Kultur der Stadt**. Berlin: Suhrkamp, 2015.

Whyte, W.H. **The Social Life of Small Urban Spaces**. New York: Project for Public Space, 1980.

"Wanting to plan urbanity is a contradiction in itself… The only thing possible is to offer spaces in which urban qualities can unfold." (Siebel 2015, 435).

Historical precursors

The rigid pursuit of modernist urban planning principles led to outcomes that, in the 1970s, were increasingly criticized as technocratic and inhumane. Various architectural and urban scholars as well as practitioners became interested in identifying and deciphering elements and underlying principles that could better describe "the urban" and might inform a more human-centered design approach. *A Pattern Language* by Christopher Alexander et al. (1977) is one such an attempt at creating urban design guidelines that adhere to the idea of human-centered design. The book is a collection of patterns – recurring "urban problems" and their possible solutions as informed by Alexander's practice as an architect and planner. Together, the patterns form a language meant to enable people to communicate with built environment professionals, facilitating co-production and empowering communities to design for themselves.

"At the core … is the idea that people should design for themselves their own houses, streets and communities. This idea … comes simply from the observation that most of the wonderful places of the world were not made by architects but by the people." (Alexander et al. 1977). Together with the works of other critics, such as Kevin Lynch (1981) and William H. Whyte (1980), *A Pattern Language* represents the search for alternative rationalizations of planning that could reconcile expert knowledge and formal design with the embedded knowledge and perspectives of the users. Interestingly, the notion of codes was only introduced by Alexander much later. *Generative Codes* (Alexander et al. 2005) proposes "a system of specific steps" for creating the socio-spatial fabric of a desirable neighborhood. Here, the focus shifts even more away from using generic design principles to achieve good urban design outcomes and instead towards structuring open, multi-stakeholder processes and negotiated outcomes.

Urban coding in contemporary planning

The 1970s demand for more user orientation and involvement in urban planning resonates in contemporary planning.

Nina Pawlicki (2017) **Construction of community model in Moravia, Medellin**.

Although reasons for planning insufficiencies and failures are often local and very specific, some general critiques persist: firstly, planning is often translated into formalistic, static, and rigidly linear approaches, which do not provide mechanisms to allow for unforeseen developments and dynamic adaptations. Secondly, planning processes tend to remain under the control of "rule-setting" bureaucrats, planning experts, or privileged and powerful political or market actors while not sufficiently including the broad majority of urban dwellers in decision-making. The level of participation guaranteed by most planning laws is often perceived as insufficient and bureaucratized. At the same time, increasing housing and living costs generate pressures on and threats to social cohesion; citizens demand more radical action to address air pollution, traffic congestion, and the effects of climate change. In these contexts, citizens have frequently lost trust in planning technocracies and demand more meaningful participation. Finally, most planning schemes – at least in the region known as the Global North – still follow classical zoning approaches, which often generate monotonous, monofunctional urban enclaves that do not fit the "messy" reality of what we perceive as desirable, diverse, and inclusive urban spaces. In their recent manifesto *The Quito Papers* (UN-Habitat 2018), Richard Sennett, Saskia Sassen, and others build on historical critiques to call for cities to engage with and strategically improve the

Philipp Misselwitz (2017) **Co-design and implementation of a community staircase in Moravia, Medellin.**

informal, improvised structures and practices that already exist. As Sennett puts it: "What we need to do is think of the city as a more open system, which accumulates complexity, and in which those complexities have to be worked with, rather than simplified" (quoted in Greenspan 2016). *The Quito Papers* advocate strategic improvement in the form of retrofitting urban textures over expert-planned ideal planning utopias – an approach that is more suitable for the capacities and resources of local municipalities and that creates the basis for more inclusive, participatory change.

Defining "urban coding"

Multiple alternative planning initiatives across the world have already begun to test such approaches, and the notion of *urban coding* has been referred to by many of these initiatives. Although a precise definition does not exist, urban coding could be understood as an umbrella term for the search for alternatives to classical deterministic planning in both research and practice. Mikoleit and Pürckhauer's (2011) publication titled *Urban Code: 100 Lessons for Understanding the City* is a compilation of observations, formulated as lessons, about the workings of public space in the Manhattan neighborhood of SoHo. The development of the "St. Pauli Code" in Hamburg is a recent example in which "urban coding" is used to refer to a concrete planning process. Here, the citizen-based network PlanBude grew out of a protest

DECODIFICACIÓN
DECODING

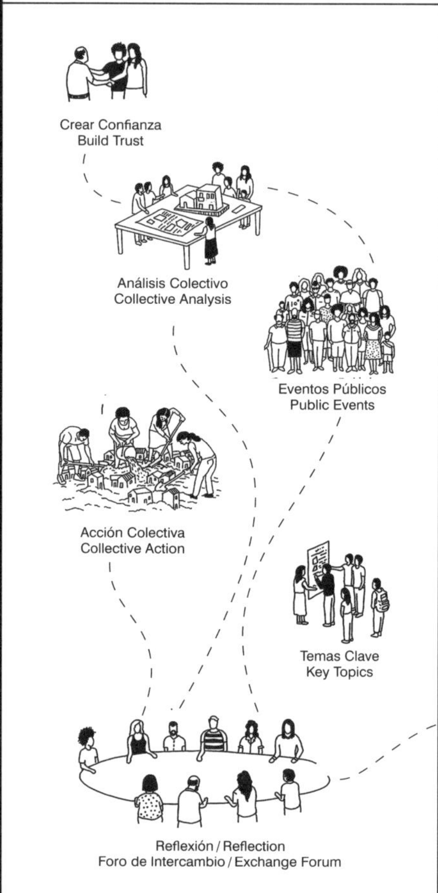

Un análisis social y espacial es la base co-producida de un proceso integral de transformación y planeación urbana.

A co-produced social and spatial analysis is the basis of a holistic urban transformation and planning process.

DEMANDAS
CLAIMS

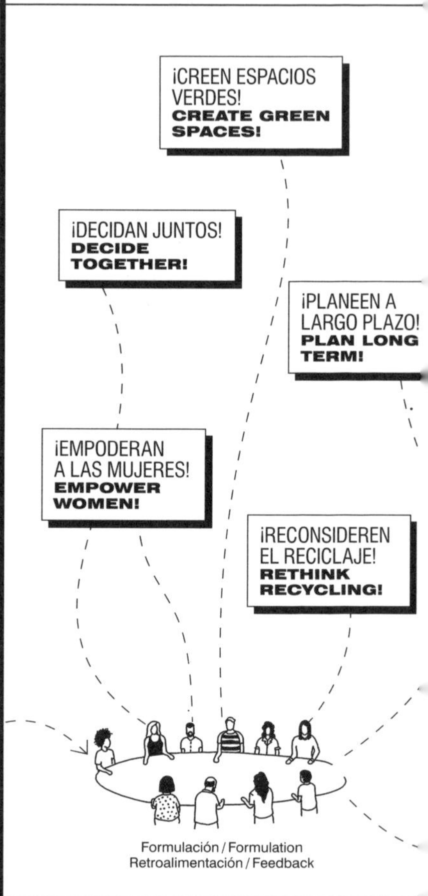

Demandas socio-espaciales, dirigidas a urbanistas, políticos y habitantes, para iniciar y guiar transformaciones urbanas.

Socio-spatial demands directed to city planners, politicians and residents, to initiate and guide urban transformation.

Moritz Ahlert (2017) **Towards a Moravia Code**.

HERRAMIENTAS
TOOLS

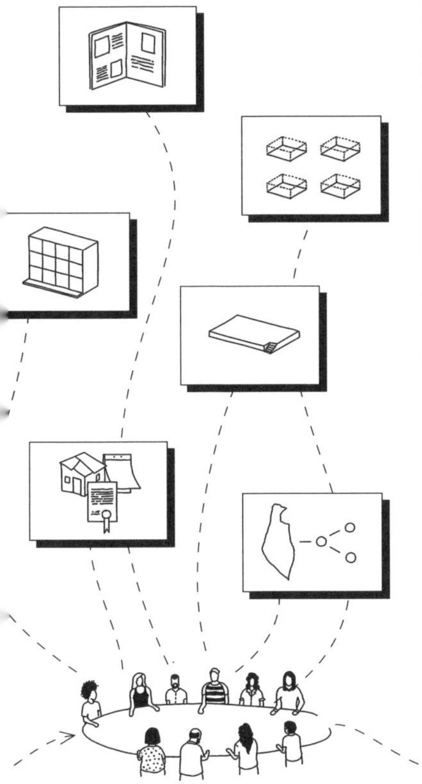

Formulación / Formulation
Retroalimentación / Feedback

Estrategias espaciales, políticas y económicas para cumplir con las metas articuladas en las demandas.

Spatial, organizational, economical and political strategies to achieve the goals formulated in the claims.

ESCENARIOS
SCENARIOS

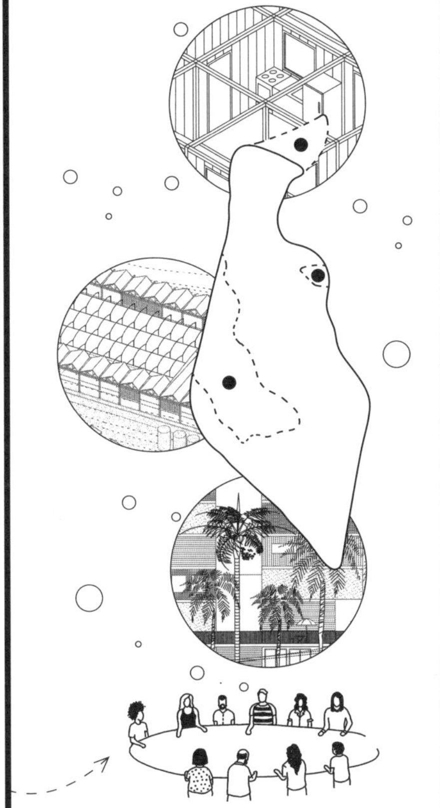

Diseño / Design
Retroalimentación / Feedback

Proyectos de transformación basados en la combinación de demandas y herramientas.

Site-specific transformation projects based on a combination of claims and tools.

against the planned demolition of the modernist ESSO Buildings located in Hamburg's inner-city district of St. Pauli. Eventually, citizens, planners, and municipal representatives agreed to cooperate in an open, community-led planning process that resulted in the formulation of the St. Pauli Code as an alternative vision for transformation in the neighborhood. Through this process – multiple events, workshops, and discussions – consensus was built by defining core qualities that should characterize the transformed neighborhood. The resulting richly illustrated 300-page document became the basis for architectural and urban design competitions; "That's only possible when you've got a good network among the city authorities and the local people. Simply setting up as a temporary office and using the tools developed in Hamburg doesn't cut it. Networking and trust among the locals are absolutely crucial" (Czenki et al. 2017).

In collaboration with a broad consortium of partners in both Berlin and Medellín, Colombia, an Urban Design Studio at TU Berlin similarly – and inspired by the St. Pauli Code – used urban coding as a principle for formulating alternative approaches to neighborhood planning, resulting in the formulation of a "Moravia Manifesto" (Ahlert et al. 2018). As in Hamburg, the project emerged as a response to a planning conflict – the proposed demolition and replanning of an informal neighborhood in the center of Medellín. Based on the experience of working in Medellín, four generic principles of urban coding were formulated that may also apply to other, similar approaches and help to fuel a more general debate on planning. These are as follows:

Critical appreciation of the existing

Urban coding approaches start with an acknowledgement of urban neighborhoods as a complex physical, social, and cultural texture shaped by its inhabitants over years, sometimes decades, that is expressed as multiple identities. This situated urban ecology should provide a starting point for any transformation process. The process needs to build on local strengths and resources that already exist, including the informal practices and coping strategies of its inhabitants. The challenge, however, is to navigate an appreciation of local qualities without becoming localist. Moreover, being defensive of change and linking local issues to the broader horizons of city and society often only consolidates the destructive local power dynamics or refusal of state authorities to address the local problems that created the need for transformation in the first place. Urban ecologies are multi-scalar, and while they include local systems, they also include broader social, economic, and environmental systems. As empathetic outsiders, planners can help to co-produce complex needs analyses, bringing together the situated urban knowledge of locals and the expertise of the technocrats and urban administrators managing broader urban systems.

Planning by doing

Conventional deterministic planning processes are time-consuming; it often takes years before changes affect everyday life on the ground. If they exist at all, participatory elements in planning law are rarely enough to build trust between the multiple stakeholders involved. Urban coding represents a shift from "planning to implement" to "intervening to plan." In the Moravia neighborhood of Medellín, concrete local interventions became the starting point for the more complex processes of analysis and planning later on. These interventions were prompted by external actors – including activists, architects, universities, and NGOs – and proved to be beneficial. Formal design criteria introduced in this manner facilitated the participatory building process, deepened local understanding of the work of "professional coders" – i.e., architects and planners – and helped to build trust among participants, which was necessary for all further work. The retrofitting of an informally planned communal staircase in Moravia as a public space addressed pressing access problems, but also served more broadly to inspire trust in the possibility of co-producing change. Design thus becomes more than the solution to a specific need. At the outset of planning processes, it can create tangible physical anchors and trigger transformation. Subsequently, it can convert "abstract" planning into a step-by-step laboratory approach for interventions in which small-scale built structures and concrete initiatives test what seemed impossible. Every intervention becomes a stepping-stone toward change, which inspires if it succeeds and provides useful lessons if it fails. It therefore shapes thinking by doing.

Co-producing through joint decision-making

The step-by-step implementation approach needs to be sustained by a decision-making structure that mediates between bottom-up and top-down. Blueprints for such planning bodies rarely work and local solutions must be found. Often, local structures of representation already exist and can be empowered to guide local residents to meaningful participation. However, co-producing decision-making cannot be limited only to the local level, but should mediate between local concerns and the opportunities and constraints offered by the broader landscape of the city as a whole. Planners and urban professionals can help to navigate the conflictual interface between local and citywide actors, between "insiders" and "outsiders," and between the various forms of urban knowledge that lie between the expertise of the lived everyday and the equally important technocratic expertise and data required in municipal decision-making. Widespread global experiences with local participatory budgeting also show how co-production can include decisions concerning finance and investment.

Defining values for change

While classical deterministic planning relies on a comprehensive master plan that fixes and regulates the future, urban coding proposes a different approach. Here, transformation goals are defined in terms of the values and qualities that should characterize a future neighborhood. This scenario – frequently named "the Code" – should be defined in a participatory process; it should be ambitious and formulated as clearly as possible while simultaneously remaining open to the trajectories and modalities with which the goals can be achieved. Urban coding is a balancing act of the need to be flexible and strategic as well as clear, committed, and accountable. Accordingly, it should transgress the simplistic binary between formal and informal, which forces us into an impossible and limiting choice.

Problems of scaling up

Urban coding is a broad concept. In our view, however, its principles indicate the directions in which planning should be reconfigured in order to guide co-produced transformation-to-sustainability processes in urban areas. It can be thought of as a set of instruments that help to steer incremental change and hence practically address the "how" and "who" missing from many global agenda discussions.

Nevertheless, multiple challenges remain. Despite alternative planning approaches (some, but not all, using the term "urban coding") in many cities around the globe, as well as a growing interest in and enthusiasm for co-production in general, the framework conditions for such planning efforts are often missing. Local activism can jump-start projects, but securing government or state support is another matter altogether. The inertia inherent in existing institutions and their methods remains strong. In many cases, it remains difficult to secure the minimum funding required to start such processes. Scaling up – and this should be the aim – will only become possible if a broader ecosystem for alternative and open urban planning initiatives can bring about a robust range of new financing options and well-established governance structures that include all stakeholders, from the state to local citizens.

This text is based on the writing of Jöran Mandik and Nija-Maria Linke[1] and Philipp Misselwitz, Florian Köhl, Christian Burckhard and was edited by Philipp Misselwitz.[2]

Endnotes

1 Submitted as coursework at TU Berlin in 2017.

2 Misselwitz, P. Köhl, P., and Burckhard, C. "Urban Coding: From Closed to Lively Cities". In Ahlert et al., **Moravia Manifesto**.

#B.26

CURATING EVOLUTIONARY LANDSCAPES

Brugmans, G. and Strien, J. **Urban by Nature**. Rotterdam: IABR, 2014.

Burnham, J. "Systems Esthetics." **Artforum** 7, no. 1 (1968). Available at http://www.volweb.cz/horvitz/burnham/systemsesthetics.html Accessed July 25, 2017.

Corner, J. "Ecology and Landscape as Agents of Creativity." In **Ecological Design and Planning**, edited by Thompson, G. and Steiner, F., 81–107. New York: John Wiley & Sons, 1997.

de Roo, G.; Silva, E.A. **A Planner's Encounter with Complexity**. Aldershot: Ashgate Publishing Company, 2010.

Loenhart, K.K. "Superfast Jellyfish. Matter, Agency and Emergent Properties of Landscape." In **GAM 07. Zero Landscape. Unfolding Active Agencies of Landscape**, edited by Technische Universität Graz, Fakultät für Architektur. Graz: Technische Universität Graz, 2011, 142–159.

Morton, T. "Zero Landscape in the Time of Hyperobjects." In **GAM 07. Zero Landscape. Unfolding Active Agencies of Landscape**, edited by Technische Universität Graz, Fakultät für Architektur. Graz: Technische Universität Graz, 2011, 79–87.

Mostafavi, M. "Why Ecological Urbanism? Why Now?" In **Ecological Urbanism**, edited by Mostafavi, M. and Doherty, P., 12–55. Baden: Lars Müller Publishers, 2011.

Jackson, J.B. "Concluding with Landscapes." In **Discovering the Vernacular Landscape**, by Jackson, J.B., 145–157. New Haven: Yale University Press, 1984.

Pollak, L. "Constructed Ground: Questions of Scale." In **The Landscape Urbanism Reader**, edited by Waldheim, C., 125–140. New York: Princeton University Press, 2006.

Prominski, M. "Designing Landscape as Evolutionary Systems." **Design Studies** 8, no. 3 (2005): 25–34.

Waldheim, C. "Landscape as Urbanism." In **The Landscape Urbanism Reader**, edited by Waldheim, C., 35–54. New York: Princeton University Press, 2006.

The design of evolutionary systems is a conceptual and methodological tool, originating in the field of landscape architecture, that brings temporal and ecological aspects into the spatial planning and design professions. It proposes an open-ended, process-oriented approach in order to deal "with the problem of determinacy versus indeterminacy, the integration of time in design, and systemic openness for changes in the design environment" (Prominski 2005, 25). Starting from the mid-twentieth century, planning and design broke with the idea of a static blueprint as the outcome of rational-technical decision making and started to develop methods for dealing with uncertainty, evolution, and complexity (de Roo and Silva 2010). Planners and designers are increasingly confronted with conditions of high uncertainty, rapid change, and insufficient data. The concept of evolutionary landscapes is a contribution that "expresses comprehensively the ability of design to deal with uncertainty, complexity, uniqueness, and value conflicts" (Prominski 2005, 25). In order to contextualize this concept, the following shifts in landscape theory, aesthetics, and ecology since the end of the last century should be considered:

From static landscapes to evolving landscapes

The traditional perception of landscape is based on an idyllic image seen as the opposite of the built environment. Furthermore, due to the lasting influence of Romantic painting, landscape has long been seen as something static. This kind of

The projects selected are on a regional or city-wide scale. In their approaches, they propose new kinds of relationships between the city and nature, and use landscape-based systems as *evolutionary landscapes* – that is, they use landscapes as active agents in their own development.

Biesbosch Stad, Netherlands[1]
Situated in the delta of the Biesbosch River in the central Netherlands, the area is a former polder region and one of the last tidal freshwater landscapes in Europe. Its current situation can be described as "intertwined in a network of relationships made up of human and nonhuman factors" (K. Loenhart 2011, 156). It is an area that has undergone an immense transformation from a tidal landscape to agricultural farmland. As the rivers were drained and dikes built, the boggy ground was deprived of water and sank down around the courses of the former rivers, leading to riverbeds lying higher than the former shores had been. This resulted in a bizarre inversion of the landscape.
The task defined by the Rotterdam Municipality as part of the Architecture Biennale 2005 in Rotterdam was twofold: to provide room for water in the re-naturalized delta, and to create mass housing. The designers had to respond to the uncertainties posed by the site, such as the constant threat of climate disturbance, heavy flooding, and the demand for housing. Proposing a *reflexive landscape practice*, the designers

static, green, arcadian image of landscape does not fit the contemporary landscape, which needs to be understood as an evolving system (Prominski 2005).

From object aesthetics to systems aesthetics

The idea of a simple world with isolated static objects has become obsolete. Systemic approaches in different disciplines have shifted the focus from the single object to its relationships and interactions with its surroundings, as well as to the processes involved. Systemic thinking also has an aesthetic dimension: as early as 1968, art critic Jack Burnham "argued for a 'systems aesthetic,' which means a shift from objects to systems, from pictures or sculptures to more open forms of art" (Burnham 1968, cited in Prominski 2005, 32). Timothy Morton argues for an aesthetic that denies any distance between the observer and the world of objects (2011). New forms of aesthetics focus on relations and interactions instead of on a product or object.

From restorative ecology to a new, radical ecology

Ecology has promoted an analytic, science-based account of natural processes and has been mostly used in a conservationist or restorative approach towards natural landscapes. This restricted view of ecology has hindered the integration of ecological knowledge in design. James Corner (1997) argues that landscape architecture must overcome this understanding: "A truly ecological landscape architecture might be less about the

broke through the existing dikes to allow the water to spill out in case of flooding. The materials from the dikes were then placed onto the old riverbeds, forming a new urban settlement structure. This created an inversion of the previous situation, with people now living on the dikes rather than behind them.
The team of Desvigne Paysagistes is anticipatively engineering the landscape with reference to its ecological, agricultural, infrastructural, and industrial past, while using elements of the landscape such as soil and water as future agents. Rather than designing an absolute, finished landscape, the team thus manages a network of agents, including natural elements and local stakeholders, leaving future relationships completely open. The landscape structure here serves as a highly flexible and adaptive framework.

55,000 hectares pour la nature / 55,000 hectares for nature[2]
Agence Ter's long-term strategic framework plan for Bordeaux focuses on the blurred edges "between city and the 'non-city'" (Agence Ter, n.d.). These spaces are a result of decentralization and an increase in municipal associations, both of which are leading to a wave of urbanization in such transitional areas.
The rapid changes are leading to socially unstable situations and highly uncertain futures. The edges are therefore being treated as "important issues for tomorrow" (Agence Ter, n.d.), on which new concepts for

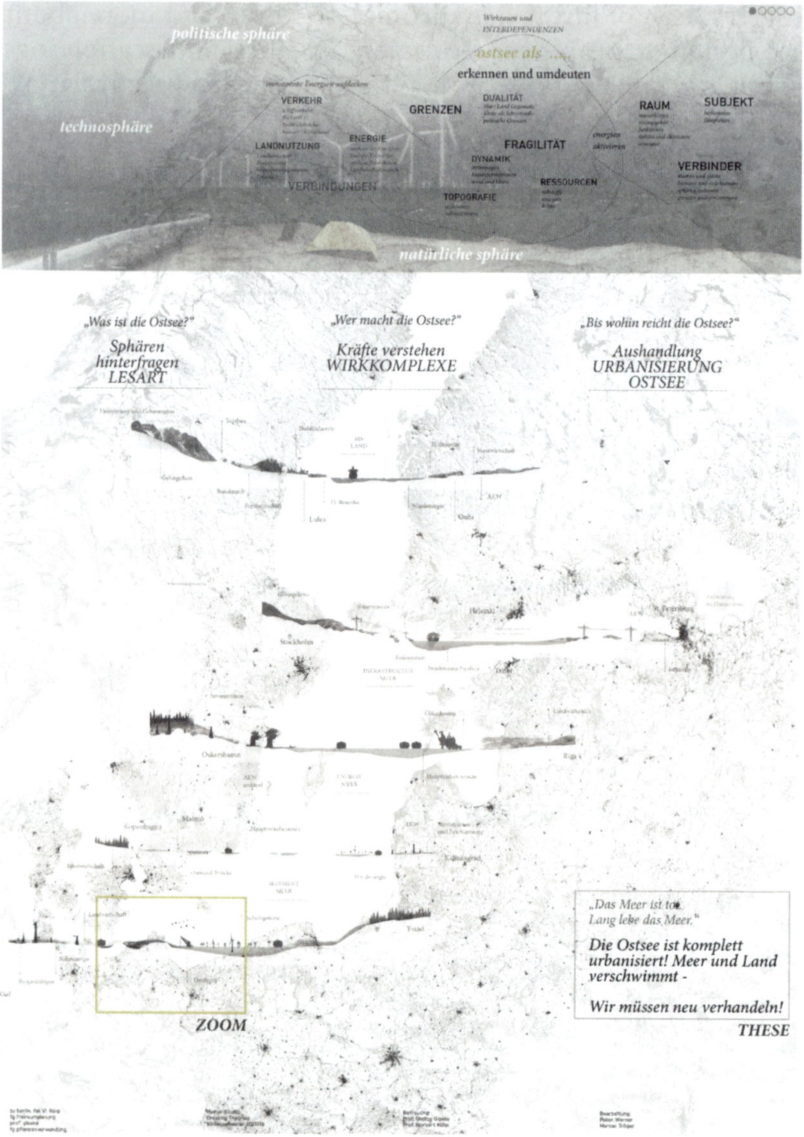

Tröger, M.; Werner, P. (2018) **The Baltic Territorial Study: Challenging the romanticized view and revealing new power relationships and aesthetics**.

construction of finished and complete works, and more about the design of 'processes,' 'strategies,' 'agencies,' and 'scaffoldings' – catalytic frameworks that might enable a diversity of relationships to create, emerge, network, interconnect, and differentiate" (Corner 1997, 278).

The designing of evolutionary systems is an attempt by the profession of landscape architecture to come to terms with the aforementioned shifts, but it can also be fruitful for other fields of spatial planning and design. In accordance with theoretical developments such as landscape urbanism, ecological urbanism, and urban metabolism, landscape is in turn considered "the basic building block of urban design" (Waldheim 2006, 37), a multi-scalar network of ecological relations (Mostafavi 2010), or a "complex, vast and interactive system that continuously works to meet the needs of its inhabitants" (Brugmans 2014). Landscape is thus no longer regarded as the opposite of the urban, and takes a central role in interdisciplinary approaches to spatial planning. Evolutionary landscapes are by definition multi-scalar, meaning that this approach has the ability to organize the landscape on a regional scale but can be also used for small-scale projects (Pollak 2006, 129).

Evolutionary landscapes can be best described as an open approach. Until now, the debate has mostly focused on the conceptual and theoretical levels rather than the methodological level, and there is no clear path for implementing the method. As shown in the example projects (Prominski 2005),

connecting nature and urbanization are to be tested. Landscape-based interface systems are being used to create a new *liveable scaffold* in these contested, highly dynamic, and uncertain areas. The landscape architects from Agence Ter focus on the composition of the different mixtures of urban and natural elements, regarding the edges not as a line but as a layer comparable to the ecotones between two ecosystems. Four types of edge are described: forest, water, agricultural, and infrastructural, all heterogeneous and highly adaptive.
The framework comes with a process- and action-oriented timeline, jumping between scales and showcasing possible implementation on various levels; identifying and prioritizing overall landscape edge situations, especially in fragile areas, developing territory guidelines as part of a master plan, and zooming in until the step of operationalization is reached. However, it does not focus solely on the creation of open systems: it sets clear goals and frameworks for implementing the reworked edge situations step by step.

What is this Baltic Sea? A littoral negotiation between the Baltic Sea and its sediment landscapes[3]
This project challenges the widespread, romanticized view of the Baltic Sea by decoding its vast ecological and infrastructural use on both a global and local scale. The Baltic Sea is portrayed as a highly infrastructural, interconnected, and urbanized

Tröger, M.; Werner, P. (2018) **Littoral Negotiation: Tactics and new sediment landscapes in Mecklenburg-Vorpommern**.

experimentation and adaptation within the constraints of a specific project and context seem to be more important than an overdetermined and inflexible methodological framework. At the very least, the aspects of temporality, open-endedness, and unpredictability described below have to be taken into account while designing evolutionary systems.

As evolution is a temporal process, it is crucial to take into account both time and the different temporal scales. The uncertain future "is not seen as something that has to be resolved, but as an integral part of the design" (Prominski 2005, 32). Therefore, this method does not ultimately lead to a finished proposal, but rather to a framework: a set of rules, parameters for growth, or formal and organizational guidelines aiming for a balance between targeted intervention and open-endedness. As *evolutionary* in this context refers to partly unpredictable processes, one pos-

space, where the spheres of ecology, technology, and culture merge, creating highly dynamic, vulnerable, and unstable littoral interfaces and thus breaking the old dichotomy between the ocean and land. The project develops a radical strategy around those interfaces based on models and statistics of the expected global sea level rise between now and 2100, which will result in drastic consequences for the Baltic region.
The authors seek an alternative way of dealing with those growing uncertainties by working with the power and needs of the sea. They develop a negotiation strategy around the identified core processes, which reveal hidden landscape structures deep inland, constantly dynamizing the ocean-land continuum and serving as a provocation to fixed attitudes towards the sea.
This results in a resilient and dynamic framework of spatial categories and tactics – referred to as fortresses, mediators, and migrating spaces – for the German Baltic Sea coast.
The framework helps increase resilience by fostering sediment landscapes based on a new sediment economy and profiting from those upcoming forces. They have been translated into prototypes, where the introduced dynamics, aesthetics, and identities will be integrated into design strategies over time.

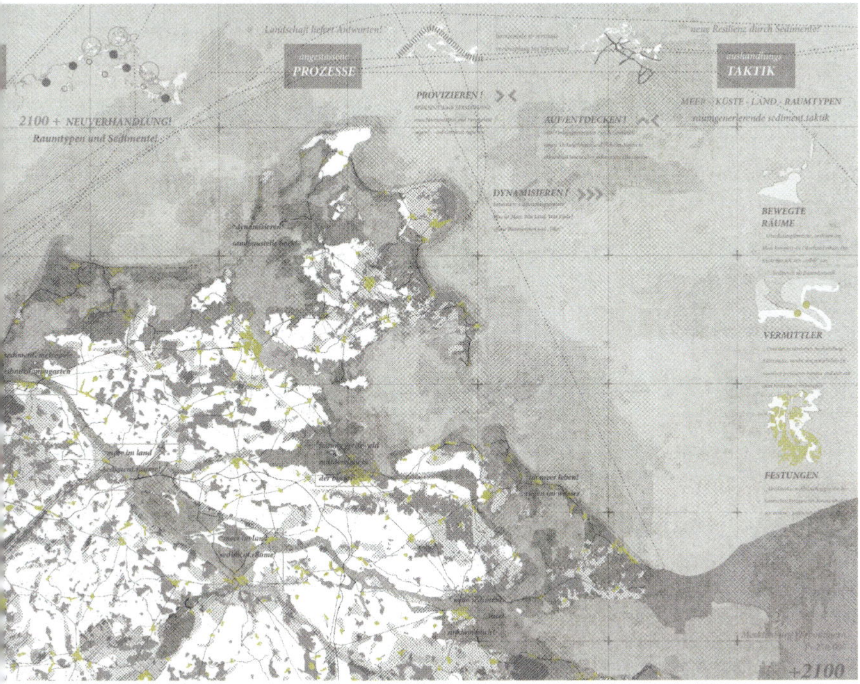

Endnotes

1 Research by design project for the Architecture Biennale, Rotterdam, 2005. Landscape Architect: M. Desvigne Paysagistes.
Tiberghien, G.A., Corner, J., and Desvigne, M. **Intermediate Natures: The Landscapes of Michel Desvigne**. Basel: Birkhäuser Architecture, 2009.

2 Action-oriented master plan as livable framework for Bordeaux, 2014. Landscape Architect: Agence Ter.
Agence Ter and Diedrich, L. **Territories: From Landscape to City**, Basel: Birkhäuser Architecture, 2008.
Agence Ter "55.000 ha pour la nature." [Online]. n.d. Available at http://agenceter.com/de/projets/bordeaux-55-000-ha-pour-la-nature/ Accessed July 25, 2017.

3 TUB Students. "Crossing Theories_Resilience and Metabolism as Design Strategies." Project for the Master's Studio at the Technische Universität Berlin, supervised by Giseke, U. and Kühn, N., 2017/2018.
TU Berlin Fachgebiet Landschaftsarchitektur/Freiraumplanung. "Crossing Theories." [Online]. n.d. http://fg.freiraum.tu-berlin.de/lehre/dokumentation/ Accessed December 20, 2018.

sible strategy for achieving this balance is to provide "a rigid structure which consists of instructions ... as well as of a formal order" (Prominski 2005, 32). In such a case, the design mainly consists of a set of tools or instructional steps, which can be implemented as needed and are developed in close connection to the existing conditions and specific characteristics of the site.

The strengths of this emerging methodological approach are manifold. First of all, these kinds of landscapes and territories are able to adapt to changes over time; in times of uncertainty, this attribute is an invaluable feature. Furthermore, this method highlights the processual nature of landscape as well as the need to integrate ecology, in a new and creative way, into the design process.

When attempting to deal with long-term temporal scales, design disciplines must yield control of the final outcome. Additionally, they face a lot of external challenges: political changes can endanger the continuity of the project, and further social or natural transformations might even lead to the collapse of a landscape system and the designer's framework. However, in an approach featuring systems-based aesthetics and evolutionary trends, even a radical collapse of the landscape – requiring further adaptation of the design approach – would be seen as a turning point in a continuous process.

This text is based on the writing of Rickmer Niehuus and Marcel Tröger and was edited by Xenia Kokoula.

#B.27

CO-DESIGNING AND BUILDING

Giseke, U., Kasper, C., Wieck, K., Harroud, T., and Mansour, M. "Transdisciplinary Design." In **Agriculture for Growing City Regions: Connecting Urban-Rural Spheres in Casablanca**, by Giseke, U. London: Routledge, 2015.

Hannemann, J.-C. "Canaan." In **Out there. Landscape Architecture on Global Terrain**, edited by Lepik, A., Giseke, U., Keller, R., Rekittke, J., Stockmann, A., and Werthmann, C. Berlin: Hantje Catz Verlag, 2017.

Kraus, C**. Designbuild Education**. New York: Routledge, 2017.

Meyer, F. "Mehr Praxis. Was Design Build Projekte in der Architekturausbildung vermitteln können." **Baunetzwoche** 490 (2017): 7–17.

ACSA, ed. **Proceedings: Working Out: Thinking While Building. Papers from the 2014 Fall Conference**. Washington, D.C.: ASCA Press, 2015.

Steiner, D. "Design-Build. The Design Build Movement." **Arch+** 211/212 (2013): 154–159.

The compound word *designbuild* describes the merging of the design and the implementation phases of a project executed by the same group of people. Kraus (2017, 2) distinguishes between the commercial practice (usually referred to in the hyphenated form *design-build*) and the non-commercial approaches used to collaboratively find spatial solutions for social or humanitarian challenges. However, the hyphenated and the compound form are often used interchangeably. Knowledge transfer and participation are essential elements of the emerging practices described by the more general term *live projects*, which also encompasses designbuild projects. The method is rooted in academic and educational practice, but private organizations and offices also increasingly apply it in their work.

Steiner (2013, 154 onwards) traces the roots of designbuild to modern architectural education and especially to the teaching practice of the Bauhaus in the 1920s. At the beginning of the 1990s, the hands-on principle of the Bauhaus was further developed at US universities, especially through the pioneering work of the Rural Studio at Auburn University, USA. Today, numerous universities cooperate with local welfare organizations to design and build essential buildings in deprived neighborhoods. In 2003 the exhibition *Just Build it: Die Bauten des Rural Studio* in Vienna reported on these projects and helped popularize designbuild projects in continental Europe. Over time, designbuild has become more professional and has gained appeal as a new form of multifaceted learning and building – with profits for the

(RE)_Create Taipei, Basurama, 2016[1]
(RE)_Create Taipei is an open-space project developed within the framework of World Design Capital Taipei 2016. The large number of homogeneous, plasticky playgrounds in the city encouraged the Spanish office Basurama to develop new visions of playing in Taipei.
Their design was developed using locally sourced waste, which was a chance to support environmental education while being both sustainable and economical.
Together with City Yeast and the support of local residents, professionals, and students, Basurama decided to design two temporary playgrounds made of upcycled materials. Close participation workshops made sure that the design harmonized with the needs and habits of the users.
The Bubble Station was used as a portable office and meeting space for their work. This temporary object was constructed out of old plastic bags donated by private individuals in Taipei.
The first playground, the Kids Ambition Park, was built using old cooling tanks (giant tanks of water from industrial refrigeration systems). The tanks were provided by the Liangchi Group, which is based in Taipei. The tanks were cut open and equipped with different materials (sourced from unwanted park equipment) to challenge the kids' senses.
The second project, the Swings Park, used leftover lampposts. The material was provided by the Parks and Street Lights Division

executor (students, office), the client, and the prospective user (Steiner 2013, 154 onwards).

Depending on the actors involved, it is possible to distinguish between three main approaches within the designbuild method. The most common approach is the implementation of the method for educational purposes, involving teachers and students in collaboration with local communities. Designbuild within academia can also be part of research projects with an action research component, set up as "an iterative process of thinking, acting, and reflecting" (Hannemann 2017, 68). Thirdly, private offices can independently initiate or implement designbuild projects, focusing more on the social communicative processes in urban neighborhoods.

Basurama.org (2016) **Water Tank Playground, Basurama, Taipeh**. View from above.

Basurama.org (2016) **Water Tank Playground, Basurama, Taipeh**. Detail.

Over the past fifteen years this educational approach has become an essential teaching method in many design faculties, allowing students to experience the complex processes of planning and design practice. The practical knowledge concerning construction procedures, techniques, cultural crafts, sustainability, and resources/materials is shared among the participants, who include students, teachers, and local people, with the aim of merging expert or disciplinary knowledge with local knowledge.

and collected in Taipei's Lamppost Landfill. All the lampposts were welded together to form an experimental sculpture for people of all ages (Basurama 2016).

A Jam Manufactory for Naxií, TU Berlin, 2012[2]
The designbuild project *A Jam Manufactory for Naxií* took place in San Jerónimo Tecoatl in Oaxatl, Mexico in 2012. On a site of about 2000m², the interdisciplinary academic designbuild team realized the construction of a kitchen house for the production of jams and conserves, the building of an assembly hall for the community, and the development of the surrounding grounds into a productive terraced garden. The project was cross-funded by many organizations, including the STO Foundation, Adveniat, the Lions Club, and private donations, and was further supported by the DAAD. The designbuild team consisted of twenty-five students and teachers from TU Berlin and UNAM (the Autonomous National University of Mexico) supported by Cocoon. Local stakeholders, such as the women's cooperative Naxií (Union de Mujeres Unidas) and the NGO CAMPO (Centro de Apoyo al Movimiento Popular Oaxaqueño), played an important role in implementing and preparing the project and supported the international team during the construction. The design was developed during the winter term at TU Berlin and implemented during the spring break. The design needed to be adapted upon arrival because of the different

Simon Colwill (2012) **Jam Manufactory for NAXII**. Oaxaca, Mexico.

circumstances encountered on the steep site. The construction was realized in six-and-a-half weeks by the designbuild team, supported by local craftsmen who also produced the adobe masonry. The finished buildings, play equipment, and terraced garden achieved better working conditions for the jam manufactory and enable better-structured apprenticeships. The interdisciplinary designbuild team experienced a new building culture and the local people realized that it is possible to achieve a high building quality even when using the traditional adobe masonry construction method. The community supported the designbuild team by hosting them in their houses and providing for them throughout the construction phase.

EMMA Generator Geneva, Raumlabor, 2011[3]

EMMA is a multifunctional object/transformation generator made of seven tables. It can be a "structure for dinners or the cinema, for building an imaginary city with children, or for round table[s] or performances" (Raumlabor 2011).

Its main goal is to connect the residents of a neighborhood. The building process of the generator is implemented by different actors – guests, schoolchildren, and local residents – and elements were added over time and adapted to the requirements of the project (Raumlabor 2011). Every participant receives a construction plan with simple technical building instructions for the modules, which were

Urban Lab Medellín Berlin Team (2018) **Urban Lab Medellín Berlin – TALLER TROPICAL MORAVIA**. An open workshop and community garden for the informal neighbourhood of Moravia in Medellín, Colombia. A new space for educational, cultural, and community activities and programmes focusing on environmental issues.

developed for easy assembly. Modules could be assembled into chairs, tables, and shelves, as well as into walls and shelters. The goal is to constantly test and improve the construction methods. The main material (wood) for the 2011 project came from Europallets and screws were provided by the local home improvement center, in addition to a stock of existing screws from previous projects. The geographic reference frame for the material is always the city/the urban neighborhood in which the generator is to be established. It is delivered by bike or car depending on the size of the objects. Constructed elements can be reused in new generator projects or can be used in one project over a longer period (Raumlabor 2011).

Die Laube im Prinzessinnengarten (The Bower in the Prinzessinnengarten), Prinzessinnengarten, Achitectuul and fatkoehl, 2015–2017[4]

The *Laube* (bower) in the Prinzessinnengarten was built as a temporary, experimental wood frame structure in the Prinzessinnengarten (Princesses' Garden) urban garden in Berlin using the design-build method between 2015 and 2017.
Co-founder of the Prinzessinnengarten Marco Clausen, Florian Koehl of fatkoehl architects, and Christian Brukhard of Architectuul made the project possible through their own initiative. In 2013, the privatization of the community garden was prevented at the last minute and the garden became a symbol of bottom-up urban

development. The project was neither initiated nor financed by an investor, nor had it developed in an academic context – it resulted from the initiators' own social motivation. The building is intended to serve the community and to be used non-commercially. It provides a space for events and workshops, a meeting point for the neighborhood, and a platform for debate, especially on issues of environmental education and social urban development. The designbuild method suited these aims as a way of building cost-efficiently without a builder-owner. The building developed from an experimental wooden structure without walls, windows, or doors, which made it possible to experiment with different building envelopes for noise, thermal insulation, and light protection.
The development process of the Laube went through two distinct designbuild stages. Due to previously accumulated knowledge, the research stage was cut rather short. First, the architects designed the structure and approached the IKEA Foundation as a first investor. After receiving a building permit from the borough in August 2015, a call for volunteers to join the building process was launched through different media. A month later, twenty architecture students and other volunteers started building the foundations, which were completed after seven weeks. The second designbuild stage commenced with the process of designing the wooden structure in detail. The emphasis was on an

Social and humanitarian projects in particular give young students and teaching staff the opportunity to deal with complex questions and reflect on their own professional aims (Meyer 2017, 7 onwards). The designbuild method is also used to test spatial solutions for future challenges, such as those associated with climate change. When implemented within a research framework, design solutions can reveal knowledge gaps, generate further research questions, and serve as a platform for conceiving and debating further necessary transformations within a community (Giseke et al. 2015, 97).

The non-educational approach in offices is less common. It often focuses on social processes in urban neighborhoods and aims to have an impact on urban space. Participation processes are an essential component of this approach and aim to forge stronger social bonding, foster political engagement, and promote environmental education. The built object is often only the starting point for initiating these processes.

The steps for the implementation of a designbuild project differ from regular design procedures in key aspects. Often, a request is made by a community or organization facing a specific challenge. In collaboration with this group, universities or private enterprises then organize a funding and sponsoring plan, which can be an elaborate process. An intensive research phase is essential in order to take actors, cultural backgrounds, climate conditions, and other particularities into account. This phase is important to facilitating the complex process of building on the

easy-to-build and flexible, modular building approach. After the *Deutsche Bundesstiftung Umwelt (German Federal Environmental Foundation)* provided funding for the second stage, a local wood retailer joined the project. In the spring of 2016, a local woodworking class, volunteers, and architecture students from TU Berlin all worked together on the wooden structure. The students also researched cladding systems to add to the construction in the TU's designbuild course and subsequently built a selection of options. The restricted space and the ongoing operation of the community garden made it difficult to erect the ten-meter-high structure. Instead of using heavy construction site equipment, alternative labor-intensive techniques had to be employed. In June 2017 a terrace and an extendable room were added to the building, which was officially opened afterwards (Prinzessinnengärten 2017).

Coproducing Housing Solutions: Medellín / Berlin, TU Berlin, 2017[5]

As part of the one-year student project *Coproducing Housing Solutions: Medellín / Berlin* by the Habitat Unit at TU Berlin, a designbuild project was executed during the spring semester in Medellín over the very short time frame of two weeks. The project was initiated by the student Albert Kreisel, who lived in the barrio of Moravia for a year. During this time, he engaged closely with the local community and discovered site. The actual design phase must be based on the outcomes of the research phase. It usually takes place within a series of workshops and, for the most part, directly on site. During the design phase, plans are never static, but flexible and adaptable. This high level of flexibility is the main difference between designbuild and regular building projects – it supports the intensive and often unpredictable interplay between actors, techniques, materials, and so on. The last step of the process is the opening and handing over of the constructed object or space – ideally to a previously informed and active local community.

The main strength of designbuild projects lies in the direct connection between practice and real life. Participants witness the different steps of building processes and become aware of complexities and possible obstacles. This experience provides an orientation for a professional future and fosters appreciation and empathy among actors. Moreover, the method is crucial for developing alternative, low-priced, and potentially more socially just approaches.

Designbuild projects often deal with complex circumstances and have to integrate a host of different disciplines in order to generate the exchange of knowledge. Ecology, economy, and construction technology are just a few examples of the disciplines that may be involved. In this context, communication on equal terms is crucial to supporting every participant as they experience and deal with new situations, actors, skills, techniques, and fields of knowledge. Furthermore, a project can function as a platform for

that there was an urgent need in the neighborhood for the renovation of a public staircase. After teaming up with Max Storch and Tobias Schrammek as the architecture collective Urban Oasis, the three looked for academic, financial, and strategic partners. In cooperation with the Universidad Pontificia Bolivariana (UPB) and TU Berlin, they started a student project that included both a spring and a summer school. The project was funded by the magazine Arch+ and the Alfred Herrhausen Gesellschaft and was supported by a variety of mostly local partners within Medellín. Most importantly, the project engaged with the local community in the Moravia neighborhood, especially with the community leaders.
The spring session was held in March of 2017 over the course of two weeks. The UPB and TU students and the local community were supported by practicing designers from Raumlabor and fatkoehl architects, which both have a lot of expertise concerning designbuild projects. Urban Oasis designed the infrastructural part of the staircase – the steps and the waste water management – with the support of employees at Raumlabor and fatkoehl. Local construction workers, pupils, neighbors, and community leaders carried out the construction work on the stairs. The student groups were split into specialized teams and assigned to different aspects and parts of the staircase. The facades of the adjoining houses were

experimenting with regional, sustainable, and environmentally friendly materials, and pave the way for regular design projects or public investments to make use of these resources. These practical experiences can also reveal valuable insights in the context of research projects.

On the other hand, the complexity of designbuild projects can also be a limitation. While the design and construction phases are short, the overall coordination – including funding, participation processes, and research – is complex and requires significant resources. Long-term management and maintenance by the local community can become a challenge once external partners and sponsors withdraw from a project, which underscores the importance of cultural aspects in establishing continuity. Extensive research in advance and during the process is necessary for participants to be prepared for the individual challenges and unknown parameters of different cultural contexts. Under these conditions, interdisciplinarity may be neglected in favor of staying within a limited time frame. Another common critique is that the designbuild method usually focuses on small-scale solutions and cannot adequately address broader structural or institutional problems (Steiner 2013, 154 onwards). The issue of upscaling can be addressed in action research projects that have a larger scope.

painted by three different artist collectives, some based in Moravia itself and others from within the broader Medellín context. The construction material was purchased by the municipality, while paint and lighting systems were contributed by local companies. Community leaders and some of the local residents were heavily involved with the building process.

Endnotes

1 Basurama. **(Re)_create Taipei**. [Online]. 2016. Available at http://basurama.org/proyecto/re_create-taipei/ Accessed December 13, 2018.

2 DBXchange. **A Jam Manufactory for Naxií**. [Online]. n.d. Available at https://www.dbxchange.eu/node/399/ Accessed December 13, 2018.

3 The building process of the transformative object took place 2011 in Geneva. See also: Raumlabor (2011): **EMMA Generator, Geneva**, https://raumlabor.net/emmagenerator-geneve/ accessed 13.12.2018.

4 Prinzessinnengärten (2017): **Die Laube** https://prinzessinnengarten.net/die-laube/ accessed 13.12.2018.

5 Urban Lab Medellín (n.d.) **Berlin Urban Lab Medellín Berlin**. [Online]. n.d. Available at https://urbanlabmedellinberlin.com/ Accessed December 13, 2018.

Despite these shortcomings, the method is an important tool for raising awareness and for bridging academic and non-academic knowledge. Its success is highly dependent on individual, case-specific, and location-specific factors, including cultural, social, and environmental ones.

This text is based on the writing of Andreas Horn, Jonas Wulf, Bente Jacobsen and Nathalie Dennstorff and was edited by Xenia Kokoula.

Undine Giseke is Professor of Landscape Architecture and Open Space Planning at TU Berlin. The chair focuses on the interactions between urbanization processes and open space systems by considering their multiple spatial, social, and natural dimensions. It teaches the theoretical fundamentals and design methods of landscape architecture within the international context. From 2005 to 2014, Undine Giseke led the inter- and transdisciplinary research project "Urban agriculture as integrated factor of climate-optimized urban development" in Casablanca. The research focused on urban-natural interactions, urban metabolism, and systemic design.

Martina Löw is Professor of Sociology at TU Berlin. Her areas of specialization and research are sociological theory, urban sociology, space theory, and planning sociology. She has developed concepts for understanding cities in the light of planning decisions, social-/cultural architectural interventions, and spatial appropriation. She is currently Head of the "Re-Figuration of Spaces" (DFG) Collaborative Research Center.

Angela Million is Professor of Urban Design and Urban Development (UDUD) at TU Berlin. With an interest in spatial qualities and the spatial knowledge of people, the department is committed to integrated scholarship that crosses disciplinary boundaries and researches theory and practice in urban planning and design. Current research projects are on educational spaces and cities as educational settings, built environment education and the participation of children, the scholarship of teaching in urban design, visual communication and cartography, and industrial, retail and multifunctional infrastructure development. She is currently the head of the DAAD-Global Center of Spatial Methods for Urban Sustainability SMUS.

Philipp Misselwitz is Professor of the Habitat Unit at TU Berlin – a globally networked research and teaching center focused on the study of urbanization processes in the Global South. His current studies focus on user-driven urban development processes and co-production in housing, rural urbanization processes, and translocal spatial production, as well as transdisciplinary teaching methodologies in the urban design field.

Jörg Stollmann is Professor of Urban Design and Urbanization (CUD) at TU Berlin. CUD research and design projects explore the complex history, politics, ecology, and economy of the urban towards more equitable and liveable environments. Collaborative and community-based design processes are investigated, developed, and tested in practice. Among the chair's research foci are urban landscapes, spatial commons, participatory development, and the mediatization and digitization of planning and the urban everyday.

Andreas Brück worked as a researcher and lecturer at the Chair of Urban Design and Urban Development (with Prof. Million) from 2011–17. Since 2018, he has been the Managing Director of K LAB – a unit dealing with the visualization and communication of the urban – at TU Berlin's Institute for Urban and Regional Planning. His main research interests range from the envisioning of urban tomorrows to incremental urbanism and the dynamics of urban movements and transformation. He is currently Guest Professor for Urban Planning at the Dessau Institute of Architecture (DIA).

Emily Kelling has been a researcher and lecturer at the Chair of Sociology of Planning and Architecture at TU Berlin since 2013. She teaches on the master's programme in Urban Design. Her independent research focuses on informal housing, international housing policy, urban inequalities, and urban design.

Xenia Kokoula is an architect and urban designer with professional experience in the field of landscape architecture in Switzerland and Germany. She has been teaching design studios and theory seminars on the master's programmes in Landscape Architecture and Urban Design at TU Berlin since 2011. Her research focuses on the role of power, knowledge, and affect in the processes of production of urban space.

Áine Ryan joined the Habitat Unit at TU Berlin in 2016. She teaches on the master's programme in Urban Design. In 2009 she joined ANCB The Aedes Metropolitan Laboratory, then newly formed, where she shaped the programmatic content and coordinated the Universities in Residence. She remains involved as the editor and as a project coordinator. Her independent research has focused mainly on spatial expressions of cultural practices. She recently commenced doctoral research on the representational approach to design.

imprint

Special thanks to Xenia Kokoula and Tom Jones for their perseverance and tireless support!

Cover: Felix Holler, based on a concept by Paul Klever and Luca Mulé
Marker typeface: TU Berlin Medium

Editors: Undine Giseke, Martina Löw, Angela Million, Philipp Misselwitz, and Jörg Stollmann
Editorial team: Xenia Kokoula, Tom Jones with Paul Klever, Luca Mulé, Anna Neuhaus, and Julia Schlütsmeier-Hage
Copy-editing: David Skogley, Jessica Glanz
Design concept: Paul Klever and Luca Mulé
Design elaboration and setting: Felix Holler, Stoffers Graphik-Design
Lithography: Stefan Rolle, Stoffers Graphik-Design
Printed in the European Union

The book was made possible with the support of the German Academic Exchange Network (DAAD), TU Berlin, and the School of Architecture and Urban Planning CAUP at Tongji University.

Bibliographic information published by the Deutsche Nationalbibliothek. The Deutsche Nationalbibliothek lists this publication in the Deutsche Nationalbibliografie; detailed bibliographic data is available on the Internet at http://dnb.d-nb.de

jovis Verlag GmbH
Lützowstraße 33
10785 Berlin

www.jovis.de

jovis books are available worldwide in select bookstores. Please contact your nearest bookseller or visit www.jovis.de for information concerning your local distribution.

ISBN 978-3-86859-571-0